White Rajah

To Din

Contents

White Rajah

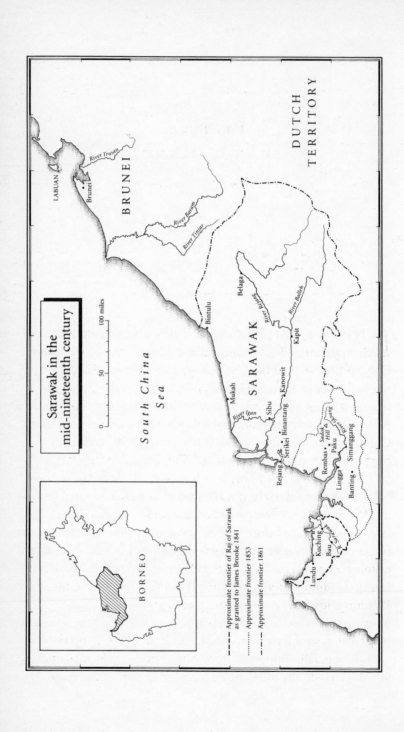

Sarawak in the mid-nineteenth century

BRUNEI

River Truan

LABUAN

Brunei

River Barum

River Tinjar

DUTCH TERRITORY

South China Sea

100 miles

50

0

Bintulu

Belaga

SARAWAK

River Rejang

River Balleh

Kapit

Mukah

River Igan

Sibu

Kanowit

Binantang

Serikei

Rejang

Rembas

Sadok Hill

Paku

Simanggang

Lingga

Banting

River Lupar

River Batang Lupar

Lundu

Kuching

Bau

River Sarawak

BORNEO

- - - - Approximate frontier of Raj of Sarawak
          as granted to James Brooke 1841
·········· Approximate frontier 1853
— · — · — Approximate frontier 1861

Preface

In 1949, in a small, bleak Sarawak town called Sibu, a minor British governor was blatantly murdered in a most public fashion. Duncan Stewart had been in the job just eighteen days, the new ruler of a mix of Malays, Dayaks and Chinese in the swampy little state that hugged the north-west coast of the huge island of Borneo. As he walked with gubernatorial aplomb down a line of flag-waving Chinese schoolchildren, a young Malay named Rosly bin Dhobie stepped briskly forward and stabbed him, almost casually.

The incident figured only briefly in the UK newspapers but in Sarawak, understandably, it was regarded as a great event. A major interest was that Stewart carried on and finished the dutiful inspection of the children before anyone noted what had happened. With blood oozing between the fingers clasped to his side, he walked calmly back to his car, took off the plumed hat that was part of tropical dress uniform and asked quietly to be taken to the hospital. Pictures show the young assassin swaggering eagerly away into martyrdom, his escort hard-pressed to keep up with him. His eyes blaze with youthful moral rectitude. Rosly would be hanged – on a gallows specially imported from Singapore – after a swift trial unhampered by any too-delicate scrupling over his democratic and judicial rights. A picturesque element in the courtroom was the daily attendance of a body of Dayak 'tribesmen' in full traditional wargear, who declared themselves there to support the government. Quite who the government was, however, was the whole issue. The British newspapers omitted to even mention *which* flag the children had been waving – British or Sarawakian.

In 1945 the Japanese occupation of Sarawak had come to an abrupt end, but servants still had to be reminded to show respect by cupping their hands to their brows or hearts in Malay fashion and not by bowing and hissing as the Japanese did. Nominally in charge was the somewhat vague, effete and well-intentioned Rajah Vyner, third in a dynasty of British rulers, drawn from the Brooke family, that stretched back a hundred years. His position was distinctly odd, as a British subject who was independent ruler of a British-protected territory which paid tribute to the neighbouring state of Brunei, most of whose land it had swallowed anyway. Rajah Vyner Brooke determined that Sarawak's future lay in a constitutional adjustment with the Colonial Office, as a regularised, sanitised and bureaucratised colony, since the British alone could bring the investment needed to rebuild the shattered economy and ruined infrastructure of the little state. The Brooke philosophy of patch, make do and mend was simply no longer equal to the task. But his people were far from in agreement. Many wanted a rajah of the British Brooke dynasty to remain as their ruler; others wanted independence; very few declared themselves eager to be swallowed and digested in the maw of the British imperial machine despite its shameless use of bribery and intimidation. Rajah Vyner's heir, Anthony, continued to campaign against the Rajah's cession of the territory to Britain and was finally banned from Sarawak.

There was plenty of time for all this to pass through the fevered head of Duncan Stewart as he was transported by flying boat to Singapore and, in the course of five days, his condition passed relentlessly from 'satisfactory' to 'doing well' to 'giving cause for concern' to 'deceased'. The British authorities put it about that anti-colonial posters had been ripped down throughout the colony and that Malays had fled into the jungle to avoid the righteous wrath of Dayaks. A hundred years after the founding of the state, the myth of Malay duplicity and Dayak loyalty was still doing its job. As he looked up at the changing brown, yellow and white faces that gazed down on him with concern, Duncan Stewart, like all of us, probably asked the question 'Why me?' To answer that, he would have to go back to the beginning of the romantic and mysterious status of Sarawak, whose final victim he was, and the start of all the confusion, fighting and wrangling – the curious and disquieting Englishman named James Brooke, who had created the tangled daydream of Sarawak and was the first and greatest of its white rajahs.

JAMES BROOKE AS A CHILD: BRITISH MUSEUM

Chapter 1

Beginnings

A childhood portrait shows a rather knowing James Brooke pouting cherubically in lace and napped velvet. From the first he was unutterably spoiled. His early years were blessed with an ample private income and hushed legal respectability, and his youth conditioned by the measured flow of imperial tribute into family coffers, for the family was 'above pecuniary excitement'. James Brooke was born on 29 April 1803 and raised in Benares, India, as the fifth child of Thomas Brooke, an official of the Honourable East India Company and a wealthy High Court judge. Thomas is described in terms such as 'not really clever', 'precise', 'old-fashioned' – probably euphemisms for withering dullness and lack of imagination – but as 'a good talker', meaning that he had been well finished. These qualities may have made him an ideal servant of the law but they contrast rudely with those applied to his swashbuckling son.

Curiously, the two always seem to have got along very well. Thomas Brooke was an affectionate and kindly parent, like the long-suffering father in a Jane Austen novel. If he had a fault it seems to have been that he was simply too indulgent and forbearing. It was a fault that, for most of his life, James would show too. Only at the end would he learn how to be cruel.

Understanding India is important for understanding the Brookes. It was the forge in which they hammered out their ideas of ruler and ruled. India became, to the whole Brooke dynasty, an enduring and terrible example of how *not* to run a country. It was too large, too professional, not based on a loyalty that was purely personal – indeed, they believed that loyalty should be almost familial, and retain the rough-edged feel of the home-made. When it later came to appointing officials in his own private kingdom of Sarawak, James would always show a suspicion of both academic brilliance and bureaucratic regulation. For him a committee was a thing that kept minutes and wasted hours.

A brother, Henry, died young in the army, leaving James sole beneficiary of four sisters. Two of these would also perish early, not in India but in the dangerously pestilential environment that was nineteenth-century England. Both of his surviving sisters would marry into the Church, Emma to the Reverend Charles Johnson, to provide the stuff of future rajahs, while Margaret wed the Reverend Anthony Savage and remained childless.)

Benares must have been an odd place to grow up in. Its principal business has long been death and the large-scale disposal of the bodily remains of the Hindu pious, burned to the purity of ashes and scattered to cosmic dissolution in the murky but holy water of the Ganges. Secrore, the European quarter, was carefully sited upwind of the fat pall of smoke and a brisk carriage ride away from the sites of incineration, but domestic arrangements behind the classical Georgian façades and velvet curtains were necessarily more flexible than those of bourgeois England. India leaked in through a hundred cracks. Thomas Brooke had been married before and, though described officially as a childless widower, he had an illegitimate son, born in 1784, whom he publicly acknowledged. Charles William Brooke was openly raised in the same household as his half-brother, 'little James', 'the sweet baby', and became a lieutenant in the 17th Native Infantry, rising to the final rank of brigadier-general. He would be that rare thing, a brigadier-general killed in action.

As a young man he writes constantly to his father, a typical young man's letters full of the gossip of wars, promotions and his urgent need for parental money. He even extravagantly requests his own elephant – he simply cannot manage without one, he declares – and is sent it promptly, a sure sign of just how doting a father Thomas Brooke could be. Charles William married Charlotte Marshall, and it is fortunate that he found children 'sweet', for he produced ten of them himself and remained on the very best of terms with his young half-siblings. The relations between his own mother and his stepmother are open to question, but he writes guilelessly to the former of 'dear Mrs. Brooke' as he wallows in the typical dreams of home of the exiled Anglo-Indian. 'My prospects are now so good that a few years hence I hope to return to England with a fortune which will render unnecessary my revisiting this country – with what joy shall I give up what are termed "the luxuries of India" for a cottage and a snug fireside. This I am determined to do.'[1] He goes on to fantasise, in the beating Indian heat, of being buried up to his chin in snow. Very English. Very much the sort of thing James would later write from Sarawak. Yet the ethnicity of Charles William is unclear. A codicil of 1835 to Thomas's will left Charles William the sum of £1,000 to provide a pension for a lady called Moher Bibee of Arrah in Bihar; '*Bibby*' was a term often used for a local mistress. In the East India Company, Eurasian faces often lurked behind impeccably British names. And despite all the talk of her brother as being a member of the Bengal Council and his complexion as 'like the inside of a bivalve shell', James's own mother, Anna Maria Stuart, was herself almost certainly illegitimate. Shame at that time lay not in having illegitimate children – such things were passed over lightly – but rather in not doing right by them. Company India was above all an opportunity for origins to be rewritten, a place for the enrichment of younger sons and the rehabilitation of the ambitious who were of doubtful, or – just as bad – regional, origins.

A contemporary description of Anna Maria casts her as

A very shy and retiring woman, not handsome or even pretty . . . for her mouth was rather screwed-up and a little

MRS THOMAS BROOKE – MOTHER OF JAMES BROOKE: BRITISH MUSEUM

underhung, but her complexion was perfectly lovely, and she had soft blue eyes and delicate features . . . Mrs. Brooke was a woman who, as the fashion was in those days, dressed much older for her age than people do now, but she always seemed to have on the best and the most proper thing . . . I never saw her in anything gay or startling. She was like her style of dress, and a very sweet lovable person: one who never raised her voice, nor should I think she had ever uttered an angry word in her life.[2]

James clearly adored her.

It is probably a sign of how deep was James's relationship with his mother that he stayed in India until the relatively late age of twelve before being shipped 'home' to be educated. Normal practice would have been to send him away at half that age. It was decreed that he should divide his time between Reigate, with his grandmother, and Bath, in the boisterous household of his guardian, Charles Kegan, friend of his father. Here he found himself again congenially surrounded by adoring female company, petted and made much of just as at home. But for the rest of the time he had to suffer long bouts of unaccustomed indignity and austerity as a Norwich schoolboy.

For knowledge of this period of James's life we are dependent on Spenser St John, a professional diplomat who was both James's secretary and friend. Often known as 'the Saint', he was a devilish sprite; one of James Brooke's chief claims to be an unusual human being must be that he managed to inspire unquestioning trust in himself and his vision in such a determinedly sceptical and deflating spirit as Spenser St John. St John summed up James's childhood tartly: 'The want of regular training was of infinite disadvantage to young Brooke, who thus started life with little knowledge, and with no idea of self-control'.[3]

Things did not go well at school. James was a boarder at King Edward VI Grammar in Norwich and, while he liked drawing, he was notoriously unattracted by 'gerund-grinding'. Biographers abhor a vacuum and so created unreliable legends of him as unable to tell a lie and recognised as the natural leader of his peers. Like much else in his life story, such tales have a decidedly derivative and second-hand look about them. The truth about James is that his later greatness was not prefigured in any prodigies of childhood and it astonished those who had known him earlier.

It was probably at Norwich that he learned to sail, an accomplishment that would set the course of his later experiences and henceforth come to symbolise for him escape, adventure and freedom. All his life, James would believe that everything would be all right if only he could lay his hands on the right kind of boat. It was during his two years here too that he formed the first of the passionate friendships that would swirl in such deep and powerful currents beneath the official surface of his existence. His friend was a boy named George Western and when, after one holiday, he returned to find that Western had gone to sea, he was devastated and resolved to leave himself. Borrowing money for the stage-coach, James decamped, not as it turned out to 'sea' but to cosy Reigate and his grandmother, where he lurked in the garden until spotted by servants and brought into the house. Thence he was referred back to stern Mr Kegan, and was only saved the burden of much further education by the return of his indulgent parents from India shortly afterwards to take up genteel retirement in Bath. A private tutor was engaged for James, a 'wayward pupil', to torment and terrify.

Brother Henry had served in the Bengal Army, as did Charles William, so it was almost with a sense of the inevitable that in 1819 James Brooke became an ensign in the 6th Native Infantry. He was sixteen years old. By 1821 he had become a lieutenant and then, doubtless through family influence, Sub-Assistant Commissary General , 'a post for which he was totally unfitted'. But there was plenty of time for pig-sticking, shooting, jokes and japes, for which he was most fitted. It was the sort of exuberant, clubby male atmosphere where James always felt most at home and excelled. His superiors noted piously that 'Lieutenants Brooke and Fendall during their attendance at Cawnpore were attentive, and willing. They possess excellent abilities, and will, we hope receive an early impression of the necessity for steadiness and decision.'[4] That hope was not to be fulfilled.

The Honourable East India Company of the time was in full expansion. It was in theory a joint stock company, instituted solely for the pursuance of trade. But trade had led to the need for overseas forts and storehouses, dockyards, towns of native workers and distribution networks. These had to be protected, militarily and legally, and all this had to be paid for by taxation and duty. Little by little, it was dragged unwillingly into the business of colonial administration, and an early version of domino theory assured that possessions were constantly added to protect those already under its sway. Moreover the British government exerted influence through a Board of Control and a well-named Secret Committee, so that the Company's aims could no longer be distinguished from those of Whitehall. In the year of James's birth, almost the whole of India had been successfully brought under its rule with the crushing of the Mahrattas. Company forces had contributed to the routing of Napoleon through campaigns in Mauritius, Réunion and Java, where James's future hero, Stamford Raffles, held the island in its name for five years. And now it was time for a war with Burma, the next obstacle to growth.

James was permitted to duck out of normal duties to raise and organise a body of irregular volunteer cavalry to serve as scouts in the campaign. He had found his niche – a big fish in a small pond, operating on the margins of established order – and this was the kind of position to which he would gravitate all his life. Much later he would relate with relish a story that, at a demonstration of their abilities to his superiors, he ordered the new forces to charge, which they did, but they forgot to come back and were never seen again. He liked to order them to charge a lot; indeed one wonders if they ever practised anything else *but* charging.

James Brooke first saw action against the Burmese in January 1825 in Rungpore, Assam. After 'a few inspiriting words', he charged. Even his greatest detractors have never been able to question his physical courage at this point in his life. The Burmese, in their well-defended and superior position, were astonished. They fled, and James was mentioned for conspicuous gallantry in dispatches. Soon after, he met the Burmese Army again.

A few days after, the general in command heard of a strong
stockade being in front, and sent out Lieutenant Brooke to
reconnoitre, but he was not able to return in time to prevent
the advance-guard from falling into an ambuscade. As the
foremost company turned a corner in the road, they were
received by a volley which knocked over a number of men.
In the midst of the confusion, Brooke came galloping up,
and putting himself at the head of the men, charged and
'foremost, fighting, fell.' When the affair was over, and the
enemy driven from their stockades, Lieutenant-Colonel
Richards asked after Lieutenant Brooke, whom he had seen
fall, and he was reported dead. 'Take me to his body,' was his
reply, and they rode to the spot. 'Poor Brooke!' said the
Colonel, getting off his horse to have a last look at him; and
kneeling over him he took his hand. 'He is not dead!' he
cried, and instantly had him removed to camp.[5]

His active military career had lasted some two days; his convalescence would last five years.

It might seem unnecessary to spend as much time poring over his
medical file as scholars have, but there are two versions of James's
injuries, and the version chosen casts a slant over the whole of the
rest of James Brooke's life. The first has him wounded in his passionate parts, neatly explaining his lack of sexual interest in women,
his failure to marry and produce an heir, his chaste 'romance' with
the heiress Angela Burdett-Coutts, and provides an instant refuta-
tion of any suggestion of unconventional sexual tastes. Since all this
follows from an honourable and tragic wound on the field of battle,
early biographers passed rapidly over it with averted eyes and a
little tutting over the missed opportunity for the love of a good
woman. The other version has him shot in the lung, the slug not
removed until he arrived back in England, where it was proudly preserved by his mother in a glass case on the mantelpiece. It is
supported by anecdotal evidence from the family, some of the
sources now lost, and by Spenser St John. Most of all it is supported
by James Brooke's own later recognition of an illegitimate son,

whom he claimed to have fathered well after this incident – though this remained a family secret until the 1950s.

The two explanations cross in the vexed question of James's sexuality, which it is premature to discuss in depth at this point. But, to anticipate, if he was physically normal why was he not romantically involved? He had charm and wealth. Soon he would be a Byronic national hero. So he was not short of the standard aphrodisiac ingredients to stir the hearts of female admirers, but he was simply not interested. As family friend Kegan Paul put it with some astonishment, 'He was one of those men who are able to be the close and intimate friends of women without a tinge of love-making.'[6] For earlier biographers it was unthinkable that a hero of the British Empire could be homosexual, a skeleton to keep firmly in the imperial closet, so the issue has been demurely fudged and even recently 'latency' has been deployed like gauze over the lens to avoid focused discussion. It was even seriously suggested in 1960 that the choice of Sir Steven Runciman to compile an official history of Sarawak, including a life of James Brooke (*The White Rajahs*), was compromised by the writer's own alleged homosexuality. Not only was James Brooke to be above reproach, so were his biographers.

Yet it remains one of the tenets of the contemporary West that sexuality is at the heart of identity, so if James was homosexual we would wish to know it. But *if* he was, what were his motives in claiming to have fathered an illegitimate son and what was really going on offstage in the backrooms of his life? These are the reasons that James Brooke's wound has so fascinated enquirers, albeit with a great deal of manly throat-clearing and evasion. Yet in a sense the interest is misplaced, for these are not either/or questions, nor can we blandly imagine, as an earlier age might, that the physical state of his loins directly determined that of his heart or his head. James Brooke could easily have been impotent yet heterosexually attracted. He could have been both homosexual and impotent through injury. He could have been homosexual and the physical father of a son. Yet other combinations are possible that belie the confidence of the simple generalisations. The question of James Brooke's wound is, after all, something of a blind alley if we want to use it as a route to know the man. The real question is that of love. Did he fall in love? Who with? And what was the nature of that love?

Many years later, in the 1920s and 30s, when the Brooke raj was firmly established, the Ranee, wife of Rajah Vyner – third, last and least of the rajahs of Sarawak – was a writer, permanently short of cash like all the Brookes, and a society flapper, if not indeed an out-and-out slapper. As a source of money, Sylvia Brooke wrote her life story, but lived so long that she was reduced to writing it again . . . and again, so that – to add novelty – each version had to be made slightly more scandalous than the last. In the final version, *Queen of the Headhunters* (1970), she reveals how she determined to write a treatment of the life of James Brooke for the motion pictures, of which she was an ardent fan. In her honour, her husband had constructed Kuching's first cinema, the Sylvia, and opened it sensationally with a showing of *King Kong*.

Sylvia wrote a synopsis of the life of James Brooke as *The Great White Rajah* and sold it to Warner Brothers. She was called to Hollywood. Arriving at the Beverly Hills Hotel, she found a large script personally rewritten from her draft by Errol Flynn and entitled *The White Rajah*.

> Flynn had turned my synopsis into a ridiculous story about a girl who dressed up as a boy and followed James Brooke through the jungles of Sarawak . . . The thing was an absurdity, and I wrote and told Warner Bros. so. They must have passed my letter on to Errol Flynn, because a few days later, I had a letter asking me to dinner.
>
> This was an evening I shall never forget . . . suddenly the staircase became brilliantly floodlit. On it there appeared Errol Flynn himself in a pair of white close-fitting trousers that showed every nerve and muscle of his body. Slowly and gracefully he descended, giving me plenty of time to appreciate his entrance – and him. He flashed a smile at me that would have sent a thousand fans into hysterics and then he started to make me a drink. The lights slowly dimmed

and I could only just see him across the room. We had no time for conversation before the lights blazed on again, to herald the arrival of Lillie Damita. She also wore white; a gorgeous creature holding an enormous Persian cat in her arms. She greeted me briefly, and proceeded to lie on the floor and play with the cat. It was the most sensual and feline exhibition I have ever seen.

After these preliminaries, we went in to dinner and I at last had a chance to ask him why on earth he had written such a fantastic story around James Brooke . . . He said that he had always imagined that the First White Rajah was like him – and I agreed that he was perfect for the part. I then asked him if he was aware of the fact that James Brooke had been severely wounded in India, and deprived of his manhood. That he had once become engaged to a girl who had thrown him over when he told her that they could never have any children. By this time, Flynn was frowning furiously.

'Another thing,' I said; 'James Brooke was the first white man ever to set foot in Sarawak. Do you think for one moment that the primitive and savage Dayaks would have allowed an English girl to follow him through the jungle? They would have taken her head and smoked it, and there would have been an end of your story.'

He took my criticism with a laugh and a shrug of his shoulders. 'You cannot have a motion picture without love,' he said.

'And you cannot have James Brooke with it,' I replied.[7]

Love (or its absence) was central to the concerns of Somerset Maugham who confirmed the general view of James's love life when he visited the senior Sarawak government officer, A. B. Ward, on a tour east of Suez.

Mr. Somerset Maugham, the author and playwright, also came on a visit [to Sarawak]. He was said to be looking for 'copy.' He certainly found it in a manner he had not bargained for.

Whilst returning from a trip to Simanggang [Sri Aman], by some inexplicable mischance the policeman in charge of his boat failed to take shelter from the approaching tide, and in about the most dangerous part of the river, they ran into the bore, a roaring wave at least eight feet high.

The boat was instantly overwhelmed, and the occupants precipitated into the water. For nearly half an hour Somerset Maugham and the rest were whirled along with the tide, tossed and buffeted by the surging water, desperately clinging to the boat which turned over and over with the action of the current. At last, helped by some of the crew, Maugham managed to reach the bank utterly exhausted. Dyaks took the shipwrecked party into their house, revived them with drink and provided them with sarongs.

Luckily all escaped injury, but English literature nearly lost one of its most brilliant writers that day. In conversation with Somerset Maugham I suggested that the history of Sir James Brooke would make a good film story. He said no; there was no love interest in the first Rajah's life.[8]

In fact, nothing could be further from the truth. The life of James Brooke was full of love, concrete and abstract, general and particular. He inspired love. He felt love. It entered into many of the crucial decisions he had to make. Love in its many forms will occupy us a lot in trying to piece together his life.

Whatever its nature, the wound festered in James Brooke's body as it has in the minds of scholars ever since. In 1825 he rejoined his parents in Bath. The most reliable version of events has the slug cut out through his back. Abscesses formed and so, in an age before antibiotics, the wound was kept open for a year by regular 'probing'. The agony must have been indescribable. Powerful opiates were prescribed. He was awarded a pension of £70 a year for life by the Company, apparently written off as an invalid at twenty-two.

His recovery was slow, relying on the devoted nursing of his family, especially that of his father. Later, like so much else in the empire, it would be attributed to the almost magically beneficial effects of an ice-cold bath every morning. How he spent his time is unclear, but from his later writings he must have started reading about the east and especially, perhaps, the work of Stamford Raffles, notably *The History of Java*. Raffles appealed as the enlightened and affectionate ruler of an island whose inhabitants he admired and whose well-being he saw as the only justification for empire. It is not clear whether the two ever met. Raffles repeatedly visited Company headquarters in Calcutta during James's childhood, but no legend of their coming together exists. Either way, he would be the blueprint for James's own rule; indeed, there would be an air of 'following Raffles by numbers' about the early years.

But life was not all reading. Attempting to return to duty in India in 1829, James was shipwrecked off the Isle of Wight and suffered a relapse. His leave was extended by six months, but employees of the Company were forbidden to be absent from their posts for more than five years. He had to return by 30 July 1830 or forfeit his commission. First the weather conspired against him. Storms lashed the coast, preventing the departure of his ship, the *Castle Huntley*, until March. Then it was becalmed, arriving in Madras on 18 July, leaving only twelve days to reach Calcutta. But no ship was available. It simply could not be done. He applied for temporary employment with the Company in Madras as a way of getting around the regulations, but was refused. Unknown to him, his father was pulling strings with the directors in London and had persuaded them to allow a loose interpretation of the rule. But it was too late. Piqued and petulant, James had already resigned his commission in India rather than wait to be dismissed.

His ever-dutiful father petitioned the Company again and it was agreed that the decision could be reviewed. But James never bothered to take this up, and he never expressed the least regret over this business of the botched absence note. 'I toss my cap into the air and my commission into the sea,' he wrote happily, 'and bid farewell to John Company and all his evil ways.'[9] Like many a man before and since, he cordially detested his employer and was glad to have an excuse to go. 'I am like a horse that has got a heavy clog off his neck . . . Here goes a puff of my cigar, and with it I blow the Company to the devil or anywhere else so they trouble me no further!'[10] Perhaps he had ingested this anti-Company feeling, like so much else, from Stamford Raffles, himself betrayed and persecuted by small-minded Company officials. Anyway, he had other reasons to stay aboard the *Castle Huntley*. Captain Marryat, who knew him later in Sarawak, wrote in hushed tones, 'If the private history which induced him to quit the service, and afterwards expatriate himself, could with propriety, and also with regard to Mr. Brooke's feelings, be made known, it would redound still more to his honour and his high principle; but these I have no right to make public.'[11] Sadly, he gives no clue of what this 'private history' might be.

James now gleefully set off on a jolly cruise to the Far East. He was young, newly restored to health – in fact back from the dead – financially secure and, Somerset Maugham's later views notwithstanding, perhaps a little . . . in love?

Chapter 2

The East

Hitherto we have known a deal about what James Brooke did and the milieu he moved in, but his own thoughts and views have been lacking. It is at this point, at the beginning of one of the longest 'gap years' in history, that he gains a voice of his own, for he became a prolific letter writer and journal keeper. Henceforth we are deluged with his words, and the sudden explosion of documentation reflects that strange sense of his contemporaries that James Brooke the man was so little prefigured in James Brooke the boy. The new James, indeed, had opinions on just about everything and felt moved to share them with just about everyone. The shyness of his youth melted away before this new public persona and increasingly in these letters and journals he now wrote in the declamatory and opinionated language of the election address. The journals especially, as published later by Henry Keppel and Rodney Mundy and drawn on by early biographers Gertrude le Jacob and Spenser St John, are revealing. We should not think of them as simply a dumping ground for the public person's subjectivity and the secret location of his sense of privacy. They are much more than that, and constitute a sort of deliberate mirror in which he can posture and dramatise himself Byronically, as a passionate creature of delicate scruple. Their later partial publication argues that he always saw them as such, as does their style, steeped in public self-consciousness. They are full of ringing phrases and fervent declarations of principle.

The journey took him from Madras to Penang, to Malacca, to Singapore, to Canton, and everywhere James Brooke looked and larked and opined how bad it all was. It would be spring 1831 before he rejoined his family in Bath, whence came not one word of paternal reproach. In Madras, the Europeans are scorned as 'provincials', while 'The natives are despicable, and here, as at every other place I have seen, have been corrupted by their intercourse with Europeans. They lose their particular virtues arising from their habits and their religion, and become tainted with the vices of those around them . . . No rational Englishman can observe the deterioration of the native character arising from their intercourse with the whites, without a blush.'[1] The notion that locals must be protected from Europeans would become part of Sarawak thinking.

On the Company island of Penang he visited the water-powered Chinese bakery, one of the great sights of the place, and found it 'rude and clumsy'. The island should be developed by European settlers, he decided, or if not by land grants to natives. Once again it was the short-sightedness of the Company that was at fault. 'It appears to me pretty certain that territorial possessions of the East India Company are considered as second to their China trade – the revenues of India are confused with the accounts of tea, the resources of India are not fully developed, or at any rate are imperfectly known, the grasp of monopoly stunts improvement, and the exigencies of war and the necessities of peace are readily defrayed from the profits of commerce . . .'[2]

In Singapore, the island colony founded by Raffles, he looked for evidence to bolster the stance of disliking the Chinese that he had assumed from the literature.

They are the first race of people I ever met with whose appearance positively displeased me. Their habits are the most filthy, their faces the most ugly and their figures the most ungraceful of any people under the sun. They appear cut out of a log of wood by the hand of some unskilful savage. Their mouths are wide, their noses snub, their eyes small and set crooked in their heads. When they move they swing arms, legs and body like a paper clown pulled by a string; and to sum up, all their colour is a dirty yellow, nearly the colour of a Hindostani corpse. Yet with all these drawbacks, they are industrious and good tempered, cheerful and obliging.[3]

In short, the world afforded him ample grounds for a growing sense of his own superiority, further bolstered in Canton, where the resident British traders were confined to their factory (trading station) by those 'ignorant and presumptuous barbarians' – the Chinese. Again, the supine Company was to blame. 'The maxim seems to have been to pick up any crumbs the Emperor may bestow, and bear kicks, insults and degradation to any extent he may command. What indeed is national honour, or national independence when compared to tea?'[4] A jape involved himself and shipmates disguising themselves as Chinese at the Feast of Lanterns, in order to penetrate the city, declared out of bounds to Europeans. 'Being once in, the whole party threw off disguise and broke some of the lanterns, which were accounted precious. They barely escaped with their lives, and how escape was possible is the marvel.'[5] James would always have a high tolerance for such japes.

It was in Canton that James fell ill with a bad attack of influenza and was nursed by John Cruikshank, the Scottish surgeon of the *Castle Huntley*. They would become affectionate friends for life. The matter has been minutely studied by Dr J. Walker in the *Borneo Research Bulletin*. Post-modernly attuned to the hidden discourse of sexuality and empire, he has devoted a good deal of effort to spotting, between the lines, James Brooke's 'boyfriends', yet the results are sometimes questionable. Attraction is not seduction, nor is seduction love. To equate them is to reduce the rich, polyphonic music of James's emotional life to a single note.

There may well have been sexual attraction on James's part –

later evidence shows he was sensitive to male beauty – but this was no mere passing relationship of the flesh rather a deep and loving friendship. John Cruikshank named one of his sons 'James Brooke' and after his father's death the boy went, at the age of fifteen, to serve in Sarawak where, to avoid confusion, he was known as 'Fitz'. Another, hopelessly alcoholic, son briefly had a job fixed for him as Government Medical Officer in 1860. There is no suggestion whatever in this long relationship of untoward seaborne yo-heave-hoing or jolly rogering. This was an attachment that hailed from a heady mix of mutual youthful exuberance, sudden freedom and the solidarity of shipmates abroad in the world. It certainly matured into something akin to love, but there is no good reason to assume that this required physical expression.

Then there was young James Templer, the mate, succeeded by his younger brother John. John's wife wrote later:

> My husband's older brother James was mate in the *Castle Huntley*. Brooke took an enormous fancy to him, and during a period of four or five years spent a great deal of the time he was in England at my father-in-law's house at Bridport, where a room was always called 'Brooke's room.' Here he made the first acquaintance with my husband, and they soon became great friends, the younger man worshipping in Brooke all the grace, romance, talent and sentiment too, as being so especially attractive at that period of his life . . . On James [Templer] giving up the East India Company's service and going to Australia the friendship with John was intensified, and one may almost say transferred, although Brooke always maintained that he had never met so delightful a companion as James.[6]

When he came to write his biography of James Brooke, Spenser St John remarked, 'One judicious friend had advised me to say nothing disagreeable about [John] Templer and the young Rajah: I would carry out that wish as far as possible,'[7] since, as he stated some time before, he had no wish to reveal 'the Rajah's *own* private life'. The whole *Huntley* period is strongly marked by a strange – almost Californian – touchy-feeliness that is indeed suggestive of more than 'much merriment and vast foolery'. But it was clearly a golden time of liberty and optimism that the band of young ship-mates would never forget, an innocent time free of responsibilities when they made their friends for life, a time of endless undergraduate conversations, when they knew exactly how to set the world to rights, the time perhaps that James had in mind when – a broken and bitter old man – he wrote poignantly 'that the young hope more than they fear, and that the old fear more than they hope . . .'[8]

We are perhaps too used to the sanctimonious tone of the Victorians as the clear sign of high-Gothic hypocrisy, and over-eager to translate every high-blown expression of esteem into a mere mask for the furtive snap of elastic. Going to bed together is far from the only 'disagreeable' matter that can occur between two men. In later years James and John Templer had a dramatic and certainly disagreeable falling-out over the state of James's mind that led to a total rupture of relations. And let us not pretend that we can easily read the discourse of Victorian sexuality, which is a language very different from our own. Two basic signposts show us that we are moving in an alien erotic and moral landscape that would fundamentally affect James Brooke's affections and actions in a way it is hard for us to imagine. The first is that boys at that time were regarded as sexually mature and could legally marry at fourteen (girls at twelve). The second is that sodomy was both an unquestionable sin and a capital offence.[9] There were regular moral frenzies against the crime, and something like 80 per cent of those convicted were actually hanged (unlike other capital offences, where the figure was a mere 12 per cent).

But, outside the main group of friends, were there other entanglements of other kinds with a more clearly homoerotic backwash? Perhaps, with the benefit of evidence from his later years, there were. For example, in 1831 James wrote to Cruikshank rather ruefully of a younger crew member called Stonhouse:

I cannot help having some hope that Stonhouse may value my acquaintance a little more than I give him credit for; but the real truth is, I have been too complying with his slightest wish, and have shown him too many weaknesses in my character for him to respect me much. Now, you will say, I write as if I were sore, and it is true; but the same feelings that make me so would also make me very ready to acquit S. of all intention to hurt me, for you know how well I liked the boy. I expect nothing from men, however; but if they will give me their affection or show me kindness I am doubly pleased.[10]

James spent several days before his death burning papers, but a problem of quite another order is that his closest circle of friends have clustered round and carefully censored even the remaining material, so that while the truth about his love life clearly lies beyond the evidence as we have it, it is impossible to know with absolute certainty what that truth was. They were evidently sensitive about it. When Spenser St John – after all a lifelong friend – took his final leave, the scene was described as follows. 'I ran down to Torquay, once more before leaving, and in the beginning of April 1867 I saw him, and as I leant over him I felt it was for the last time. As I neared the door he called me back and I saw the tears falling and then I could see how he also felt that it was one last adieu.'[11] But deliberately excised from the published version of this passage as 'too sensational and Nelsonic' and 'contrary to British taste' are two chaste kisses.

There are, of course, many kinds of love, sentimental, physical, blatantly sexual, and James Brooke seems to have been an emotional man capable of them all. Yet erotic love seems to have required a seed of compassion around which to crystallise and in which to hide itself. For him, pity does not lead to a purgation of eroticism into pure sentiment – quite the reverse: it stokes the fires of desire into what may be termed 'compassionate lust'. Sometimes, the balance comes down on one element in the pairing and sometimes the other. While his correspondence with Cruikshank and the

Templers does *not* suggest a physical relationship but something compounded of large amounts of mutual affection and respect that is increasingly rooted in nostalgia for lost youth, indications from his later life, involving not his equals and co-evals but very much younger, poorer, more vulnerable boys, are a different matter. These will be considered in due course but the cumulative evidence is that, where they were concerned, James Brooke was a skilled dissimulator, hiding the sensual in purely avuncular benevolence. St John remarked smoothly, 'He would often endeavour to defend his system and argue that boys should not be thwarted; and certainly he carried his system into practice with all the lads that came under his control, and certainly also with very markedly bad results.'[12] We shall see how badly later. Thus perhaps of significance is another passage in that letter to Cruikshank about the Penang pool. 'Let me hear from you from the old ship,' it ends. 'Present my affectionate remembrance to her. Tell me how she looks and feels and what sort of folk are aboard. I pity you the job of carving in the cuddy and saying pretty things to the ladies. Take care of the "mids" [midshipmen] and be kind to them, as you always were, for you know the "mids" of the *Huntley* are under my especial care.'[13]

Chapter 3

The Schooner

I dreamed that honours decked my head,
I dreamed of conquest hardly won.
Welcome to me the gory bed
If bright and brief the course I run.

What peril that I would not court,
What danger that I would not brave,
A Child of Fortune's wildest sport
To grasp at power and find – a grave.

How, step by step, I could not creep
While tytled fools, at will, ascend,
Better to sink in one great leap
Than struggling live for such an end.

But vain the wish I might procure
A place in rank, a star decked breast,
Obscurity I can endure
Better than share among the rest.

In vain my ardent soul aspires,
In vain my spirit strives to soar,
Till sickened hope herself expires
And one by one those dreams are o'er.

Then thus the sparkling bowl I drain,
Thus, thus defy the will of Fate,
Tho' all my fondest hopes are vain
I'll dream at least I shall be great.[1]

Thus James Brooke, poet, in the early 1830s, back from near death, back from the east and trapped in 'the whirl of renewed affections' in Bath, but dreaming romantically of greatness elsewhere. 'I have dined out two or three times, but I feel the irksomeness of civilized society greater than ever, and its bonds shall not hold me long. My own family speak to me of the years we are to pass together, and that it always makes me sad to think that in my inmost heart I have determined to plunge into some adventure that will bestow activity and employment. I have thought much of "the schooner."'[2]

'The schooner' is the shorthand name for a vivid daydream he has hatched with his old friends of the *Castle Huntley*. He will learn navigation. They will sail away together under his leadership to adventure, battle, wealth, distinction, an all-boys' adventure writ large upon the real world. Meanwhile he moped at home, raging at 'The growing, desperate, damned restraint – the consciousness of possessing energies and character, and the hopelessness of having "a fair field and no favour" to employ them on . . . If I say that I fret or fume, the fools turn on me and say, "You have fine clothes and fine linen, and a soft bed and a good dinner;" as if life consisted in dangling at a woman's petticoat and fiddling and dancing.'[3]

He shows all the signs of frustration: drinking too much, smoking too much. Despite his pampered condition, he feels himself one of the oppressed of this earth, with a horrible sense of time drifting away, and sees, staring him full in the face, 'a youth of folly and an age of cards'. He is afflicted by a sense of his own unappreciated

greatness and, like many who puzzle that their abilities are so
strangely unrecognised, turns to politics, writing a pamphlet in support of Reform. Then another pamphlet, 'A Justification of the
Foreign Policy of Great Britain Towards Holland'. He will stand for
Parliament – but he lacks the money. He and Cruikshank will go
whaling in Greenland. Wait, no. He will run off to Australia with
Kennedy of the *Castle Huntley* and become a farmer. After all, he
has read some botany books. 'My schemes may be *wildish*, but not
quite visionary.'

The old crew visited each other, caroused and reminisced –
Cruikshank, Kennedy, sulky Stonhouse, Wright – in Scotland,
Bath, Ireland. He will go to the Azores. No, better – up the
Amazon. He will go to war against Holland. If only he had a ship.

His father was increasingly unwell and James became relentless
in his wearisome nagging for a vessel. Finally Mrs Brooke threw herself into the family disagreement, taking the part of her son.
Thomas, who had already had to buy one son an elephant, caved in
at once and bought James a ship and merchandise. So in early 1834
James proudly wrote to Cruikshank, 'I have a vessel afloat, and
nearly ready for sea – a rakish slaver brig, 290 tons burden – one
that would fight or fly as occasion required, and made to pay her
expenses. The Indian Archipelago, the north-east coast of China,
Japan, New Guinea and the Pacific is the unlimited sphere of our
adventure.'[4] Long-suffering Thomas had not given way without
some barbed and sniffy remarks:

> Supposing gain by traffic to be one of your objects, I
> conclude you will agree with me, that about trade you are
> quite ignorant, and that there is no pursuit for which you
> are less suited. Is it the intention to plunge into the
> China mania? This is not trade; it is mere speculation;
> and, after all, are not traders for the greater part a tribe of
> smugglers? The speculation has so little of the mercantile
> character, and is so much like a gambling concern, that I
> know not whether a preference is not to be given to a
> gaming-table.[5]

But there were other reasons to concede the ship. Love had intervened again in the life of James Brooke, and it was love that moved the family to action.

> About this time, he passed through that ordeal which
> punishes most men – he fell in love and became engaged.
> What were the causes which induced the lady or her family
> to break off the engagement I do not know, but it was
> broken off, and Mr. Brooke appeared to look on it as final;
> and from that time he seems to have withdrawn from all
> female blandishments. He never spoke of it to us, though an
> occasional allusion made us think that his thoughts often
> reverted to this episode in his history. I notice in one letter
> it is stated that this lady, whose name is given, died shortly
> afterwards.[6]

That letter does not survive. Jacob gives a more Mills & Boonish version:

> In or about this year, 1833, it seemed as if Brooke's whole
> nature might be charmed into the willing loss of an
> adventurous future, for he became warmly attached to a lady,
> the daughter of a Bath clergyman. She had been at school
> with his sister Margaret, and these two, as girls, had felt
> drawn to each other. It would seem that she returned
> Brooke's affection, and that an engagement followed, but
> that, in consequence of the families on both sides seeing
> grounds for objection, she felt it right to break it off, and
> Brooke appears from this time to have taken ambition as his
> only bride.[7]

We cannot but speculate on what these 'grounds' might be and how they tie up with Marryat's 'private history' (see p. 18 above). Jacob suggests they may involve Brooke's growing unitarianist doubts on the dogma of the Trinity. A modern mind would – more crudely but not necessarily more accurately – suspect them to lie in his enthusiasm for midshipmen. Strangely, there is another explanation. In 1858, James Brooke publicly acknowledged an illegitimate son. Recent revisionist students have supposed the mother to be a housemaid, adding class exploitation to colonial outrage in the catalogue of Brooke crimes, though there seems to be no clear reason to think she was not the clergyman's daughter of this early romance. From the age and date of death of this young man, as recorded on his gravestone in Plumtree graveyard, Nottingham, he must have been born in 1834, possibly conceived in 1833, the year of the breaking-off of the engagement. So perhaps we do not have to look too far for the cause of Thomas Brooke's sudden change of heart on the question of the schooner plan. After all, he had the oldest reason in the world to get the boy out of town fast.

Thomas was right about his son's nautical and mercantile skills: the trip was a disaster. In James's life, 'trade' was always just the excuse for indulging his thirst for adventure. Kennedy and Wright from the *Castle Huntley* fought endlessly on the way out. James, it seemed, interfered constantly in matters of discipline. Finally, the ship and cargo, become wearisome, were sold at a heavy loss in Macao and James returned to England. But again, if there was family recrimination it went unrecorded. At the end of 1835, Thomas Brooke died and left the children £30,000 apiece, despite the understanding that James's schooner was a deductible anticipation of his inheritance. With his pension and other assets James was now in a position to live in gentlemanly ease for the rest of his life.

But the money was burning a hole in his pocket. Within three months he had bought a real schooner, the 142-ton *Royalist*. The previous fiasco was now reckoned useful training, and this time his preparations were more considered. Over the next two years he studied charts and read books, notably Raffles on the Malay archipelago and George Windsor Earle on Borneo. He undertook shorter cruises, to break in the crew and the vessel. The problem with the previous voyage, he now saw, had been not his own interference but the opposition to it from others. Henceforth he would always demand to be master of his own vessel and any questioning of his authority would be counted disloyalty. Before he sailed again to the east he wrote his letter of farewell to Cruikshank:

> For my temperament and mode of thinking, there is nothing which makes prolonged life desirable, and, I would fain be doing something to add to the amount of happiness, especially in the way of life suited to my wild habits, wild education and ardent love for an undue degree of personal freedom . . . Could I carry my vessel to places where the keel of European ship never before ploughed the waters – could I plant my foot where white man's foot never before had been – could I gaze upon scenes which educated eyes never have looked on – see man in the rudest state of nature – I should be content without looking for further reward. I can, indeed, say truly that I have no object of personal ambition, no craving for personal reward: these things sometimes flow attendant on worthy deeds or bold enterprises, but they are at best but consequences, not principal objects.[8]

So it was the love of adventure, the urge for distinction and a vague sense of social duty that drove him on. But duty is in the eye of the beholder. Towards the end of his life, he described it more dramatically: 'I was twenty years younger, and forty years lighter of heart when I left England for the shores of Borneo. I had some fortune, more ambition and no outlet for it. There are thousands and thousands of our countrymen whose hearts like mine are higher than their positions.'[9]

Enormous self-confidence was an essential part of his mission, for James Brooke took himself seriously. He published a prospectus to his trip in the *Athenaeum*, speaking of resisting Dutch influence in Borneo, reasserting British claims to Marudu in the north, and the founding of colonies, as though this young tourist were creating, in fevered imagination, a whole new British imperial policy in the east. Trade was fine, he concluded, but it was better for trade to follow unforced from colonial possession than the other way round. Looking for a justification for British interference in terms of 'tender philanthropy', he homed in on the existence of slavery and paganism in the east. 'Not a single voice is upraised to relieve the darkness of Paganism, and the horrors of the eastern slave-trade.' He did not yet know about headhunting, whose eradication would later replace slavery as chief argument for the civilising nature of his mission. Once he was actually established in the east, the abolition of domestic slavery would be politically too hot to handle and he would leave it severely alone.

The British government yawned complacently, but Dutch agents pricked up their ears. To them this sounded like that terrible man Stamford Raffles come back to life. According to the article, the final goal of this mass of geopolitical bar-room speculation was to be a private gentleman's voyage of exploration and the collection of natural history. Yet the whole subsequent train of events in Sarawak is there to be read in advance, and messianic tones already shine through his discussion of the possibility of founding a settlement at Marudu and spreading 'inferior posts over the Archipelago'.

James also had views about the treatment of his crew. In an age where naval discipline was notoriously brutal, he preached kindness. He later summed up his views on discipline as follows: 'It was necessary to form *men* to my purpose and, by a line of steady and kind conduct, to raise up a personal regard for myself and an attachment for the vessel . . .'[10] This too would be Sarawak policy. As a young man, James was never unkind where it could be avoided.

Kennedy and Wright of the *Castle Huntley* were aboard, a token that this was finally the realisation of the 'schooner' dream, but again it all turned sour. The voyage as far as Singapore took some five months, full of squabbles and bouts of seamanly drunkenness and petulance. James's journal reads like the script of a soap opera, scored with stories of the crew's wearying personal animosities.

The two men were not suited to pull together. The Captain's system of discipline irritated the men almost to mutiny and Brooke had many worries, small and great, disappointments

and disagreements, that culminated at last in an open
quarrel . . . James wrote to Cruikshank: 'The story you want
is a long one, and coming from one of the parties involved
must be partial, but I can say that I do not think on the
whole that the blame of any disagreement rests on me.'[11]

After nine weeks in Singapore, they signed on some new crew,
including eight sea gypsies, a Danish doctor and a half-Malay interpreter. On 27 July 1839, they set sail for Sarawak.

Chapter 4

First Impressions

Borneo did not loom large in the British imagination at the start of the nineteenth century, having somewhat declined from its early position as candidate for the earthly site of El Dorado. There had been previous attempts to establish a presence in the huge ridge-backed island of green forests and brown rivers, but they had all faded dankly away and been engulfed by the endless mists and swamps. One Signor Pigafetta touched on Brunei in the north of the island in 1521 during Magellan's circumnavigation of the globe but the tardy British did not arrive until the end of the seventeenth century. In 1773 the East India Company had founded a settlement at Marudu, following their dramatic rescue of the Sultan of Sulu (Philippines) from a Spanish kidnapping, and this was the claim that James Brooke toyed with reanimating. A further vacillating British presence had flickered indecisively at Banjermassin to the south, generating the usual mixture of wars, corruption, debt and disappointment, while under Raffles the languidly uxorious and eccentric Alexander Hare had run a plantation with scandalous use of convict labour supplied from Java, before being evicted by the Dutch. What Borneo was known for was piracy, as James would find to his eternal cost. Local vessels being excluded from legitimate trade by Portuguese, then Dutch, monopolies, their crews had turned to the obvious alternative. Annual visits, using the monsoon wind, by Illanun marauders from the Philippines supplemented local efforts. During his rule of Java (1811–16), Raffles had mounted raids on the pirates of Borneo, but it was a credo of long standing among the English that the only real weapon against piracy was freedom of trade, and they were probably right.

The northern half of Borneo was nominally under the rule of the Sultan of Brunei, though the Sultan of Sulu claimed Marudu as his own, and the rest of Borneo was under Dutch hegemony – but then the Dutch had sought to construct flimsy paper claims to the entire Malay archipelago in order to exclude outsiders. They still regarded Singapore as rightfully theirs, so they were especially suspicious of British intentions. After all, under Raffles the British had blandly walked into all the Dutch possessions and simply taken over, to prevent them falling into Napoleonic hands. Should they care to, they had the military power to do so again at any time.

Rule, anyway, did not amount to very much, since authority was fragmented between the different rivers and their hinterlands as these were the only routes of communication. The typical pattern was to command the mouth of a river and so its trade – or rather the raids on the upriver inhabitants. In the devastated feudal economy, the best business to be in was simply taking money off others by violence. In the coastal towns, administration was largely in the hands of Malays, while commerce was split between Chinese entrepreneurs and an old Malay merchant class. Inland, the 'Dayaks', whom later ethnographers would shatter into a dozen distinct local peoples, were regarded more as a natural resource than a body of citizens. They lived by farming, collecting forest produce and warfare, and heeded or ignored the greater administration as they thought fit. The important distinction for James Brooke was that between warlike Sea Dayaks – to be broken – and pacific Hill Dayaks – to be protected. The royal house of Brunei, in the city known as Borneo Proper, divided its time equably between the traditional demands of fornication, murdering its relatives and Islamic piety. A ruler depended on male kinsmen for his power, yet on his

Rajah Muda Hassim, Governor of Sarawak: British Museum

death the throne often passed to the senior of these, cutting out his own son, so that the art of succession to Brunei kingship depended on choosing exactly the right moment to slit the throats of one's brothers and nephews, i.e. when they ceased to be valuable supporters and became rivals. Within the royal house, discussions of kinship rapidly become unintelligible because of multiple in-marriage, but when James Brooke arrived the Sultan was Omar Ali Saif Udin, allegedly semi-imbecile and blessed with supplementary thumbs, nephew of the former incumbent who had been known as Api – Fire – on account of his incendiarist propensities.

Api's brother, Rajah Muda Hassim, both uncle and cousin of the new sultan, had been appointed Regent and was known as a mild, indecisive and highly agreeable person. It was him that James Brooke had come to see. Since the British were familiar with the term '*rajah*', they assumed his name was Muda Hassim and called him such. *Rajah Muda*, however, 'Young Rajah', is a self-contained title for the heir presumptive, something like Crown Prince, just as *Rajah Tua*, 'Old Rajah', was the title for a ruler who had handed over power to a successor. In later years, the precise meaning of these terms would come to haunt James Brooke. Since the Malays were very polite and did not want to embarrass this foreign visitor who thought he spoke some Malay, it was years before they told the British what their correct names were.

They arrived in Sarawak on 15 August 1839 and began a series of gun salutes that showed both their peaceful intentions and the size of their ordnance. Strengthened by breakfast, they were received in the audience hall that was little more than a shed on poles, open to one side and hung with cloth. It was very much a building in the Brunei style. The Brooke party was placed on the left and the local party of Hassim, twelve of his brothers, the governor, Makota, and local Malays on the right. Bruneians wore silk, Malays velvet. Seats were offered and the reception began.

The dress of Muda Hassim was simple, but of rich material, and most of the principal men were well, and even superbly, dressed. His countenance is plain but intelligent and highly pleasing, and his manners perfectly elegant and easy. His reception was kind, and, I am given to understand, highly flattering. We sat, however, trammelled with the formality of state, and our conversation did not extend beyond kind enquiries and professions of friendship. We were presented with tobacco, rolled up in a leaf, each about a foot long, and tea was served by attendants on their knees. A band played wild and not unmusical airs during the interview, and the crowd of attendants who surrounded us were seated around in respectful silence. After a visit of half an hour, we rose and took our leave.[1]

James was pleased. It had gone well.

He had not come empty-handed. The *Royalist* was stuffed with presents: gaudy silks of Surat, scarlet cloth, stamped velvet, gunpowder, a large quantity of confectionery – sweets, preserved ginger, jams, dates, syrups – and, a final afterthought, a huge box of Chinese toys for the children.

Rajah Muda Hassim was very friendly. When the year before a British ship, the *Napoleon*, had come to grief on the rocks and her crew been driven to take refuge in the jungle, he had sent for them, housed and fed them, saved as much of their cargo as he could and returned them to Singapore at his own expense. This was not what might have been expected. According to British preconceptions about Bruneians, he should have murdered, enslaved or ransomed the crew, and stolen the cargo. This is exactly the policy that his nephew would later adopt towards British sailors. The astonished Singapore merchants had taken advantage of James's voyage to send the prince a substantial present, together with the thanks of the Governor of Singapore for his humane behaviour. The basis of a very helpful misunderstanding, crucial to the Brooke raj, was being laid.

James, desperate as ever for distinction, made much of the fact that the *Royalist*, ex-Royal Yacht Squadron, had the privileges of a man-of-war. It could fly the white ensign and receive a naval salute.

HALL OF AUDIENCE, SARAWAK: BRITISH MUSEUM

With the vessel, James also bought the right to wear a special semi-naval uniform and was so proud of it that he later had his portrait painted flaunting it. His ship was heavily armed. He arrived with all kinds of official documents as a messenger from the British authorities – yet he claimed to be just a private person. St John comments, 'It was natural for the Malay chiefs to doubt whether any man would give himself the trouble to make so long a voyage at so great an expense, merely to explore a country, survey its coasts and collect specimens of natural history. They expected every moment to hear that Mr. Brooke was an agent of the British government or at least the chosen envoy of the Governor of Singapore.'[2]

Hence the strange conversations that followed with the Bruneian princes. Should they trade with the Dutch? Would the English send trade? If the Dutch attacked them would the English intervene? And – more poetically Malay – of the English and the Dutch, which was the cat and which the mouse? The Dayaks, with their own concept of *bejalai* – where young men, 'brave bachelors', go travelling in search of cash, adventure, and heads – would have understood exactly what James was about. He himself seemed to find it not at all odd to be asked his views on such arcane matters. He adored being interrogated on questions of state – he had his long *Athenaeum* article to quote at them – so he warned them, without the slightest hint of irony, that the Dutch should at all costs be avoided as they had never yet established themselves in a Malay kingdom without ending up taking it over.

Rajah Muda Hassim was in Sarawak to put down a rebellion of local Malays. The rebel Malays just outside the town were alleged to be in alliance with the Sultan of Sambas, across the border in Dutch territory. A different version of the quarrel had it that Prince Usop, another uncle of the Sultan of Brunei and enemy of Hassim, had sold Sarawak to Sambas, so that the Bruneians of Hassim's faction desperately needed a counter-alliance with the English to keep the threat of the Dutch and Usop at bay. They had no idea they were entering into a political alliance not with a government but with a spoiled young man from Bath squandering his inheritance.

There followed a period of exploration. James was so obsessed

Mr Brooke's First Residence, Sarawak: British Museum

with the fact that his were the first European feet to touch this spot
that he foolishly walked barefoot. Quite soon the European feet
would swell up with infection and he would be lame. Never mind.
James's reluctant hosts took him, by river and sea, to meet some of
the exotic headhunting and piratical Dayaks he had been hearing
about. He was charmed by their openness, frankness and wildness.
The women were bold and bare-bosomed; the almost naked men had
fine muscular figures and suffered themselves to be measured. Even
his first encounter with smoked human heads in his first longhouse
seemed simply exotic and no more than a little naughty. The savagery of the practice, he assures us with instant expertise, is
exaggerated. His infatuation with adolescence was being fatally
extended to include whole supposedly 'child-like' peoples. They
were all becoming midshipmen under his especial care and already
he was leaping to judgement, forming the stereotypes that would
anchor Brooke rule. The Malays were natural gentlemen but, when
bad, could be sinuous and duplicitous, and they were lazy. The
Dayaks were naturally honest, chaste, passionate and faithful, people
of the land, not the town. It was like the difference between cats and
dogs. Repeatedly, the Dayaks are explicitly compared to hunting
dogs with a bad master. The master may be changed for a good one
but the dogs will take time to learn not to snap and bite. But they
were a good breed and would be won by kindness.

He saw his first Chinese settlement and immediately knew all
Chinese to be thrifty and industrious rather than poetic. The pink
and white lotus flowers whose beauty enthralled him were grown to
feed pigs.

And there is no reason to think that the judgements of locals
were not just as rapid and their friendliness not as genuine. James
was not the first westerner to be entranced with the warmth and
politeness that is the idiom of social exchange in the Malay archipelago. He became firm friends with Hassim, somewhat revising
his first haughty opinion that he was a 'semi-savage', exchanging
knives with him as though they were both little boys; and while he
would later come to see the cruelty and rapacity of Prince Makota,
he at least appreciated his intelligence and culture. Makota, after

all, wrote four-line, *pantun* poems, even about James Brooke. Sarawak was beginning to civilise James a little, to make him a little less unthinkingly English. Foreigners were no longer all rogues or fools, as they had been when seen from the *Castle Huntley*.

James believed Hassim's statement that there was no war, just 'a little child's play' among his subjects. While it was being sorted out he would complete his exploratory programme with a short trip to the neighbouring islands of Sulawesi and Singapore. On the last night, the *Royalist* sailed downriver to leave on the early tide, accompanied by a small boat of Malays. During the night the boat was attacked by Dayak pirates and several Malays were wounded. Having frightened off the pirates, James took the wounded back to Kuching, where Hassim was so overjoyed at his return that he served an allegedly 'English dinner', clearing the plates and pulling the corks with his own royal hands.

James would be absent some six months. After the warmth of Sarawak, Sulawesi proved a disappointment and the inhabitants a sad contrast with 'his' fine Borneans, though, since Raffles had collected natural history and found relics of ancient Hinduism, James needs must do the same here. Raffles had been interested in orang-utans. So for James too orang-utans became something of a fixation in his writings. On board was Betsy, a specimen presented by Hassim. The Dayaks had worked out a theory that orang-utans were once people who had fled to the forest because they had been terribly shamed as men and there declined from the state of humanity. He sailed on.

And then, in Singapore, Raffles's city, out of the blue, he found the recognition he had so long craved. He was lionised by the merchants. 'I am really becoming *a great man*, dearest mother; the world talks of me! The rulers of England threaten to write to me! Newspapers call me patriotic and adventurous! The Geographical Society pays me compliments! Am I not a great man?'[3] But the Governor, Mr Bonham, was not about to pay compliments; indeed, he was upset to hear of James's civilian dabbling in politics and James – ever ready to fly off the handle – sulked, fretted, reverted to the propounding of wild schemes. He would go to Manila, to China. Instead, in August 1840, he abruptly clapped on sail and steered for Sarawak again.

RIVER SARAWAK AND TOWN OF KUCHIN: BRITISH MUSEUM

Chapter 5

Change

When James Brooke returned to drop anchor in the Sarawak River, little had changed. The town of Kuching was still a sad and dilapidated collection of thatched huts under the temporary occupation of a vast and useless retinue of Bruneian nobles and their servants. Some of the Dayak troops had come over from the rebels to Hassim, and a useful contingent of Chinese had arrived, but the war still dragged on. The Bruneians intrigued to lure James into the fighting on their side, and he agreed to visit the front. He received their Dayak allies on board. 'They ate and drank, and asked for everything, but stole nothing.'

The war was perhaps not a very honourable one. Its basic cause was the rapacity of Prince Makota. Pangeran Indera Makota was to play the villain in James's drama, largely because, as the existing governor, he stood in the path of the Brooke raj and so was required to embody all the wickedness it was to replace. The British, following James, referred to Makota biblically as 'the Serpent'. It is noteworthy that in their relations with Borneo the British switched easily between their two dominant biblical myths of the wild – the notion of Sarawak as a paradise to be preserved from corrupting 'outside' influence, and as a wilderness to be roundly civilised.

Dayaks fitted neatly within the first myth, Chinese within the second. Makota had been such a corrupting influence, squeezing trade and exploiting the poor inland Dayaks till there was no room left for the Malays to do the same. So, they went into rebellion.

Legend has it that, when James Brooke was riding a horse in Singapore, his mount kicked and cracked a stone brought in ballast from Sarawak, and the break showed the dull gleam of antimony ore. It was explained that this was one of the few commercial exports of that backward place and Singapore had a stranglehold on it. In the trade, indeed, the ore was known as 'Singapore stone' and in Malay its name is *sarawak*. The metal had only a few sources but there was a steady demand for it. Natives used it to colour their sarongs and as a cosmetic to add mystery to their beautiful brown eyes. Westerners turned it more brutally into type metal, tin cans and bullets. Makota was determined to dominate this valuable export, and it was this resource that had led to a direct confrontation with the local Malays.

As Commander-in-Chief of the Brunei forces Makota avoided making any rash moves by making none at all. Warfare consisted largely of the erection and dismantling of wooden fortifications, the actual work being done by the Chinese and the Dayaks. As soon as one was completed, it was dismantled again to be put up somewhere else. The fortifications served largely for the beating of gongs and the shouting of insults. 'Like the heroes of old, however, the adverse parties spoke to each other: "We are coming, we are coming," exclaimed the rebels; "lay aside your muskets and fight us with swords." "Come on," was the reply; "we are building a stockade and want to fight you." And so the heroes ceased to talk but forgot to fight.'[1] Hassim's army was not impressive to James's eyes. There were two hundred Chinese armed with swords, spears, shields and a primitive sort of two-man musket that was an iron tube using powder to fire a metal slug. 'Powder is poured in, the end knocked on the ground, and the slug with another knock sent on the powder, without either ramming or cartridge.' When it comes to firing, 'one holds the tube over his shoulder, the other takes aim, turns away his head, applies his match and is pleased with the sound'.[2] There was not, he implied, likely to be much effect beyond the sound. Sarawak combat would later be revolutionised by the British use of efficient military rockets. There were 250 Malays, loyal to the Bruneians, some with muskets and a few swivel guns, and Dayaks with not much at all. A sort of armour would be constructed out of rattan, or hide, or metal plates – some indeed ingeniously adopted the lead lining of tea-chests – but this was only effective against poisoned darts. The most important weapon was sharpened bamboo stakes, which played havoc with bare feet.

All in all, James reckoned on three hundred actual fighting men, but more effort was spent in preventing the allies from falling on each other than was devoted to attacking the enemy. There were endless plans that came to nothing, assaults that were broken off when there was a risk of imminent success. In two months of warfare no men were lost and only five of the enemy even claimed dead. James, however, saw this warfare as a great evil. 'It is the slow poison which wastes the strongest frame, the smouldering fire which does its work of destruction slowly but surely. Year after year it is protracted; few fall in open fight, but prisoners and stragglers are murdered; and whilst both weak parties, gradually growing weaker, hold their own ground, the country becomes a desert.'[3] He sent in some 6-pounders and breached the enemy fort from the safety of his own, but could not persuade the Bruneians to follow it up.

Seeing the effect, I proposed to Makota to storm the place with 150 Chinese and Malays. The way from one fort to the other was protected. The enemy dared not show themselves for the fire of the grape and the canister, and nothing could have been easier; but my proposition caused a commotion which it is difficult to forget, and more difficult to describe. The Chinese consented, and Makota, the commander-in-chief, was willing; but his inferiors were backward, and there arose a scene which showed me the full violence of the Malay passions, and their infuriated madness when once aroused. Pangeran Usman urged with energy the advantage of the proposal, and in the course of a speech lashed himself

to a state of fury; he jumped to his feet, and with demoniac
gestures stamped round and round, dancing a war-dance
after the most approved fashion; his countenance grew livid,
his eyes glared, his features inflamed; and for my part, not
being able to interpret the torrent of his oratory, I thought
the man possessed of a devil, or about to 'run a-muck.' But
after a minute or two of this dance, he resumed his seat,
furious and panting, but silent.[4]

Having thus spent all their passion in rhetoric and dance, no one
actually attacked. Instead they bickered among themselves, pos-
tured and delayed. James returned to Kuching in outrage. He even
took his guns back and, since they would not let him take complete
charge, refused to participate at all.

It must be asked what were James's motives in returning to
Sarawak and becoming involved in this depressing struggle. He
himself invokes 'my reluctance to quit the Rajah in the midst of difficulty and distress and his *very sad face* whenever I mention the
topic.'[5] Doubtless friendship bound the two, but there are other
considerations. First, there is James's ambition to insinuate himself
into Sarawak affairs, to be a big fish again even in a small tropical
pool. What better opportunity could be offered to gain that fame he
always hungered for than by winning the war? He had enough of
what might be politely termed 'self-confidence' to imagine he could
take over such an enterprise. Then there is his simple passion for
adventure and his state of terminal boredom in Singapore and the
absence of anything better. Again, James argues that his participation in the war at least ensures that humane treatment is afforded to
women and children. But there is another focus of interest in
Sarawak. It is love again.

One of Hassim's many younger brothers was called Prince
Badrudeen. He was energetic, bold and manly, and James was very,
very taken with him. From some time in 1840 they appear
inseparable. The young prince accepted James as his mentor in all
things, adopted western customs, drank wine, dressed in European
clothes. James's concern with Badrudeen shows a pattern of attraction

that will repeat itself regularly throughout his life: the flattering attention, the seeking-out of the company of the new, young find, the
selfless bestowal of patronage, the concern with his education and
development, the breathy descriptions of his qualities in letters to
others and usually – finally – the emotional retirement of the loved
one to become a Sarawak official. In 1843 James wrote to his mother,

> I wish you could know the Pangeran Badrudeen, who with
> the amiable and easy temper of his brother Muda Hassim,
> combines decision and abilities quite astonishing in a native
> prince, and a directness of purpose seldom found in an
> Asiatic. As a companion I find him superior to most of those
> about me, and there is something particularly interesting, in
> sounding the depths and shallows of an intelligent native
> mind, and examining them freed from the trammels of court
> etiquette.[6]

He also wrote to Templer about Badrudeen's cleverness and his
being 'fitted by nature to govern' and described him as 'an exception – a striking and wonderful instance of the force of good sense
over evil education'.[7] At the end of his life James lamented of
Badrudeen, 'My love for him was deeper than anyone I knew.'
Badrudeen played no small part in attracting James's attention to
the muddy backwater that was Sarawak.

In return for James's continued help in the war, Rajah Muda
Hassim now offered him the whole state of Sarawak. 'The country
was offered to me. The only inquiry was, whether the Rajah had the
right and the authority to make over the country to me, and this I
was assured he had. The government, the revenue (with slight
deductions for the Sultan) and one of his brothers to reside here in
order to ensure the obedience of the Malays were all comprehended
in this cession, freely and without condition.'[8] We may speculate on
which brother was to be chosen to stay with James.

It is a standard part of most of the founding charters of colonisa-
tion that the native rulers fell over themselves to give their countries
away to Europeans. They did not even have to have a language in

common to do it. Francis Drake had Californian Indians begging Queen Elizabeth to take them over quite unambiguously in signs. We should not forget that Hassim still thinks he is dealing with the British Navy rather than simply James Brooke Esq., so that an alliance with James is, for him, perhaps the only way of swiftly ending the war and returning from this tedious exile to Brunei, where he can be sure his enemies are already plotting. Yet it is hard not to believe that the suggestion came from James rather than, as he insists, the other way round.

There is plenty in the previous writings of James Brooke to show that he had designs on Sarawak. What was lacking was a single individual who embodied his vision of what it was to become, a glittering, ideal specimen around whom this romantic vision could crystallise. Then, suddenly there is Badrudeen. Amongst what James sees as the mass of idle and cowardly Malays of the army, the prince stood out as the glorious exception, the only one ready for vigorous measures. Badrudeen was the new improved Sarawak incarnate, and his role in the war proved it.

The fighting was hardly being prosecuted with passion. 'We found the grand army in a state of torpor, eating, drinking, and walking up to the forts and back again daily; but having built these imposing structures, and their appearance not driving the enemy away, they were at a loss what next to do . . .'[9] No problem, James would show them what to do. The solution was, as always, that they should charge, even if this had to be on foot rather than on horseback as in India, and it was Badrudeen's 'overawing presence' that would make them. But the Malays wrong-footed James, turned things around and refused to attack, urging that they dared not risk Badrudeen's precious royal life. 'Badrudeen insisted that if I went he would likewise go and the Malays insisted that if he went they would not go . . .' So Badrudeen and James retired and directed the artillery from a place of safety; all went well until the surreptitiously advancing assault troops betrayed themselves by making the mistake of praying too loudly – attracting the attention of all three old muskets in the hands of the defenders – at which they prayed still more loudly and swiftly retired.

At the front, everyone built more forts and James looked for more things to charge.

> A Dayak came running through the jungle, and with gestures of impatience and anxiety begged me to assist the party attacked. He had been sent by my old friend the Temonggong of Lundu, to say that they could not hold the post unless supported. In spite of Makota's remonstrances, I struck into the jungle, winded through the narrow path, and after crossing an ugly stream, emerged on the clear ground. The sight was a pretty one: to the right was the unfinished stockade, defended by the Temenggong; to the left, at the edge of the forest, about twelve or fifteen of our party, commanded by Illudeen, whilst the enemy were stretched along between the points, and kept up a sharp shooting from the hollow ground on the bank of the river. They fired, and loaded, and fired, and had gradually advanced on the stockade as the ammunition of our party failed; and as we emerged from the jungle, they were within twenty or five-and-twenty yards of the defence. A glance immediately showed me the advantage of our position, and I charged with my Europeans across the padi-field; and the instant we appeared on the ridge above the river, in the hollows of which the rebels were seeking protection, their rout was complete. They scampered off in every direction, whilst the Dayaks and Malays pushed them in the river. Our victory was decisive and bloodless: the scene was changed in an instant, and the defeated foe lost arms, ammunition etc. etc whether on the field of battle or in the river, and our exulting conquerors set no bounds to their triumph.[10]

This minor victory was a turning point. It emboldened James to neatly sidestep the Bruneian administration by using the political power of religion, which might have been thought to count against him as an infidel. He and some of the Malays on either side, who were sharifs (locally *sherip*) – descendants of the Prophet – imposed

LUNDU DAYAK: BRITISH MUSEUM

a parley on their own initiative. Interestingly, these are precisely the people who would later be a constant source of trouble to him and whose influence he would most deplore and seek to control. The terms were simple: the rebels would surrender if their lives were spared – but James lacked the authority to guarantee this. Instead he placed them royally under his personal protection, persuading the Chinese and the Malays within the Bruneian forces to promise that there would be no plundering of the area – which, urged on by Makota, their commander-in-chief, they attempted to do the very next day. Risking everything, James had his men fire over their heads and browbeat Hassim into sparing the lives of the rebels. Hostages were taken, arms surrendered, the forts burned. The four years' war was over and James Brooke had imposed his personal peace on Sarawak, but Makota would be henceforth his personal enemy. James's own struggle for power had just begun.

It started with a peaceful visit by a fleet of Illanun (Philippine) pirates with a few allies from Halmahera in the Moluccas to the east. James was fascinated by their accoutrements and wild dances, by the huge warboats with fifty oars. He noted the constitution of the crew, most being mere slaves, and remarked, 'The Datus, or chiefs, are incorrigible; for they are pirates by descent, robbers from pride as well as taste, and they look upon the occupation as the most honourable hereditary pursuit. They are indifferent to blood, fond of plunder, but fondest of slaves . . . A few severe examples and con-stant harassing would soon cure this hereditary and personal mania for the rover's life.'[11] This would be the business of the next few years.

A very odd deal was struck with Hassim. James received some sort of warrant as Resident, though this referred only to his right to stay in the country and 'seek profit'. This, it was explained, was mere political expedience, to avoid giving fright to the Sultan back in Brunei. He was now to go to Singapore and bring back a cargo to stimulate trade. He would receive a shipment of antimony ore in return and they would build him a house while he was gone. This would be James Brooke's last attempt at direct trade, for he early came to recognise that his father had been right about his mercantile limitations. He would talk readily enough about the expansion of British trade to rally support among merchants at home, but 'As a man of commerce I am a fool – fit to talk about the national debt but as for saving sixpence I cannot do it.'[12] Anyway, James was always happy to be bad at business, as a sign of his own gentlemanly quality, for deep down he had much the same distaste for trade and the same love of roving as his pirate visitors. He knew that what called them to arms was above all the lure of sheer excitement, relief from the boredom of a regular existence, the dullness of the kind of life he was seeking to impose on them, so he would often admire them as he fought them, a very gentlemanly concept of war that served also to disguise the imbalance of armament on the two sides.

There now came an obscure period in the affairs of Sarawak. James returned with a new vessel, the *Swift*, and a cargo which was joyfully carried away by Hassim. The promised house had not been built. The promised antimony had not been collected for shipment. In fact, nothing much had been done and nothing much would be done for another five months. James noted with astonishment that the Bruneians were now even unwilling to profit from his extensive views on the country and how it was to be managed. He was 'clipped like Samson' and paid back in the coin of empty courtesies. His trump card of course was his armed vessel in the harbour, but he was reluctant to use it, thinking still in terms of going on to Brunei, where such an act would count against him. The crisis, when it finally came, was precipitated by the threat to the upriver Dayaks.

In accordance with ancient usage, a fleet of a hundred Malay vessels from the Skrang and Saribus Rivers was to be permitted by the Bruneians to sail upstream to murder and plunder Sarawak citizens in return for a cut of the profits. James was simply appalled – 'the idea of letting 2500 wild devils loose in the interior of the country is horrible'[13] – and demanded the fleet's recall. There was no response. He took to his man-of-war. Hassim sulked and took to his harem. But he reluctantly called back the marauders, and both agreed to blame all on Makota. James again took a great gamble and

Saribus Dayak: British Museum

upped the stakes in a blatant demonstration of his own security of tenure. He sent what antimony ore he had been able to gather to Singapore, and dispatched the *Royalist* to Brunei on rumours of a British ship being in distress there. He was so annoyed with the Bruneians that he even sent Badrudeen away. Apart from three companions he was now quite alone and undefended, and he settled down to write a description of the Malay fashion of chess-playing, as a metaphor for the political power of which he was deprived. He had now adopted a Dayak boy called Situ and a 'passionate' Buginese from South Sulawesi, Sika.

The *Royalist* returned with the news that the Sultan of Brunei had been hostile and clearly meant to ransom the British seamen, so James threatened British action against the unimpressed Bruneians. Hassim as usual dithered and delayed. The atmosphere became ever tenser. Was James ruler or was he not? And then, out of the blue, as if magically summoned by James, the East India Company steamer *Diana* sailed into the river from Singapore and belched arrogant black smoke over the town. It was the first steamer ever to enter the river. James basked in its 'reflective power'. The cavalry had arrived. Now he could charge again.

Following physical violence on a respectable Chinese and an attempted poisoning both of which James also laid at 'the cunning and diabolically intriguing' Makota's door, he felt his 'little treasury of grievances' had given him the excuse he was looking for. The rebels, Malay and Dayak, whose lives he had saved from the recent war offered support, so that he now had a local constituency.

I landed a party of men, fully armed, and loaded the ship's guns with grape and canister; after which I once more proceeded to Muda Hassim and protested my kindness towards him, exposed Makota's machinations and crimes, his oppression and his deceit, and threatened him with an attack, as neither Muda Hassim nor myself were safe, while he continued practising these arts . . . After this demonstration, affairs proceeded cheerily to a conclusion. The Rajah was active in settling; the agreement was drawn

out, sealed and signed; guns fired, flags waved; and on 24th
September 1841, I became the governor of Sarawak with the
fullest powers.[14]

He was careful to point out that he was acting against Makota,
whom he replaced, not Hassim, whom he was protecting, and so in
accordance with respect for Bruneian sovereignty. James always
considered his actions to be genuinely for the benefit of locals –
whether the locals realised it or not – so that his interests and theirs
would naturally coalesce. It was a fundamental tenet of his rule
that Brookes governed only by consensus, Bruneians by unprincipled oriental despotism. But this was hardly the free entreaty or
'election' by grateful natives that Brooke history would record.

Chapter 6

The Rule of Law

J ames Brooke was thirty-eight years old and finally had the country he had dreamed of and that he saw as his unquestioned right. He quite unlawfully assumed the title of Rajah – locals referred to him simply as the Tuan Besar – the Big Lord – and began his rule and his new life in a legalistic high moral tone. The hundred-odd wives and children taken as hostages at the end of the civil war were now released and restored to their families. Some had already been taken as wives by Hassim's brothers – a great honour, James was assured – and he let that rest. He reappointed the state officials, the Datuk Patinggi, Datuk Temonggong and Datuk Bandar, who had gone into rebellion and determined that they should be paid an annual salary instead of filching for themselves. They were not particularly impressive individuals, but James always sought to cloak revolutionary change in the mantle of the restoration of tradition. And he owed them a debt for their support against the Bruneian faction. He had become the champion of the Kuching Malays against the Bruneians, but now he must do something for the Dayaks against the Malays. '"Divide and govern" is the motto. I must govern each by the other, and when I am rich enough, procure a body guard of fifty Bugis [Buginese from Celebes].'[1]

He set about demolishing the infamous system known as *serah* which weighed particularly heavily on the Hill Dayaks, who had been driven into disaffection along with the Malays. According to this, Bruneian and Malay nobles and their relatives had the right to appropriate any Dayak property they took a fancy to. They could confiscate a Dayak boat by cutting a notch in the gunwale. Should another Malay demand the same boat, the owner had not only to yield it up to the first but to pay compensation to the second for his disappointment. They could buy up forest produce at any price they saw fit, and if insufficient quantities were delivered by villagers they might seize their wives and children and sell them into slavery. Should they resist, other Dayaks would be set upon them – which might happen anyway, as part of the practice of issuing licences to devastate tribes beyond the reach of normal exploitation. This combination of practices had reduced the province to misery. Of course, the Hill Dayaks (Bidayuh) suffered more than the Sea Dayaks (Iban) as the latter were the principal devastators.

> The Dayaks or wild tribe of the hills are, taking them generally, one of the most interesting and easily to be improved races in the world. You must be careful, however, not to confound these Hill Dayaks with the predatory tribes of the coasts, for although they likewise have many excellent qualities, yet they are *great pirates* and head-hunters. These, (the Hill Dayaks) are an industrious, quiet and strictly honest people, in which last particular they present a striking contrast to the South Sea Islanders. Their wars, one against another, do little mischief, even to themselves, save that the fear of surprise, prevents their cultivating an exposed ground . . . Though industrious, they never reap what they sow; though their country is rich in produce, they are obliged to yield it all to their oppressors: though yielding all beyond their bare sustenance, they rarely can preserve half *their children*, and often – too often – are robbed of them all, with their wives. This may appear to you

somewhat an exaggerated picture, but I have not given it
the colour which it merits.[2]

James determined that this was to end. Ancient laws were now to
be respected and be protected from abuse. Native religion was to
suffer no molestation – but this, in fact, only affected the Malays.
Dayaks were held to be children of nature, without true religion,
since their most cherished beliefs were dismissed in the eyes of
civilisation as mere childlike superstition.

It was to be indirect government:

> The experiment of developing a country through the
> residence of a few Europeans, and by the assistance of its
> native rulers, has never been fairly tried; and it appears to
> me in some respects more desirable than the actual
> possession of a foreign nation; for if successful, the native
> prince finds greater advantages, and if a failure, the
> European government is not committed. Above all, it
> insures the independence of the native princes, and may
> advance the inhabitants further in the scale of civilization
> by means of the very independence than can be done when
> the government is a foreign one, and their natural freedom
> sacrificed.[3]

It is also cheaper.

The antimony mines whose control lay at the bottom of the
vexed war were taken over by James to pay for government,
together with a rice tax. Although he dreamed of mineral wealth –
gold, diamonds – and had already sent home 'the Brooke Diamond'
(which turned out to be not a diamond at all but a relatively value-
less opal), he was ironically unaware of the value of the noxious
crude oil that seeped from the ground far to the north, ruining the
soil. The Victorian age, after all, lubricated its smoke-belching
engines with green, renewable palm oil, not fossil poisons. Anyway,
this area was not yet part of Sarawak, which at the moment com-
prised about three thousand square miles of profitless swamp, jungle

and river. Expansion lay in the future, notably under the next Rajah, Charles, but from the first James had an eye on the border. And mineral wealth was only thought of as a source of salvation in much the same way as a man dreams idly of winning the lottery, for Sarawak had precious little to offer the world and, in the early years, James alternated between wildly talking up his province's resources and a more sober acceptance of its financial situation. Moreover, his own fiscal management scarcely represented an advance.

> Mr. Brooke calculated that the revenue of the country was about £5,000 a year. How he arrived at this estimate, I do not understand, as the whole income of the country consisted of a few hundred bushels of rice, a little profit from opium and the net proceeds of the antimony. I can readily imagine that he was incorrectly informed by his treasurers, who were such poor accountants, that on examining his books, I found that all expenditure was put under the head of revenue . . . Dollars valued at 4s 2d and reals worth 3s were treated as equivalent coins, and added together . . . Thus Mr. Brooke never really knew what was the true state of his affairs. What he did know was, that every now and then he was informed that there was a balance against him, and he drew bills on his private fortune, until it began gradually to vanish to nothing.[4]

James would be more or less broke for the rest of his life. Whatever colonial model he fits, it is certainly not that of self-seeking commercial exploiter.

Yet the imperial ambition is there to be read between the lines. He sent home fretting that he had no knighthood, he asked for a rifle with eight barrels ('with Dayaks it would be invaluable') and a magic-lantern show of Napoleon on his white steed at Waterloo. James often seems to talk most clearly about himself when writing of others. Thus he gave advice to his mother on moving house, but it is hard not to feel he was writing about his plans for Sarawak. 'I would rather have a cottage, a freehold of my own, and all entirely mine own, than a mansion and park on lease for five hundred years, with a vile landlord somewhere or other, with big prying eyes, and an intelligent agent, close at hand to see you did not convert oaks into firewood.'[5]

He was, as yet, still a mere tenant of the Sultan of Brunei, but that tenure would soon be changed into freehold. James Brooke described his takeover of government in terms of resigned altruism, *noblesse oblige*, selflessness, the urge to do good. Likewise with his Dayak boy, Situ. James writes:

> Last night I received a strange and embarrassing present, in the shape of a young Dayak boy of five years old – a miserable little prisoner, made during this war, from the tribe of Brong. The gift causes me vexation, because I know not what to do with the poor innocent; and yet I shrink from the responsibility of adopting him. My first wish is to return him to his parents and his tribe; and if I find I cannot do this, I believe it will be better to carry him with me than leave him to become the slave of a slave: for, should I send him back, such will probably be his fate.

And, later:

> Situ, my Dyak boy, seems content and happy; and judging by his ways and his fondness for tobacco, he must be older than I at first supposed. In pursuance of my desire to restore him to his parents, I made every enquiry as to their probable fate; but I have learned nothing that leaves me any hope that I shall be able to do so . . . Supposing my endeavours to restore the child fail, I have resolved to keep him with me, for many reasons. The first is, that his future prospects will be better, and his fate as a freeman at Singapore happier, than as a slave in Borneo; the second that he can be made a Christian. I can easily provide for him in some respectable household, or take him to England, as may hereafter be most

advantageous for him: and at the former place, he can always be made a comfortable servant with good training. Yet with all this, I cannot disguise from myself that there is responsibility – heavy moral responsibility – attached to this course, that might be avoided: but then, *should* it be avoided? Looking to the boy's interests – temporal, perhaps eternal – I think it ought not; and so provided always I cannot replace him where humanity and nature dictate, I will take the responsibility, and serve this wretched and destitute child as far as lies in my power. He is cast on my compassion; I solemnly accept the charge; and I trust his future life may bear good fruit, and cause me to rejoice at my present decision.[6]

All this is very noble. But it is written by James in those oddly public journals – both *to himself and to the world* – in elaborate self-justification, at the time when he is deciding whether or not to quit Sarawak or to stay. Such minute, late-night examinations of conscience, blind to the major unconscious issues that we would see lying beneath them, are characteristic of James Brooke. They are as much a façade as a self-revelation. His relations with Situ are cast in exactly the same terms of chest-beating morality as his relations with the whole of poor, suffering Sarawak. He will take in the devastated, orphan province, protect it, train it up, give it the means to earn a living – if only as a servant – and give it back its self-respect, regardless of the cost to himself. Above all, he will give it love. 'And the greatest of these is love.' No wonder, then, that it becomes a matter of deep concern whether Situ and other boys were – as claimed – objects of selfless love or active lust to James Brooke. To debauch Situ would be to metaphorically debauch innocent Sarawak in general. He would be no longer the founder and protector of a model state but the abuser of innocent trust. 'Sarawak, indeed, is like a foundling which at first you protect with hesitation and doubt, but which foundling afterwards repays you your cost and your trouble.'[7]

We will never know whether, as Rajah, James boiled daily in the clammy sheets of unrequited lust, engaged in a little vague scout-masterly fumbling, sublimated desire under a stiff rictus of avuncular benevolence or reached a sensible standing arrangement with one or more of his young men. Even if nothing 'actually happened' in those long, steamy Sarawak nights it does not get James off the hook for a modern reader, who sees him quivering on the brink of either sexual exploitation or the imperial egotism it represents. In a post-Freudian age a conscious thought denied merely invites us to look for an unconscious one that is deeper and more 'true'. For contemporary biographers, goodness can rarely be accepted at its face value; it has to be unmasked as something else, the lower the better, and James apparently anticipated this. 'It requires a man of enlarged mind to confide in the generosity and disinterestedness of his fellow mortals,' he noted. The post-imperial Westerner, having lost his epistemological nerve, no longer has that enlarged mind and is prey to uncertainty in a way that James never was. It cannot be denied that James Brooke really did seek to do good *as he saw it*, but his lack of self-doubt may arouse discomfort nowadays. For there is a form of extravagant self-abasement – which he himself termed 'that species of pride that apes humility' and shared by such as Albert Schweitzer and the late Diana, Princess of Wales – that is also a mark of self-obsession and of arrogance and that is hard for us to understand except as the other side of a terrible guilt. It is quite probable that he was able, to a greater or lesser extent, to use his lust to fuel his higher altruism. As he served Sarawak, he publicly tamed and civilised the dark side of himself. But his letters still read like those of a man who burned.

The writing of laws was among the first regal acts, the declaration of the openness of trade, the introduction of a system of weights and measures and the start of that long process of finagling for the status of a British protectorate that St John characterised sharply as 'the great error of his life'. James, typically, thought that if only he had a steamer all would be well. He wrote long summaries of his doings, to be published in England. He knew more than most the value of public opinion and urged friends and relatives to agitate and appeal

MALAY CHIEF: BRITISH MUSEUM

to England on moral, commercial and religious grounds. But for seven months there was another priority.

For the British, rule is law and law is history. As the mark of rule, a lawcourt was held almost every day. It was a fine and typical Brookean blend of declared modesty – the restriction of interference to the impartial application of ancient laws – and unaware arrogance – the assumption that James obviously knew better than anyone else in Sarawak what real justice was about and could overrule the law if need be. The most important thing, he concluded swiftly, was not the administering of oaths, which were lightly treated, but the preventing of one witness hearing the testimony of the others. Inadequate rehearsal made their lies more revealing than their truths. Like the kings of old, he was Brooke the law-giver. He drew up a list of all the laws he could think of and had all eight printed in Singapore. It was a start. But he never realised that he did not just give the people justice. In a small town starved of regular diversion, he also gave them theatre.

The court sat in Brooke's own house, a rustic but imposing structure across from the Chinese bazaar. Fifty-four feet square of plank and thatch, it had been put up by Hassim in shamefaced haste, with a cutting of corners that would have been the pride of any London jerry-builder. Like many Kuching buildings, it was built on posts of the nibong palm that the English called 'kneebone', driven into the mud so that at high tide water flowed under it as at Borneo Proper. James calculated that in a year it would collapse, but then it had not been made to bear the weight of justice being seen to be done. (He was right. He ended up falling through the bathroom floor and nearly drowning.)

The *Royalist* had been stripped of fittings to trim the house so that nautical chairs accommodated Judge James and such of Hassim's fourteen brothers as could be spared to sit on left and right. The private rooms were enhanced with sofas, books and paintings. Rajah James had an artistic way with soft furnishings that was much remarked upon. He either did not know or did not

Long-Wai Dayak in War Costume: British Museum

care that the night-time scent of *chimpaka* – gardenia – that haunted his rooms, conjured up in Malays the terrors of the terrible *pontianak* ghost which lured men by its irresistible sexual attraction and then tore them apart. In the days of his successor, Rajah Charles, the courtroom chairs would be replaced with an agonising iron bench, an implacable symbol of unbending judicial virtue, but then Rajah Charles was a little mad on the whole subject of effeminacy, sewed up his sons' trouser pockets and imposed fines on his young officers if he caught them in unauthorised possession of upholstery. Health, he would declare, was all a matter of how a man 'held himself'.

Across the room were the three great ministers of the Kuching Malays, the Datuks Temonggong, Bandar and Patinggi, at their feet the litigants on cunningly crafted mats, and behind them, crammed in against the walls and spilling outside, what might be viewed either as the citizenry or the mob: betel-juice-spitting Malays, hawking Chinese, wild-eyed Dayaks – all men.

Languages criss-crossed: Malay, English, Iban, Bidayuh, obscure tongues of the Baram River, contesting dialects of Chinese. Williamson, the Eurasian interpreter brought from Singapore, sweated and laboured and hacked a rough path of sense through as many as he dared. Languages did not so much translate as overlap a little in meaning.

The stories began to form a familiar pattern. Little men were oppressed by the great, who were in turn protected by the greater. The Bruneians were so rooted in dishonesty that many of them would rather cheat themselves than be honest. Little men's weakness was transformed into debt, debt into slavery, slavery into every form of moral and physical wrong. And the slim brown backs that ultimately bore this mass of human unhappiness were those of the innocent Hill Dayaks. They spoke their wretchedness in a pure poetry straight from the pages of Ossian – of big birds pecking little birds and sharp thorns hidden in bunches of lush bananas – that brought tears to his eyes. Anger began to kindle in James Brooke and he determined to bring all, including the Bruneians, within the law.

The Chinese attended his courts and paid great attention to the proceedings. They counted on his support for protection against the Malays and it was only after he encouraged Chinese immigration in the 1850s that Sarawak would finally begin to pay its way. Better, they alone in Kuching had a liking for cold impersonal cash while others bartered in produce, and they were excellently taxable, with their taste for gambling, opium and alcohol. But James never knew that part of the fascination of his courts was not the business of justice being done, but the gambling made possible by the outcome of cases. It was even alleged that suits were wholly concocted and pressed solely to provide an outlet for this passion. And the Chinese, of course, ran the gambling and gambling was illegal. When the ex-pats of the local dramatic society happily performed Gilbert and Sullivan in later years, the exotic and absurd plots were always dangerously close to the reality of Kuching.

A big case involved the Chinese charter granted by Hassim, allowing the San Ti Qu *kongsi*, a democratic community of Chinese under a 'captain', to mine gold and antimony on the right-hand branch of the river. They objected to plans to allow another *kongsi*, the Sin Bok, to do the same on the left-hand side, invoking infringement of the original agreement as grounds for complaint. Examination of the documents showed that the Chinese translation had cheerfully converted the simple permission to mine of the Malay original into a deed of gift of the whole interior. A few face-saving concessions were made, but the claims were dismissed. James must have been aware how closely the case might resemble one involving his own elastic agreement with Hassim. It was time to finally go to Brunei.

He was accompanied by Princes Badrudeen and Marsale. James was himself moved to tears to see the grief of Hassim at parting with them. 'It is part of our better nature to feel when we see others feel.' Borneo Proper had sadly declined since first visited by Europeans on Magellan's round-the-world voyage, when it was an opulent place of silk-hung elephants that traded in heaped spices, gold, diamonds and mythical 'dragon's blood'.

On approaching the town, before the ebb had run long, it appeared to be a very Venice of hovels, a river Cybele rising from the water. For those who like it, the locality is not ill chosen. The hills recede from the river and form an amphitheatre; and several other rivers or streams flowing in, cause a muddy deposit on which the houses are built. At high-water they are surrounded; at low water, stand on a sheet of mud. On nearing it, we were encompassed by boats which preceded and followed us, and we passed the floating market, where women, wearing immense hats of palm-leaves, sell all sorts of edibles, balanced in their little canoes, now giving a paddle, now making a bargain, and dropping down with the tide, and again regaining their place when the bargain is finished. The first impression of the town is miserable. The houses are crowded and numerous, and arriving at the palace does not present a more captivating aspect, for, though large, it is as incommodious as the worst.[8]

Although the population was assessed at some ten thousand, all seemed poor, and James was incredulous that this was the famed Borneo Proper about which such romantic tales had been spun, the lost paradise of sophistication for which Hassim pined while in Kuching. All silver objects turned black overnight from the noxious exhalations of the mud.

For once, James's aims appeared clear. He wanted to reconcile the warring Bruneian factions so that Hassim and his brothers and attendants could be safely returned to Brunei Proper and got off his hands and out of his hair. His major long-term aim was to strengthen the pro-British faction in the court and ultimately ease Hassim's own passage to the Brunei throne. He also sought the release of British 'lascar' (Indian) seamen from another recent wreck. Above all, he desperately wanted a legal piece of paper, finally confirmed by the Sultan, giving him the widest rights possible in Sarawak.

He also had a hazy plan to get British hands on the coal that was rumoured to be found on Labuan Island, off the Bruneian coast. Perhaps reparations for the mistreatment of the British seamen

BRUNEI: BRITISH MUSEUM

would be a painless and face-saving way of covering the transfer of the island, since James had taken over from Raffles the idea that shame is the one thing impossible for Malays to bear.

St John, afterwards long resident in Brunei, describes Sultan Omar Ali as 'a man of about fifty years of age, short and puffy in person, with a countenance that very obviously showed the weakness of his mind which, as indexed by his face, assumed a complex map of confusion, without astuteness, without dignity, and without good sense. He was ignorant, mean and avaricious, fond of low society and of stupid jokes . . . He was, however, full of pride.'[9] The British never liked him very much.

Nevertheless, most of James's aims were achieved without opposition, even from Usop, the mooted ally of Makota. Sarawak's yearly payment of $2,500 to Brunei was doubtless a powerful argument, so that the province was now 'made over to Mr. Brooke (to be held under the crown of Brunei) . . .'.

On their return to Kuching, according to Malay custom, the Sultan's letters in their yellow silk envelopes were treated with great honour, respected indeed as manifestations of the Sultan himself.

On their arrival they were received and brought up amid large wax torches, and the person who was to read them was stationed on a raised platform. Standing on the step below him was Muda Hassim, with a sabre in his hand; in front of the Rajah [Hassim] was his brother Pangeran Jaffir, with a tremendous *kampilan*, or Lanun sword, drawn; and around were the other brothers and Mr. Brooke, all standing, the rest of the company being seated. The letters were then read, the one appointing Mr. Brooke to hold the government of Sarawak last. After this the Rajah descended from the steps of the platform and said aloud, 'If any one present disowns or contests the Sultan's appointment, let him now declare it.' All were silent. He next turned to the native chiefs of Sarawak and asked them – they were obedient to the will of the Sultan. Then the question was asked of the other Pangerans [royal princes], 'Is there any

Rajah that contests the question? Pangeran Makota, what do you say?' Makota expressed his willingness to obey. One or two other obnoxious Pangerans who had always opposed themselves to Mr. Brooke were each in turn challenged, and forced to promise obedience. The Rajah then waved his sword and with a loud voice exclaimed, 'Whoever dares to disobey the Sultan's mandate now received, I will split his skull!' At the same moment some ten of his brothers jumped from the veranda, and drawing their long knives began to flourish and dance about, thrusting close to Makota, striking the pillar above his head, and pointing their weapons at his breast. This amusement, the violence of motion, the freedom from restraint, this explosion of a long pent-up animosity, roused all their passions; and had Makota, through an excess of fear or an excess of bravery, started up, he would have been slain, and other blood would have been spilt. But he was quiet, with his face pale and subdued, and as shortly as decency would permit after the riot had subsided, took his leave. Had he been slain on this occasion, many hundreds, nay, thousands of innocent lives might have been saved.[10]

James packed Makota off into exile. It would take Hassim two years to gather up enough resolve to move back to Brunei.

Chapter 7

And So To War

In 1843 in Penang, the Company island off the coast of the Malay peninsula, James met a red-haired British naval captain named the Hon. Henry Keppel, 'whose energy and dash, and quick appreciation of the earnest purpose of Mr. Brooke, had so great an effect on the future of Sarawak'. One might add that he was hard up, Napoleonically short and Napoleonically ambitious. He was thirty-five years old but had held his first command at twenty-five and, in later years, royal favour did nothing to hinder his further advancement. He had a taste for danger and adventure that had been displayed in his recent deeds in China and was an ardent admirer of James Brooke's attempts to impose order on the boisterous anarchy of Borneo. The two men rapidly established a coalition of intelligent interests based on mutual respect and admiration.

James had already determined to solve the piracy question by belligerent means, and given his neighbours fair warning that slaving and headhunting raids on Sarawak would no longer be permitted. To his joy, inland tribes began to move down towards Kuching in search of his protection. Some had never seen the tidal bore on the rivers before and were afraid of it, refusing to drink this odd new kind of water. James loved them for their innocence and suffered them to come unto him.

Construction of a small fleet of war canoes was started. He already possessed the *Snake* and the *Dragon*, manned by 140 crew and armed with swivel guns, and the *Jolly Bachelor* was under construction, but the pirate opposition could put fleets of 150 vessels into the field. Earlier, he entertained the Skrang pirate chieftains Matari (Sun) and his friend Bulan (Moon) in Kuching and found them thoroughly delightful. Matari was 'as fine a young man as the eye would wish to rest upon – straight, elegantly yet strongly made, with a chest and neck and head set on them which might serve Apollo, legs far better than his of Belvedere, and a countenance mild and intelligent'. Apart from the pagan splendour of bare Iban thighs and torsos, he was charmed by Matari's boyish naughtiness.

'You will give me, your friend, leave to steal a few heads occasionally?'

'No,' I replied; 'You cannot take a single head; you cannot enter the country; and if you or your country men do, I will have a hundred Skrang heads for every one you take here!'

He recurred to this request several times – 'Just to steal one or two!' – as a schoolboy asks for apples.[1]

There had already been difficulty with headhunters. After a prolonged campaign in Singe, the dissident leaders were taken prisoner and briskly put to death by Hassim. It might be thought a minor matter, but these deaths would later be laid at James's door by enemies in England, anxious to show him a sanguinary despot. Trouble was also brewing with Sherip Sahib, a notorious Arab-Malay sponsor of piratical raids on the Saribus River, where one of the local leaders had boldly hung a basket high on a tree and declared it ready to receive the head of James Brooke. Wild rumours of marauders lurking off the coasts chased each other around the small town and constantly threatened the infant state. James had failed to interest the East India Company ship, *Diana*, in taking action against pirates, but he would find Henry Keppel more flexible.

James and Henry were immediately friends. They were close in age and both were men of considerable personal charm and masters of the arts of mess camaraderie. To both, fighting pirates was the stuff of boyhood and *Castle Huntley* dreams – a jaunt. Keppel's official mission was the suppression of the Illanun and Balanini raiders of the Sulu Sea who preyed on British and other shipping, but James and Governor Bonham of Singapore suggested that this remit could reasonably be stretched to include pirates from the Borneo coast and that it was obvious that the only effective way of resolving such acts of piracy lay in the devastation of their secure home bases. James had already identified the interests of Sarawak with his own. Now he would add those of Britain. Since water was the universal means of transport in Borneo, anyone travelling there with malice aforethought immediately became a pirate, so that robbers, rebels and outlaws conveniently all disappeared to be absorbed in the new classification. Crucial in all this was legislation left on the statute books from the British anti-slavery squadrons of the West African coast. According to an act of Parliament of 1825, bounties were payable to officers and men on ships that took action against pirates. The terms were staggeringly generous: £20 for every pirate taken prisoner or slain, and £5 a head for every other piratical person estimated aboard at the time of the engagement. While the freed African slaves were reduced to a state of liberated destitution, the Navy had done very nicely out of British philanthropy, and fighting against pirates was extremely popular aboard Her Majesty's vessels. Through his friendship with Henry Keppel, James Brooke effectively gained a navy to use against his enemies; and the fact that he kept no large standing army disguised the truth that his rule, as in every official British colony, relied on military force rather than that simple free choice of independent men that goes into the Brooke prospectus.

The first manifestation of this was his return to Kuching in HMS *Dido*, Keppel's own ship, a smart three-masted sloop of 376 tons, bearing eighteen 32-pounders and served by a crew of 145 men. The Admiralty was so unfamiliar with Sarawak waters that, according to the best naval charts, the voyage involved sailing

HMS DIDO AT SARAWAK: BRITISH MUSEUM

over the tops of mountains to a distance some eighty miles inland. *Dido* was by far the biggest vessel ever to enter the river, and its masts towered over the town and even most of the trees, with the sailors running up the rigging in white uniforms in thrilling displays of symmetry, the band playing and the biggest cannon ever heard firing a salute of twenty-one guns which shook the houses and echoed back and forth between the mountains. Everything was calculated to increase the prestige of the Brooke raj and Keppel – no fool – noted that the Malays now had gained such confidence that they brought out their children to greet the British. It was the visible sign of the new political order, clear proof to the locals that James's claims to be a mere private citizen were nothing but diplomatic posturing. By good fortune, the British even encountered and captured their first pirates on the way – or maybe they only shot up some innocent boats belonging to the Sultan of Riau. Already the notion of piracy was becoming a little vague. But Keppel was enjoying himself.

> The next business was my visit of ceremony to the Rajah which was great fun. The band, and the marines as a guard, having landed, we all assembled at Mr. Brooke's house, where, having made ourselves as formidable as we could with swords and cocked hats, we marched in procession to the royal residence. His Majesty having sent one of his brothers, who led me by the hand into his presence . . . His Majesty chewed his sirih-leaf and betel-nut, seated with one leg crossed under him, and playing with his toes. Very little is ever said during these audiences; so we sat staring at one another for half an hour with mutual astonishment; and, after the usual compliments of wishing our friendship might last as long as the moon, and my having offered him the *Dido* and everything else that did not belong to me in exchange for his house, we took our leave.[2]

James made sure he enjoyed himself still more. A little Dayak tour was organised, complete with human heads and savage cabaret, just as for the tourists of today. He kept open house and wined and dined the officers in what, by day, was the lawcourt.

On the arrival of Keppel, Makota finally left the town, but still cast a long shadow of intrigue, this time involving Dr Treacher, the new civilian medical officer.

> Dr Treacher received a message from a confidential slave, that one of the ladies of Makota's harem desired an interview, appointing a secluded spot in the jungle as the rendezvous. The doctor, being aware of his own good looks, fancied he had made a conquest; and, having got himself up as showily as he could, was there at the appointed time. He described the poor girl as both young and pretty, but with a dignified and determined look, which at once convinced him that she was moved to take so dangerous a step by some deeper feeling than that of mere fancy for his person. She complained of the ill treatment she had received from Makota, and the miserable life she led; and avowed that her firm resolve was to destroy (not herself, gentle creature! but) him, for which purpose she wanted a small portion of arsenic. It was a disappointment that he could not comply with her request: so they parted – he full of pity and love for her, and she, in all probability, full of contempt for a man who felt for her wrongs, but would not aid in the very simple means she had prepared for redressing them.[3]

The few opening skirmishes with pirates had already led to a marked drop in their activity. Respecting the letter of the law, James created a judicial paper trail, with a formal written request from Hassim, delivered by Badrudeen on the brass tray, in one of the yellow silk envelopes, begging Keppel to take action against pirates with the promise of Bruneian co-operation. James was even to be allowed to join the attack against the inhabitants, Dayaks under Malay leaders, of the Saribus River to the north-east. It would rely on mixed British, Dayak, Bruneian and Malay forces. Prominent among them was Subu Besi (Iron Anchor). 'His [James's] coxswain,

War Dance of the Lundu Dayaks: British Museum

Subu, we shall all long remember: he was civil only to his master, and, I believe, brave while in his company. He was a stupid-looking and powerfully-built sort of savage, always praying, eating, smiling or sleeping.'[4] Subu would go on to be public announcer and executioner of the little state.

The force of some thousand men ascended the river to the first village of Paku, the sound of gongs and cannon from the enemy announcing the preparation of resistance ahead. Cannon always counted for something in the male world of Sarawak. Even today the Iban slang for 'penis' is *cannon*. There were also spears, ululations and warriors dancing savagely on the rooftops, but this time there was no pausing and building of forts. Instead, Keppel and Brooke responded with a charge – waterborne. Like early surfers, they rode the tidal bore which swept them past screaming warriors (Keppel: 'No report from musketry and ordnance could ever make a man's heart feel so *small* as mine did at that horrid yell') and into a barrier built across the river. At the last minute, they spotted a gap and steered for it, avoided a fatal impact, but now found themselves alone on the other side and faced with fire from three forts. 'The banks of the river were covered with warriors, yelling and rushing down to secure – what I suppose they considered me – their prize,' wrote Keppel.

> I had some difficulty in getting my long gig round, and paddling up against the stream; but while my friend Brooke steered the boat, my coxswain and myself kept up a fire, with tolerable aim, on the embrasures, to prevent, if possible, their reloading before the pinnace, our leading boat, could bring her twelve-pound cannonade to bear . . . That evening the country was illuminated for miles by the burning of the capital, Padi, and adjacent villages; at which work, and plundering, our native followers were most expert.[5]

The pursuit of the routed pirates was taken up, bloody fighting in the rain-soaked, darkened jungle, hour after hour, and then – a

The Attack on Padi by the Boats of HMS *Dido*: British Museum

dawn truce. James lectured the local leaders on the advantages of trade over piracy, drawing again perhaps on his *Athenaeum* article. 'They were very humble and submissive; admitted that their lives were forfeited: and if we said they were to die, they were prepared, although, they explained, they were equally willing to live. They promised to refrain for ever from piracy, and offered hostages for their good behaviour.'[6] (James was still new to Bornean warfare. In later years he would find it much more convenient to take hostage the ancient Chinese jars in the longhouses that were fabulously valuable heirlooms.) The force pressed on towards Padi, pausing to collect the heads of slain enemies. Tombs were not spared by the Dayak in these operations. 'Why should we eat the hard-caked rice at the edge of the pot when there is plenty of soft rice at the centre?' they asked.

'The operation of extracting the brains from the lower part of the skull, with a bit of bamboo shaped like a spoon, preparatory to preserving is not a pleasing one. The head is then dried, with the flesh and hair on it, suspended over a slow fire.'[7] Although the Brooke raj would always invoke the gradual eradication of head-hunting as one of its self-evident civilising justifications, in fact to this day most of the heads in Dayak longhouses are identified as taken in the service of the Brookes, whose campaigns greatly inflated the currency of human heads. While the Malays wanted plunder, the Dayaks fought for heads, which they needed for the decent burials of prominent men and for marriage. No self-respecting woman would do anything but sneer at a suitor who brought no head. The future Rajah Charles, always something of a misogynist, would regard the Dayak women as the driving force of the whole headhunting complex, which is what justified the suffering they were subjected to when villages were razed, as they frequently were, on his orders.

A very little razing here sufficed to bring the people to truce, the yielding of hostages and the promise to attend a peace conference in Kuching. The force pressed on to Rembas, where there was a higher proportion of Malays – who might be expected to have firearms – in the population, but now the Sarawak forces too had been reinforced, by some nine hundred Lingga men who noted which way the wind was blowing.

At Rembas, the tide was not up until just before daylight; and having no moon to light us, a night attack was not considered advisable; so that we brought up about a quarter-tide below the town on the evening of the 16th . . . We advanced early in the morning, and soon came up to a succession of formidable barriers, more troublesome to cut through than any we had hitherto encountered. About a mile below the town we landed 700 of the Linga Dayaks on the left bank of the river, who were to separate into two divisions, – commanded by Sherip Jaffar and his son, a remarkably fine and spirited youth, – and creep stealthily through the jungle, for which the country was well adapted, so as to get to the rear of the town and forts, and make a simultaneous attack on the first shot being fired from our boats. The last barrier (and there were four of them) was placed just within point-blank range; the gig being a light boat, I managed to haul her over, close to the bank, and advanced so as to be both out of sight and out of range; and just as our first boat came up with the barrier, I pushed out from under the bank, and opened a fire of musketry on the stockade, which was full of men. This, with the war-yell that followed from their rear (both unexpected), together with their fears having already been worked upon by the destruction of Padi and the defeat of Paku, threw them into the greatest confusion. They fled in all directions without provoking us by firing a shot, although we found the guns loaded. Sherip Jaffar and his Dayaks were gratified by having all the fighting to themselves, and by some very pretty hand-to-hand encounters. We were much amused afterwards by their own account of the heroic deeds they had performed. Lives were lost on both sides, and heads taken. This Rembas was by far the largest and strongest place we had assaulted.[8]

But it was a humane victory. 'A few heads were brought away by our Dayak followers as trophies; but there was no unnecessary sacrifice of life, and I do not believe there was a woman or child hurt.'[9] It has been suggested that this is something of a whitewash but the figures will, of course, never be known. James Brooke always believed in teaching a firm lesson but never revelled in bloodshed for its own sake. Keppel meanwhile had begun to acquire magical powers in the eyes of the locals and was now known to command the tidal bore on the river. Before he could pass on to inflict an even tougher lesson on the Sakarran (Skrang) Dayaks, he was recalled by his superiors to China; but henceforth locals would call him Rajah Laut – the Sea King.

Scarce had Keppel departed than another British ship arrived, but this time it was the *Semarang* under the appropriately named Captain Sir Edward Belcher. Belcher was a very different proposition from Keppel, being a grumpy, sceptical damn-and-blast man, unwilling to be impressed. His task was to report back to London on James's installation in Sarawak and the state of affairs in Borneo more generally. He was particularly to pay attention to the coal deposits of Labuan. He did not think much of the mission, was not prepared to waste a minute longer than necessary over this distraction from China service, and even used the unkind word 'balderdash' of it. Moreover, he proved to be largely immune to the heroic charm of James Brooke and took a dim view of all his 'poodlefaker' endeavours.

Yet once again fate intervened and Belcher's proud vessel struck a rock as he was hurrying away to Brunei. The ship capsized and he was ignominiously obliged to stay and accept Brooke hospitality. James, moreover, housed, fed and entertained the entire crew royally while helping with the righting of the vessel.

Belcher's visit brings us a new source, in one of those adolescent midshipmen that James was so fond of, Frank Marryat, son of the writer of *Masterman Ready*, who testifies fervently to the appeal of such a romantic figure and such an enchanting place for most of the crew – apart from Belcher.

It was a beautiful starry night and, strolling through the village, I soon made acquaintance with a native Dyak, who requested me to enter his house. He introduced me to his family, consisting of several fine girls and a young lad. The former were naked from the shoulders to below the breasts, where a pair of stays, composed of several circles of whalebone, with brass fastenings were secured round their waists; and to the stays was attached a cotton petticoat, reaching to below their knees. This was the whole of their attire. They were much shorter than European women, but well made; very interesting in their appearance, and affable and friendly in their manners. Their eyes were dark and piercing, and I may say there was something wicked in their furtive glances; their noses were but slightly flattened; the mouth rather large; but when I beheld the magnificent teeth which required all its size to display, I thought this rather an advantage. Their hair was superlatively beautiful, and would have been envied by many a courtly dame. It was jet black, and of the finest texture and hung in graceful masses down the back, nearly reaching to the ground . . . As it was late I bade my new friends farewell by shaking hands all round. The girls laughed immoderately at this way of bidding goodbye which, of course, was to them quite novel. I regretted afterwards that I had not attempted the more agreeable way of bidding ladies farewell which, I presume they would have understood better; as I believe kissing is a universal language, perfectly understood from the equator to the pole.[10]

James's own attentions were otherwise engaged in the form of the thirteen-year-old great-nephew of the Bishop of Calcutta, William Brereton. 'He is a delicate and gentlemanly boy, and his age is tender; and when I think of our Charlie [Charles Johnson] I cannot help my heart expanding toward him.' In the capsizing of the vessel he had lost all but his trousers. Elsewhere James notes, 'Writing about boys, I have got a sick one with me, of the name of Brereton, a distant relative of mine – he being a great-nephew of the Bishop of Calcutta; a fine little fellow . . . I have got quite fond of him since he has been here; and somehow there is something in the position of a young volunteer of thirteen years of age, which rouses one's kind feelings; so young, yet forced into manhood, to share privations and fatigues, when yet a boy . . .'[11]

Brereton would later be engaged in the Sarawak administration and die of dysentery in the Skrang fort, at the still-tender age of twenty-four. But for the time being all was japes and juvenile disporting with the 'mids'. 'I do not know what the natives thought of the European Rajah Brooke playing at leapfrog, but it is certain that the Rajah did not care what they thought. I have said little of Mr. Brooke, but I will now say that a more mild, amiable and celebrated person I never knew. Every one loved him, and he deserved it .'[12]

Help came too late for the *Semarang* in the form of a whole fleet of British vessels – the *Diana*, the *Vixen*, the *Harlequin* and the *Wanderer* – but this huge display of British sea power did James no harm, especially since they all sailed off with him to Brunei. Here Belcher was reluctant to land, as smallpox was raging in Borneo Proper. James boldly went ashore to a big set-piece conference, Badrudeen performing with distinction – with the guns of the *Semarang* openly trained on the town to reinforce his eloquence – and Brunei's co-operation was complete. Belcher never properly visited the coal deposits that he was to assess, yet later he would write an authoritatively dismissive report of the whole of Brunei and Sarawak, denouncing the coal as unminable and the Sultan as a savage. But James used the visit to get yet another piece of paper from Brunei confirming his appointment and this time it conferred the government of Sarawak upon himself and his heirs in perpetuity. There were a few troubling clauses about confining his activities to Sarawak alone, but they would be forgotten in time. Crucially, he could no longer be dismissed by the Sultan. He had finally become a freehold rajah in his own right.

Charm. James Brooke reeked of it in a way that does not easily come across in his own somewhat inflated prose. Sarawak was bathed in it as in limpid moonlight. Charm was for James a major instrument of foreign policy. Had the inhabitants been less beautiful or James less of a dashing man's man, his little kingdom could not have thrived. Whenever charm failed, the whole state wobbled.

He was not unconscious of it. 'Do you remember when young at Bath, that people did not *understand* me? Now everyone understands me, and I really think I have acquired, or am acquiring, the most plausible and pleasing manners! I am not in the least shy or reserved to outward appearance, and I really do all I can to shake myself clear of this inherent complaint. Restraint and company I bear far better than formerly . . .'[13] So James to his mother in 1844.

The next beneficiary of the fatal charm was to be Admiral Sir William Parker, Keppel's superior officer. James made a special trip to Penang to meet him, and was delighted to find that all Keppel's anti-piratical operations met with his unreserved approval. In fact, the fleet was off to do some more pirate-bashing in Sumatra on Sir William's authority. Did James not want to come along? He did. If nothing else, the exertion might lift the melancholy caused by the news of the death of his adored mother.

The first battle, at Batu, was one-sided but the second, at Murdu, was a different affair. The locals were unintimidated Malays who owed allegiance to the formidable Sultan of Aceh, and were used to taking on and beating western vessels. Indeed, they had recently taken and plundered a merchant ship with great loss of life. James described it to Templer in vivid terms.

The rascals were prepared for us, and we had five hours as pretty fighting as you would desire. We beat the enemy from point to point, and burned and destroyed as we advanced: but the country was thickly wooded and afforded excellent cover for the enemy's musketry, which annoyed us considerably. In short, it was prettily contested, and we had several times to load and drive the enemy from their stockades. Having burned the place, we returned under a galling fire, to our vessels; and though we had accomplished

COURT OF THE SULTAN OF BRUNEI: BRITISH MUSEUM

all we were sent for, yet we could not well say that the
Murdu people were either subdued or cowed . . . I was
likewise amongst the wounded, as in charging the stockade I
got a spear thrust, which cut my eyebrow in two, a light but
very bloody scratch, which has slightly injured my beauty;
and at the same time a shot inside my right arm, which
rendered me for the time *hors-de-combat*: my eye is now well,
and my arm so well that you may observe that I write as
badly as usual . . . Behold me then a wounded hero, and I
must confess that my vanity was flattered by the crew of the
Wanderer who made a request to be allowed to cheer me
when I quitted the brig.[14]

The compliment was, if anything, made sweeter by the presence
and consternation of Keppel – fresh back from China – who
rebuked him for his rashness. There would be no lack of co-
operation from the Navy now. He had charmed them all in their
own language.

In the summer of 1844, the British Navy made its second military
intervention in the affairs of Sarawak, owing to what was effectively a military old boys' network. Sherip Sahib, who financed and
encouraged pirate raids, together with James's old enemy, Makota,
had been at work during James's absence in Sumatra, spreading
rumours that his departure was permanent and assembling a fleet of
some two hundred Dayak vessels on the Sadong River as in the
good old days. Keppel again interpreted his orders so as to favour his
friend, and assembled a small fleet of vessels that stopped off in
Kuching.

I found the place much altered for the better. Mr. Brooke
had established himself in a new house, built on a beautiful
and elevated mound, from which the intriguing Makota had
just been ejected on my first visit. Neat and pretty-looking
little Swiss cottages had sprung up on all the most
picturesque spots, which gave it quite a European look. He
had also made an agreeable addition to his English society;

and a magazine [shop] of English merchandise had been opened to trade with the natives, together with many other improvements.[15]

Pausing only to get another covering letter, requesting aid, from Hassim and an Islamic blessing from the local imam, HMS *Dido* and the Company paddlesteamer, *Phlegethon*, sailed up on the flood tide, accompanied by a flotilla of smaller ships. A series of strong forts with copious guns had been set up by the 'pirates' and, after a little military foreplay, a major engagement ensued in which the Sarawak forces suffered some losses, but finally the enemy stronghold at Patusan was comprehensively laid waste. James and Badrudeen were in attendance while Dayak warriors finished the job at close quarters, gathering in the heads and making hay with the Sherip's 'curious and extensive wardrobe'. As a precaution, many had shaved their own heads to make them less attractive to the enemy and harder to carry away if taken. Before this, James had presented Sherip Sahib with a twin-barrelled shotgun, here embarrassingly deployed against him, but now the forces managed to destroy some sixty enemy cannon and two tons of gunpowder.

The next two days were spent razing the town. But Keppel had other business.

I also had an account to settle with that cunning rascal Makota, for his aiding and abetting Sherip Sahib in his piracies. He had located himself very pleasantly near a bend in the river, about a mile above Sherip Sahib's settlement, and was in the act of building extensive fortifications, when I had the satisfaction of returning the visit and some of the compliments he would have conferred on my friend Mr. Brooke at Sarawak. Badrudeen, the Rajah's brother, had likewise been duped by this fellow, and was exceedingly anxious to insert the blade of a very sharp and beautiful kris into the body of his late friend. Mr. Brooke, however, was anxious to save his life, which he afterwards had the satisfaction of doing. I shall never forget the tiger-like look

of the young Pangeran when we landed together in the
hopes of surprising the 'Serpent' in his den; but he was too
quick for us, having decamped with his followers, and in so
great a hurry as to leave all his valuables behind, – among
them a Turkish pipe, some chairs once belonging to the
Royalist, and other presents from Mr. Brooke. Every thing
belonging to him was burnt or destroyed save some
handsome brass guns. There was one of about 12cwt. that
had been lent by the Sultan when Makota was in favour,
and which I returned to Badrudeen for his brother.[16]

It is clear here how far James dominates the perceptions of the
British, who constantly repeat his own opinions as their own direct
experience.

The forces moved on, and a running battle began that lasted
four days. This time it was the aged Kuching Malay leader, the
Datuk Patinggi Ali, who displayed the military gall that is gallantry.
'Patinggi Ali was likewise absent, in pursuit of the enemy that had
been driven from the stockades with whom he had had a hand-to-
hand fight, the whole of which – being on rising ground – was
witnessed by our boats' crews, who could not resist hailing his return
from his gallant achievement with three hearty British cheers.'[17] Ali
was perhaps learning from James, but learned only too well. A few
days later he would be killed after rashly charging the enemy while
heavily outnumbered.

The river was now too small for the ships, so the combined forces
took to the boats and pressed on, hacking their way through barri-
cades thrown across the stream. Malay boats could be ninety feet
long with a large cannon mounted at the bow and three or four
swivel guns. Dayak boats might be even longer, some ten feet broad
and manned by sixty to eighty men. Spears, poison darts, swords,
muskets, rockets and swivel guns spat death in both directions.
There were sallies, ambushes, acts of boyish heroism and noble
deaths – the different races dealing with their dead in their various
ways: burning, burying, consigning to the deep. They fired the country as they advanced and pushed ever further up the Skrang River

from one engagement to another, often in great personal danger. 'It would be difficult to describe the scene as I found it,' wrote Keppel.

About twenty boats were jammed together, forming one confused mass: some bottom up; the bows or sterns of others only visible; mixed up, pell-mell with huge rafts; and amongst which were nearly all our advanced little division. Headless trunks, as well as heads without bodies, were lying about in all directions; parties were engaged hand to hand, spearing and krissing each other; others were striving to swim for their lives . . . while on both banks thousands of Dayaks were rushing down to join in the slaughter, hurling their spears and stones on the boats below. For a moment I was at a loss what steps to take for rescuing our people from the embarrassed position in which they were, as the whole mass (through which there was no passage) were floating down the stream, and the addition of fresh boats arriving only increased the confusion. Fortunately, at this critical moment, one of the rafts catching the stump of a tree, broke this floating bridge, making a passage, through which (my gig being propelled by paddles instead of oars) I was enabled to pass.'[18]

Finally they decided to retire to the steamer at Patusan, where Belcher came aboard. What was said at Belcher's meeting with James, following his uncomplimentary report on Sarawak, went unrecorded but on the way he had fatefully engaged pirates from Halmahera – or maybe again it was just an innocent Dutch anti-piracy patrol – and even more fatefully drawn up a claim, calculated at the usual rates, for £12,000 to be paid to himself and his crew. Keppel submitted no accounts for the much sterner action they had just been through.

New alarms. Sherip Jaffar of the town of Banting, himself not beyond suspicion of piracy, had been joined by Sherip Sahib and was said to be collecting troops. Ill-health alone, Sahib asserted coyly to James's messengers, prevented his accepting an invitation

to a conference at Kuching. Meanwhile Makota was taken prisoner by Sarawak forces. In a gesture that outraged local decencies,
James did not execute him but simply favoured him with a lecture
and set him free. Perhaps the sheer diplomatic awkwardness of exe-
cuting a senior Bruneian royal prince for defending what was still
Bruneian territory had a role in this act of clemency.

The ships sailed again for Banting and, in an act of gross intimidation, sang 'Rule Britannia' lustily outside the town to the
accompaniment of fireworks. It worked. Jaffar was deposed, in due
form, by Badrudeen while Sahib fled to the Dutch border, knowing
that James would not pursue him there. As Keppel describes it:

> A second conference on shore took place, at which all the
> chiefs of the surrounding country attended . . . On this
> occasion I had the satisfaction of witnessing what must have
> been – from the effect I observed it to have produced on the
> hearers – a splendid piece of oratory, delivered by Mr.
> Brooke in the native tongue, with a degree of fluency I had
> never witnessed before, even in a Malay . . . From these
> people many assurances were received of their anxiety and
> willingness to co-operate with us in our laudable
> undertaking: and one and all were alike urgent that the
> government of their river should be transferred to the
> English.[19]

The process by which little Sarawak would grow had begun, all
quite legal and driven entirely by local demand, of course.

Chapter 8

Treachery

It was time for Hassim to be sent back to Brunei. He was a nuisance in Kuching, implying a higher authority than James himself. Moreover, James had plans for him in the capital. He was to be the next Sultan of Brunei, though the price James paid was high: separation from beloved Badrudeen, who was needed there to give the ever-vacillating Hassim a little backbone. They travelled aboard Belcher's *Semarang*, the royal ladies shaded from impudent eyes by elaborate screens. Once they arrived, Pangeran Usop, Makota's friend, fell from grace and Hassim was reinstalled as heir and principal adviser to the Sultan. Sarawak, the tail, had begun to wag Brunei, the dog.

Things were going well for James. It even seemed that his campaign at home to establish Sarawak as at least a British moral responsibility if not a formal protectorate was working. In 1845 Captain Bethune of the *Driver* arrived with Mr Wise, James's commercial representative in London, and brought a florid and empty letter appointing him Confidential Agent to Her Majesty's Government in Borneo. Never mind, it could and would be turned to use. The British were pressing ahead with the realisation of one of James's most ill-considered fantasies, the takeover of the

Bruneian island of Labuan as a coaling station, and Sir Thomas Cochrane, Commander of the Far Eastern Fleet, pledged himself to help James with the active suppression of pirates. An impressive array of ships sailed from Singapore and as they passed through Brunei a broadside through the roof of Pangeran Usop, friend of Makota and enemy of British influence, intimidated the anti-British opposition, while a raid on the 'pirate' Usman of Marudu lifted a major threat both to Brunei and Sarawak. Returning via Brunei again, James discovered that Usop had attempted a military insurrection and been driven away by brave Badrudeen. 'Pangeran Badrudeen fights like an European; the very spirit of the Englishman is in him; he has learned this at Sarawak.'[1] Badrudeen even cared for Usop's women, and chivalrously divided their lord's gold amongst them. Sultan Ali, perhaps predictably, declared himself their particular protector and seized it all back. Usop was outlawed and he and his brother were 'strangled with all the respect due to their relationship to the Sultan'. A rival American attempt to gain exclusive mining and trading rights foundered and the year ended with Sarawak finally at peace, with the British party in the ascendant throughout the whole of Borneo and trade flourishing. James even got excited about the number of plates sold in Kuching per month and began to think about designing his own flag. It was all bound to turn out badly.

'If I am lying may I be eaten by a crocodile.' Thus a solemn Malay oath. The Malays and Dayaks might have warned the Rajah to beware of the omens to be read in crocodiles, but he would not have listened. Many years later, Ranee Sylvia would write a poignant romance about a poor crocodile hunter of Sarawak whose adored young wife pined for ever more gold bracelets and so ran off, leaving him heartbroken. Years afterwards he found her remains, complete with bracelets, in the hairball in the belly of a crocodile he slew. So she had not been faithless after all, simply eaten. To this day, the Sarawak Museum exhibits similar hairballs cut from the stomachs of crocodiles, one containing a watch, another a dental plate. They are greatly appreciated by local visitors, who see in them something akin to the workings of divine dramatic irony.

The first to fall foul of crocodiles was young Williamson, the Eurasian interpreter, who was discredited owing to the excessive influence of Malay ladies in his court decisions. Quite what this meant in practice we can only speculate, but James was so outraged by it that he used the ultimate sanction, short of capital punishment, in his little country. He ceased to invite Williamson to dinner. The effect was dramatic far beyond its nutritional implications. Williamson went into a decline, others sought to act as intermediaries, a reconciliation was arranged; and an invitation to dine was again issued. But perhaps they all drank too deeply of the cup of friendship. On his way back across the river from the *astana* to the town, Williamson plunged from the little ferry into the water 'and did not rise'. The local crocodiles got him. James would be accused by his enemies of a Caligula-like act of assassination.

But James was no murderer – even a crocodile's fate was carefully weighed up, as if in the lawcourt. A man-eater was captured and brought to him, and a discussion arose concerning its fate.

One party maintained that it was proper to bestow all praise and honour on the kingly brute, as he was himself a Raja among animals, and was now brought to meet the Raja; in short, that praise and flattery were agreeable to him, and would induce him to behave genteelly in my [Brooke's] presence. The other party said that it was very true that on this occasion Raja met Raja, but that the consequence of honouring and praising a captured crocodile would be that the crocodile community at large would become vain and unmanageable, and after hearing of the triumphant progress of their friend and relative, would take to the same course with double industry, and every one eat his man for the sake of obtaining the like fame.

Having maturely weighed the arguments on both sides, taking also into deep consideration the injury which so unwieldy a captive might do in roaming over my garden and

grounds, followed by a host of admirers, I decided that he
should be instantly killed without honours; and he was
despatched accordingly, his head severed from the trunk,
and the body left exposed as a warning to all other
crocodiles that may inhabit these waters.[2]

And in Brunei a still larger crocodile, the old Sultan, was intriguing again to rid himself of the pro-English faction at court.

One night, when the brothers [of Hassim] were scattered,
the signal was given: bands of armed men left the palace,
and pulling silently in the darkness, arrived unobserved
near the houses of the different brothers. They attacked
simultaneously. The young princes had but few followers
with them. Badrudeen fought gallantly: he defended the
entrance of his house for some time, but with three or four
followers he could do little against a murderous band of
forty or fifty. Finding that he with his *kris* held his own,
and that they could not force an entrance into the house,
one of the assailants fired. The shot took effect in
Badrudeen's left wrist, and as that arm fell he received a
severe wound in the right shoulder and several wounds in
the body. His few followers were either killed or fled. He
managed, however, to gain the inner apartments, where he
found his sister, a favourite concubine, and Jaffar, a slave
lad. The latter he commanded to reach down a barrel of
powder and spread the contents on a mat. He then called
the women to sit near him, and turning to the lad said:
'You will take this signet ring (One which Mr. Brooke had
given him) to my friend, Mr. Brooke, tell him what has
occurred, let him inform the Queen of England that I was
faithful to my engagements and add,' he said, 'that my last
thoughts were of my true friend, Mr. Brooke.' He then
ordered the lad to save himself. Jaffar opened the lattice-
like flooring, slipped down a post into the water, and
swimming to a small canoe was enabled to paddle quietly

away, while the murderers, suspicious, were cautiously
making their entrance into the house. Jaffar had not
proceeded many yards when a loud explosion told him that
the gallant prince had set fire to the powder, rather than
fall into the hands of his enemies.'[3]

Hassim, suddenly decisive at the last, similarly tried to blow himself up into, or as, a hero, but inevitably botched it. A solitary
survivor of the blast, he finally blew his brains out with a pistol.
Only two of his brothers escaped the massacre, one wounded, one
insane. The news arrived dramatically in Sarawak aboard the
Hazard, whose commander had been saved from an assassination
attempt by Jaffar, who had paddled out to the ship to warn him that
the so-called emissaries of Hassim who had come aboard were in
fact to be his killers.

And to what was all this attributed? To the conflict between the
piratical mode of life and legitimate trade, or that between vas-
salage to the English and proud independence, or that between two
different notions of legitimate succession to the sultanate? No.
According to St John, it was umbrellas.

One of the customs of Brunei was, that when a non-noble
passed before a house inhabited by a royal personage, he was
obliged to fold his umbrella and expose himself either to the
hot rays of the sun or to the rain. The custom had fallen into
desuetude, but these princes determined to revive it. The
principal street of Brunei is the main river. Whenever a
non-noble was seen passing before Muda Hassim's palace
with his umbrella up, officers were ordered to pursue and
bring his canoe to the landing-place, and he himself was to
be brought before the Rajahs to be fined. This gave rise to
much abuse. The insolent followers of the princes, secure
from all punishment, beat and otherwise ill-treated the most
respectable members of the merchant class and thus
alienated from the cause the most devoted partisans of Muda
Hassim.[4]

But for James, as usual, it was all about loyalty and betrayal. The death of Hassim was a loss for the country but, as for Badrudeen, this was the stuff of the London stage – mustachio-twirling villains, wronged love, noble death and, above all, deathbed declarations and tokens of kept faith. James was desolate.

The signet, my own crest and gift to him, that Badrudeen sent to me in his dying moments, as a pledge not to be false to him in death. It is a poor, a melancholy consolation that he died so nobly; his last thought was upon me – his last request that I should tell the Queen of England how he perished. Surrounded by traitors, who still held back from his desperation, wounded to death, he applied the match which blew himself, his sister, and another wounded and faithful woman into eternity. A nobler, braver, more upright prince could not exist. I have lost a friend – he is gone and I remain; I trust, but in vain, to be an instrument to bring punishment on the perpetrators of the atrocious deed . . . My suzerain the Sultan! – the villain Sultan! – need expect no mercy from me, but justice he shall have. I no longer own his authority, or hold Sarawak under his gift . . . he has *murdered our friends*, the faithful *friends* of Her Majesty's Government, *because they were our friends*.[5]

Adding insult to injury, the Sultan also stole Badrudeen's ring, James's signet ring, from young Jaffar before he was able to hand it over to James.

James was incensed to the point of madness.

Violent passions and sleepless nights are hard to bear. I lay no blame on anyone. I look forward as much as I can, and backward as little, but I ought not and cannot forget my poor friends who lie in their bloody graves. Oh how great is my grief and rage! . . . But the British Government will surely act, and if not – then let me remember, I am still at war with this traitor and murderer – one more determined

struggle – one last convulsive effort – and, if it fail, Borneo,
and all for which I have so long, so earnestly laboured, must
be abandoned and . . .[6]

The journal ends with a jagged line teetering across the page. For
once, he has no more words. Badrudeen was for James both a breath-
ing corporeal presence and the incarnation of an abstract idea. In
what seems inevitably a homoerotic, though possibly unconsum-
mated, passion for the prince, James loved the notion that the whole
of Brunei could undergo a regeneration, that it could attain a beauty
that was at once physical and deeply moral. Badrudeen's death is the
beginning of the death of James's optimism.

The rush of immediate practical considerations overtook such
simplicities. He was now HM Confidential Agent, not a free man.
The Governor of Singapore sent over the *Phlegethon*, but under the
false impression Kuching was under attack. Admiral Cochrane
became involved, but was uncomfortably aware that Brunei was a
sovereign country. James raged of burning and deposing but it was
not until six months after the massacre that the British turned up to
actually do something. Cochrane approached Borneo Proper with a
fleet of British ships and after a little diplomatic posturing sought to
enter the town. Fortunately for later Brooke history, the Bruneians
fired on him and so relieved him of all further need for justification.
The flag had been insulted, a treaty thus violated, and there must be
a response.

The engagement was not without risk. The Bruneian forts were
formidable and the thin iron plates of the *Phlegethon* easily pierced
by local gunfire. But the defenders lacked resolve and so their forts
were swiftly taken and the guns silenced. The Sultan fled and
Cochrane toyed with the idea of investing James with his title but,
old hand that he was, knew that he could not get away with it in
England. Instead, a provisional government was established under
Hassim's brother Mohammed and his brother-in-law Munim, until
Sultan Omar Ali formally submitted, in a grovelling apology to the
baffling foreign queen he had never seen but who caused him such
annoyance.

Signing the Treaty for the Cession of Labuan: British Museum

James got yet another piece of paper giving him the title to Sarawak and the right to mine coal. In one of their most foolish acts of acquisition, the British got the pestilential and profitless island of Labuan as a coaling station and oaths of loyalty and friendship and, in return, undertook to suppress piracy along the north coast of Borneo. James nobly assumed responsibility for the dependants of the Hassim/Badrudeen camp, 'a perfect menagerie of old women and children', and shipped them back to Sarawak.

After yet another excursion with the Navy against Balanini pirates, he handed the Sarawak administration over to Arthur Crookshank, the police magistrate and a sort of nephew. (Nepotism was a Malay cultural practice that James intended to continue in Sarawak.) It was high time to pay a visit to England.

Chapter 9

Home and Away

James Brooke arrived in Southampton on 1 October 1847 after a journey that he described as 'the Inferno with a French cook and cool claret'.[1] He had been away for nine years and it came as a shock to find that he was famous. Wise, his agent, and John Templer had long been lobbying on his behalf but, more importantly, Keppel had just published parts of James's journal, to largely favourable reviews. *The Times* recommended that the government support and protect 'the heroic and indefatigable Mr. Brooke', and went on in the terms of a laudatory obituary.

> Much as we owe . . . to guns and grapeshot, we are indebted still more to the peaceful and meritorious exertions of one man, for the advances which have happily been made towards civilisation and peace amongst the Malay people of whom we speak. England owes a debt of obligation to Mr. Brooke, Rajah of Sarawak, which she will not easily repay. One volume of Captain Keppel's book contains the diary of this gentleman and we know not when we have read a history of true greatness so modestly narrated; a series of events so full of interest and striking novelty. The career of

Mr. Brooke, whilst in the highest degree romantic, has been throughout one of practical benevolence.[2]

The natives had not bowed down to guns, then, but to pure Englishness. James was the hot topic of the moment, the proof that Englishness, civilisation and progress went hand in hand. He travelled everywhere and met everyone, was endlessly lionised and became a freeman of the City of London, courted by the ancient Goldsmiths' and Fishmongers' Companies, a member of the foremost clubs. The government upgraded his appointment to that of Consul-General for Borneo at £2,000 a year, but still neither recognised it as a sovereign state nor accorded it British protection. Oxford gave him an honorary doctorate, while even the school from which he had run away and which had refused to take him back was now anxious to claim him as its own and offered a dinner in his honour. He met lords and ministers and military and merchants and churchmen and everywhere he did what he loved to do – talked about Sarawak. And finally he met the Queen.

Three minutes before eight, the groom of the chambers ushered me from my apartment in the York Tower, conducted me along a splendid gallery, resplendent with lights, and pictures, and statues decorated with golden ornaments, the richest carpets, and bouquets of fresh flowers, and ushered me into a drawing-room as fine as mortal eye could wish to see. Directly afterward Lady Westmoreland and Lady Peel, with Lord Westmoreland and Sir Robert [the ex-Prime Minister] entered with the lord-in-waiting (Lord Morley), equerries and grooms: then came the Duke and Duchess of Bedford etc., etc., and last the doors were thrown wide open, and the Queen and Prince Albert and the Duchess of Kent were ushered in, attended by the court ladies. I had to kiss hands on my presentation: her Majesty said very sweetly that she was happy to make my acquaintance. I bowed to the ground . . . and I may conclude

by saying, that, highly honoured as I have been, delighted
and pleased, yet I shall be glad when it is over.[3]

James's headquarters were in Mivart's Hotel on Lower Brook
Street, where he ran a sort of male messroom of diners and late
carousers, among them the father of his later biographer, Spenser
St John. It was here that was born the fable of his romance with
Angela Burdett-Coutts, the richest woman in England.

> One day at breakfast, a waiter brought in a letter, which Mr.
> Brooke asked permission to open immediately. He then said,
> 'This is a curious one.' It was from some lady, who,
> enamoured of his deeds, proposed herself in marriage. The
> letter continued that if Mr. Brooke had no intention of
> marrying, he was to destroy a note which was enclosed, and
> which contained her name, her address and all particulars as
> to her family and fortune.
>   The guests laughingly said, 'Have an intention to marry,
> and open the note': but Mr. Brooke immediately rose from
> the table, saying, 'I have no intention of marrying,' and put
> the letter and the enclosure into the fire. If the lady be still
> living, it will be a comfort to her to know what became of
> her communication.[4]

James's life had an odd habit of assuming novelettish forms.

Things were not going well, however, with James's London agent.
Wise was a thoroughly metropolitan and modern man, and the
Brookes would always have a country-gentry suspicion of trade and
businessmen. 'The pollution of lucre takes possession of them. It is
the devil's own go-cart, with four or five other pet vices as lackeys
hanging on behind.'[5] Wise had been hoping to float a public company that would buy out James's interest in Sarawak with himself
owning half the shares and make lots of quick money. To James's
fury, he had already sent a trading ship to Sarawak without his permission and arranged the issue of trading tokens bearing James's

head instead of a legitimate currency. 'I will become no party to a bubble,' James raged. He would sell off his antimony monopoly, or the right to trade in opium, but no more. For him speculators divided into two groups – 'the doers and the done'. 'Slow, cautious, gradual' were his watchwords, and above all it was the interests of locals that must be paramount. Never for a moment did he doubt his ability to know what those interests were, and there was always the suspicion that another's profit was a theft from them. He would never have permitted the ruthless asset-stripping of Sarawak's natural resources that followed on from independence. But James had the wit to see that the problem was more general, that, however much cold water he poured on excessive expectations, Europeans would always find this hard to believe because they were still navigating by the old mythical maps that made Sarawak a place of romance. 'Really the mania for an El Dorado is so universal that I should not be astonished if such a place was discovered – a mountain of gold with nothing wanting but pickaxes – or some other such vulgar heaven upon earth. Everything distant seems to attract the imagination; distance lends enchantment to the view – distance of time softens down the crimes and errors of the dead – and Hope, herself, is but reality at a distance. In short, distance is a great and undiscovered principle!'[6]

It could be his own epitaph. And Templer foolishly allowed Wise to see these confidential letters, where James expressed his doubts about him in such eloquent and hurtful turns of phrase. Wise would not forgive and forget – in fact he took copies, and his vindictiveness was set to become a running sore. Slandering James behind his back, Wise nevertheless showed him a sweet face in public, in the hope of exploiting the coal of Labuan, of which James was now named Governor, through his new Eastern Archipelago Company. In 1848, after a deal of bickering and the expensive bankruptcy of a trading company in which Wise had involved him, James effectively fired him, following it with the sort of nit-picking legalistic dispute he so enjoyed, over whether Wise was strictly an agent or a partner. In 1849 Wise entered into a relationship with James's enemies and set to plotting his downfall.

Ceremony of Hoisting the British Flag on Labuan: Parker Gallery

After four months James had had enough of England but, before leaving, he sat for his portrait by Sir Francis Grant RA, a painter newly fashionable by royal preferment. The painting shows him in Byronic pose, leaning on what is presumably a convenient rock, hair carefully tousled by a passing zephyr, staring into the future with a confidence that some might term arrogance. He is roguishly garbed in his Royal Yacht Squadron outfit, tight-trousered and bare-throated, knowingly swashbuckling. Behind him steam the rivers and jungles of Sarawak, while tropic clouds swirl messianically above. No wonder ladies sent him offers of marriage. The painter made him a present of the canvas; James never even bothered to say thank you.

They set sail from Portsmouth in HMS *Maeander*, commanded by his old chum Keppel. On board were his new secretary Spenser St John, William Napier, the pettish Lieutenant Governor to Labuan, and Hugh Low, botanist and Secretary to the Government. There were also Mrs and Miss Napier, who were held by the men to be a confounded nuisance when tempers grew as short as space aboard the crowded ship. Miss Napier was of mixed race and devastatingly beautiful, a terrible threat to the established hierarchy of empire. More importantly for James, there were other friends aboard.

> Mr. Brooke . . . had a large cabin, and this was the rendezvous of as unruly a set of young officers as it has been my fortune to meet. He had a nephew on board, Charles Johnson, a staid sub-lieutenant, who endeavoured to preserve order, but it was of little avail. The noisy ones were in the ascendant, led by a laughing, bright-faced lad, who, when he was a midshipman on the *Agincourt* in 1845–47, had become acquainted with Mr. Brooke, and whose fondness for cherry-brandy was only equalled by his love of fun. No place in the cabin was respected: six or seven would throw themselves on the bed, careless of whether Mr. Brooke was there or not, and skylark over his body as if he

SIR JAMES BROOKE BY SIR FRANCIS GRANT, 1847:
NATIONAL PORTRAIT GALLERY

were one of themselves. In fact, he was as full of play as any
of them.[7]

There was amazement at James's forbearance. He really seemed
to mind such youthful physical liberties not at all. James often crept
about the deserted ship at night and 'kept the middle watch [12 to
4 a.m.] with a friend'. 'Scandal' is perhaps too strong a word to use
of the effect of this behaviour on the vessel, but St John notes that
it led to 'coolness' from the officers, not perhaps improved by
James's dancing the polka with one of them. The 'friend' was, judg-
ing by later correspondence, probably that 'laughing, bright-faced
lad' Charles Grant, nicknamed affectionately by him both Charley
and Hoddy Doddy (an awkward and ungainly person). He was a
considerable catch, the grandson of the Earl of Elgin. James had lav-
ished upon him a good deal of attention and very expensive, sadly
obvious, presents – weapons, clothes, jewellery; later there would be
an Arab steed called Baby – since meeting him at the age of fourteen. The Francis Grant who had painted James was his uncle and –
in line with Brookean nepotism – it was almost inevitable that one
of James's nephews should marry Charley's sister. In 1847, before
their return to England, James wrote him a twenty-page letter, 'The
Rajah's Journal to the Hoddy Doddy',[8] while waiting for the young
sailor to join him in Singapore. It contains a fantasy description of
the mids of HMS *Agincourt* attacking a plum pudding:

> *My eyes, a rare delicious sight is here*
> *A sight of wonder but no sight of fear.*
> *Solid, consistent, majestically tough,*
> *Behold a living map of unsliced Dough.*
> *The knitted walls a precipice present*
> *With plums and cannon bristling at each vent.*
> *Bombproof and arched, the heavy summit*
> *Like Etna sprinkled with eternal snows,*
> *Like Etna towering and like Etna hot*
> *Just like emerged from out the devil's pot*
> *Conscious of strength, the smokey fabric stands,*

and frowns defiance to all mortal hands . . .
So stands Dough Citadel, a virgin post,
Uncaptured though begirt with many a host,
Like other virgin places that I wot,
Uncaptured yet because assailed not.
Smoking it stands and seems to dare the worst.
The storm is rife – not care I when it burst . . .
And youthful Doddy firmly stands his ground.
Unflinching still, he's swallowed full a pound . . .

One does not have to be a committed Freudian to detect a phallic subtext to all this. Another poem, after all, is written in affectionate terms to Charley's adolescent pimples. It is the usual amalgam of fierce compassion, ardent self-sacrifice and barely suppressed lust that occurs in many of James's letters to his young men, the forced, jokey voice of a passion that knows itself to be ultimately tragic. Charley himself gave a slightly baffled account of their relationship, though this could hardly have been a first encounter with homosexual attraction – he had, after all, served an apprenticeship in a nineteenth-century English public school followed by one in the British Navy – and he had the acuity to note the centrality of compassion in the formation of James's love. Charley had been badly bullied, and the Rajah

took a fancy to me, I can't tell why, but I think partly because I was a little fellow, for I was about the smallest in the ship. We went together to Borneo, we were together for some months, he asked me to go to [blank] which I wished for very much but we were both refused for several had to come before me. We again met about a year afterwards. I saw a great deal of him, he was on board for nearly six months, we went to Brunei together and several other places. We again met at Penang, about six months after this, and it was there I saw so much of him. We were much together and often corresponded. The long and short of this is that I knew the Rajah and I loved him. If I got into difficulties or had any rows, or anything of that sort, I went to him for advice and you know the advice he gave me in his journal. We were, as you know, for a long time together during his stay in England, and we both learned a great deal about the other, and he got me appointed to this ship . . . I have great reason to be fond of the Rajah – I am proud of having such a friend, and I am sure he is as fond of me as I am of him, for he would not have done for me what he has, nor would he have done it without intending to do what he can.[9]

In England, James regrets that he cannot visit his new passion at Kilgraston, his country seat. 'All other considerations apart, I regret not being able to come because I should like to have stored up Kilgraston for a topic of conversation on a moonlight night in the East.'[10] They seem instead to have met at James's sister's house, and James arranged for Charley's transfer to Keppel's ship, where he was irritated that Keppel would not release him to serve as his personal ADC. To overcome any doubts entertained by Hoddy Doddy's parents over this strange attachment, his mother received a bracelet of shiny Sarawak gold and his father gruff, avuncular promises, man-to-man style, of £5,000 and more to be put in trust for the boy in case of the Rajah's death. It was never paid. Nevertheless, in 1848 Hoddy Doddy left the Navy at James's insistent urging and joined the Sarawak service. In a long letter, marked 'Private and Confidential', James wrote to Charley in 1847 concerning the duties of an ADC, summing them up as, 'He is pulling the string which makes the puppets about him dance,'[11] which is presumably the explanation for the existence of a comic poem on the same theme elsewhere in his papers. He continues, 'You *must* watch the peculiarities of my disposition, and yield to them. You must frequently sacrifice your own will, and pleasure in trifles, to my wishes. You must be always kind in manner as well as in reality, and you will find that these sacrifices to me will each be without return and if that they be profitable that my heart will be more open and more confiding.' After this, the letter breaks off to resume in an altered hand and a more sententious and pompous voice on the subject of statesmen.

CHARLES GRANT WITH BLANCHES AND SUPPORTERS, 1859. PHOTOGRAPH BY
BISHOP MCDOUGALL: BRITISH MUSEUM

James and Charley seemed almost inseparable. When the Rajah travelled, his ADC, of course, travelled with him. On their next trip back to England they shared a cabin.

When the ship arrived in Singapore, there was news waiting. James was to be invested as a Knight Commander of the Order of the Bath in a flurry of official engagements. He was *Sir* James at last, a pillar of the establishment, a romantic popular figure, an accredited British official. It was the high point of his life and he could have no idea that at that very moment, back in London, a new and less happy chapter was opening. For James Brooke and the Labuan administration had attracted the terrier-like attention of the honourable member for Montrose, Mr Joseph Hume, a staunch reforming Liberal with a reputation for sniffing out British colonial oppression. Although Britain was a major imperial power, the moment of government-sponsored jingoist expansion was not yet come. Colonies had been taken inadvertently and grudgingly. They were expensive and troublesome. Hume rose in the House to question the foolish expenditure on this newly British island of Labuan and other Liberals rallied to the cause, questioning the morality of British military actions in the east. Lord John Russell, the Prime Minister, defended James Brooke, and a strategic motion to cut the new Governor's salary was swiftly defeated. So far so good. But it was the start of a long and bitter struggle.

James and his entourage docked in Sarawak to a greeting of gongs and salutes. There would be high ceremony, but James was most gratified by the relatives of Hassim, who shinned up the side of the ship and in through a quarterlight to greet him with little formality but great feeling. The sailors were most moved to be sprinkled with coloured rice, gold dust and rosewater by Inda, beautiful daughter of Datuk Gaffur, strewn from a chamber pot. The band of the *Maeander* played as James's new Sarawak flag was run up the flag-pole for the first time. It was based on the Brooke family crest, a red and purple cross on a yellow ground. But they were surprised to find two new families installed in the courthouse. In their absence, the Borneo Church Mission had arrived. Sarawak had attracted so much public attention in England that it was considered fit for evangelisation – despite James's own rather wild ideas of the Christian faith – and so the Sarawak mission had come into being, under the formidable Frank McDougall and his slight but indestructible wife, Harriette.

At the Hanover Square meeting that led to the setting up of the mission, the Reverend Francis Thomas McDougall had made his appearance with a speech that had not impressed James. 'The tone of his speech made Mr. Brooke sigh,' St John noted, 'but it was hoped his actions would be more sensible than his words.'[12] Frank McDougall was a stout man of military family, one of the most highly qualified surgeons of his day, polyglot, an excellent sailor, a former mine manager, champion jockey, rower and scholar. In fact, Frank McDougall was depressingly outstanding in just about all spheres of human endeavour. His appearance was a little frightening, with wild hair, a huge beard and a complexion so dark as to be confusing in pigment-sensitive colonial circles. Harriette, his adoring wife, was musical on both harp and piano, artistic in watercolours and needle and thread, yet combined a ruthless practicality with the highest spiritual ideals. Though raised in a house grown wealthy on the sale of insurance, she had personally intervened to save Frank from a safe, dull and dutiful life at the British Museum, going in person to secure his release from employment there and urging him to undertake this new and dangerous endeavour among the ungodly. She would always be as much a mother as a wife to Frank. Harriette had what was kindly called 'a speaking face' and was also prone to giggle. At the first of his sermons that she attended, fat Frank got stuck in the pulpit while delivering a sermon on the text 'Strive to enter in by the strait gate' and Harriette never forgot it. In later days, when Frank was a bishop, his superior wrote to him perplexedly, 'I have taken the liberty . . . to caution you, now you are a chief pastor and a father in God, against excessive hilarity of spirits. There is a mild gravity, with occasional tokens of delight and pleasure, becoming your sacred character, not noisy mirth.'[13]

They had come with a family called the Wrights, who took one

FRANCIS AND HARRIETTE McDOUGALL WITH MILDRED (ABOUT 1868):
BRITISH MUSEUM

look at Sarawak and moved straight back to Singapore. Harriette was made of sterner stuff, convinced that shadows merely enhance the interest of a scene. 'I often think that no one *really* wants to go out as a missionary, who isn't a little queer in the head,' she remarked. Sarawak life would show the truth of the observation.

James too had views about missionaries.

The truth is, there are two sorts of Christian missions – the one of unmixed good, the other somewhat dangerous. Some missionaries begin at the wrong end – by preaching Christianity or running down Mohammedanism or any other received belief. These show gross ignorance of human nature, and neglect the principles of toleration; for if we abuse another's belief, we confirm him in it, and make him a bigot, and he will rather retort abuse than hear reason. Such a mission will never succeed in any Malay country, and probably not amongst the Dayaks. The other sort of missionaries are the American, who live quietly, practise medicine, relieve the distressed, do not dispute or argue, and aim to educate the children. With the Dayaks it requires a person to foster and protect them, to teach them the arts of life, to inspire confidence, become acquainted with their manners and prejudices, and above all, to educate their children . . . If X wants a red-hot missionary crusade, to begin by telling the natives that their religion is a lie and their prophet an impostor – for though this be true, it should not be told – I want none such. If he wants a mission of reasonable and educated men, who know when to speak and when to be silent, who hold civilization and education as a means of religion, who will strive to enlarge the native mind, and to give them the outlines of our religion, its accordance with theirs in its earliest stages, to instruct the children, to benefit the adult, then the sooner they come the better.[14]

It was a decidedly pragmatic view of evangelism. James had

sworn not to interfere with the Islam of the Malays and would hold to that, but Dayaks, not subscribing to any of the world faiths, were seen as simply 'without religion' and so fair game. It was deemed politically a good idea they not become Muslims. Indeed, just as in the days of the Vikings, Christian conversion was counted the only cure for piracy and headhunting. Initially, Frank MacDougall seemed to fit in with these views.

The missionaries were At Home to the Rajah on Thursdays and were received in the *astana* every Tuesday and dined there once a month. Harriette adored being the only white lady in Sarawak. But things were far from easy for the new arrivals. Their eldest boy, Charley, had been left in England but Harriette was encumbered with a young baby, Harry, and was pregnant again. Despite Frank's medical qualifications, she found it impossible to raise children in Sarawak and in the next fifteen months she would lose three. In line with James's views, Frank opened a dispensary and Harriette a school. The Rajah immediately dumped four bastard children of Europeans on her, but at least paid for their education. The Church was being used to raise a new administrative class. James always judged the mission from the point of view of its utility to the government.

It was inevitably Frank himself who drew up the plans for the mission building, leaving the minor artistic touches of the doors, railings and arches to Harriette's more gentle brush. He knew all about building, of course, but would receive unexpected help. They had sailed from England in the perilous *Maria Louisa*, and wallowed, in God's hands, through a series of cataclysmic thunderstorms with the cargo of coal and gunpowder sweating and shifting beneath them. The ship was wrecked on the return journey and its German carpenter, Stahl, turned up in search of employment. Frank set him to work on his new building, 'Noah's Ark'. They took their biblical building metaphors very seriously and builded high and with solid foundations digged deep, for the couple had learned the lesson of the courthouse, constructed 'like a big cage' where, with kettles of boiling water, they waged constant war on ants, to whom English oak 'seemed like a slice of cake'. The solution was the ironwood that the Dayaks used for their longhouses, so hard that it blunted the tools and reduced the insects to despair. Soon the building began to take shape – offices, dormitories and classrooms below, dining room, library, place of worship and bedroom on the first floor and three more sweltering bedrooms tucked under the ironwood roof. It is still there in Kuching, looking for all the world like a mock-Elizabethan Home Counties golf clubhouse, as a solid testament to their determination and faith.

The hill was already occupied by the Adam and Eve of cobras, convenient symbols of evil and the wilderness. Adam was dispatched by Frank with a stout stick just before it could kill the carpenter. Eve was encountered late at night as Frank wandered into his dressing room with a candle and book. Having no stick to hand, he smote it this time with the book, a heavyweight copy of Robinson's sermons discussing St Paul and the viper. The coincidence accorded nicely with the McDougalls' ideas of the essential practicality of Christianity.

Harriette walked up every day to see the progress on the building, taught the children their letters in the white sand of the site and chatted cheerfully in Malay with the Chinese workers. Frank, of course, had to interfere, importing more efficient wheelbarrows to replace the hoes and baskets they customarily used to shift earth, but the workers found the wheelbarrows simply too heavy to carry. They shared their tea with Harriette and she was quite unflummoxed to find that their 'tea' was hot rice spirit.

The pirates were stepping up their raids again. Makota was in the ascendant in Brunei. The troublesome Muslim divine, Sherip Mullar, had returned to his haunts among the Saribus Dayaks. Both were plotting and there had been killings all around Sarawak. The Melanau people up the coast were suffering; they were just outside James's jurisdiction, but he would soon shift the border.

First he had to start the British settlement at Labuan, and that tied him down for a good two months. On the island, everyone was racked with fever; many were at the point of death – Indian troops and Europeans alike; some died; there were no resources; the naval

BISHOP MCDOUGALL: BRITISH MUSEUM

protection was withdrawn. James raged but was too ill himself to do much more than a little gentle inter-island diplomacy.

By the time he returned to Kuching, a hundred Malays had been slaughtered in Sadong and the town was awash with Melanau refugees. Something had to be done. James struggled to mount a campaign on his own – the Malay leaders had the right to summon their followers for war service while the Rajah provided the rice – but it came to nothing. Then the Company steamer *Nemesis* arrived. In March 1849 a pointless expedition sailed into the Saribus country and burned a few longhouses in a token manner, but the pirates were making hay elsewhere. The Navy retired and promised help for July. Rather against the odds, they kept their promise, and the second expedition was a resounding military success. The *Albatross*, *Royalist* and *Nemesis* joined a fleet of eighteen Sarawak war canoes led by James in the *Rajah Singh*. Fifty more Iban boats from the Lundu and Balau area as well as Malays from the Sadong and Samarahan Rivers met them. William Brereton, former 'mid' friend of James, was put in command of the *Tiger*, and since he was a great favourite with Harriette, she did her bit for the war effort by embroidering his standard, putting in the eyes and teeth of its tiger's head during a moonlight boat ride with Frank.

The fleet learned that a Saribus flotilla had recently set sail for the north, and rather than pursue them they decided to barricade the mouths of the rivers and quietly lie in wait for their return. A week later they did return, at dusk, and a pitched sea battle ensued in the bright moonlight and the eerie light of blue flares. In England the Battle of Batang Marau would become infamous as 'the *Albatross* affair'. Brute courage served ill against the concentrated fire and thrashing paddle wheels of the well-named *Nemesis*. 'The action was a night action; the pirates were entirely surrounded, and, after their first panic dashed at Point Marau and engaged our native force guarding it; but, failing to force a passage at once, they ran their perahus [canoes] ashore to the number of ninety, and fled into the jungle. In this encounter several of our people were wounded, and one or two killed. The remains of this large fleet, trying to escape by sea, were cut up by the steamer *Nemesis*.'[15]

In the course of five hours that night, the pirates lost a hundred boats and five hundred men against fourteen locals on the Sarawak side, but some two thousand managed to land and escape home. James could have cut them off and slaughtered them or starved them out, but instead let them go. They were badly bloodied, and – after all – he wanted them to spread the word of what had happened, so he contented himself with once more burning their stronghold at Paku. He could not guess how, later, this act of calculated mercy would be turned against him by those who would argue that these must have been harmless sailors, otherwise – had they really been pirates – they would surely have been hanged. 'I know very well that these people are to be reclaimed by punishment and by kindness, and there is no chance of their being "exterminated," though there is a certainty of all the poorer and peaceful Dayak tribes being exterminated if the Saribus and Skrang are countenanced by the English philanthropists, and encouraged to slaughter their neighbours,'[16] wrote James.

Then James turned his attention to the restive Skrang Dayaks, and burned some of their fortifications around Kanowit. The Saribus Dayaks immediately sent their submission and later so did those of the Skrang. Henceforth – except for the supporters of the recalcitrant Rentap – they would fight on the Rajah's side. James suggested strongly to Sultan Omar Ali that Sarawak should take over the administration of these rivers and divide the revenue with him. The Sultan's dominion was numinous, the revenues non-existent, and James had just eloquently demonstrated his ability to do anything he liked with the area. Omar Ali hastily accepted the offer. A fort was built and young, 'delicate' Brereton was sent to live there in terrible isolation. 'I choose Brereton to rule over these people, and I trust to God he will do it well; though young, I have confidence in him, and know that he has many qualities suited to the task.'[17] It was perhaps just as well that the basis of James's recruitments to the Sarawak service was not more widely known. But Brereton did do well, so well that he was able to organise a formal peace ceremony of 'drying the eyes and wiping the face' amongst the various peoples of the river, to finally extinguish traditional enmities.

SURPRISE OF THE PIRATE VILLAGE OF KANOWIT: BRITISH MUSEUM

James naïvely expected his recent naval victory to be lauded as a gallant triumph of British arms, of civilisation over savagery. New extracts from his journal had just been published in England and there seemed no reason to suppose they would not go down as well as the first. But they were less discreetly edited, and Wise had taken copies of the more bellicose sections that had been previously excised and eagerly laid them, torn out of context, before the public. James was unfairly portrayed as a mad, sanguinary despot who used the navy to slaughter harmless natives so that he could seize their land.

The liberal conscience, once roused, was not easily laid to rest. Hume and Cobden spoke publicly and in the House of a massacre of innocents. Mr Woods, editor of the Singapore *Straits Times*, delivered delicately filleted accounts of the action mixed with damning editorials. His implacable enmity was said to go back to the slight of being omitted from the invitation list to the investiture of James Brooke as a Knight Commander of the Bath. Wise, who had wanted to asset-strip Sarawak, piously founded the Aborigines Protection Society and used it as a stick with which to beat James Brooke. Deputations assailed the Prime Minister, and the fires were stoked the next year by the claim for over £20,000 compensation for the naval personnel who had participated in the Battle of Batang Marau. There were public meetings, petitions, calls for an inquiry, even for a trial. Hume, it seems, was just a high-principled, windy bore, his allies such as Cobden rather sharp politicians who knew a good bandwagon when they saw one. The government carried the day, but it was severely rattled. Borneo was a long way away. Who could really tell exactly what was going on? There was just sufficient truth mixed in with the falsehood to unnerve Russell. After all, James *had* killed lots of natives, *had* taken over their territory, and *had* used the British Navy to do it. The name of Brooke was taking on a bad smell and the whole business of Borneo was becoming a great deal more trouble than it could possibly be worth.

Labuan was proving an unmitigated disaster. Governor Napier fought with everyone, including James. The confused nature of the coal lease, the ill-defined rights of Wise's company and the unclear distribution of responsibilities tied everyone in a knot of mutual distrust and animosity further inflamed by chronic malaria. When Keppel had turned up in 1849 hoping for coal, there was precious little of it and he had to load it himself, the most unpopular job in the Navy. There was devious dealing in the control of the island's drink-trade. It all looked very much like local-government hands dipping into the till. Worst of all to James, it seemed that Napier had become ultimately compromised by borrowing money off Wise and he finally dismissed the Lieutenant Governor. It was scarcely legal.

The 'mean calumnies' at home came as a great shock to James. After all, he had been thinking, the worst was now over. Sarawak was established and at peace. The Dayaks had learned the error of their ways and become his friends. He could look forward to an era of steady development – 'steady' was one of his favourite words of approbation. Trade would flourish. The money would come rolling in. He himself declared:

> You must not think . . . that I *now* take these things much to heart. At first they told upon me; they appeared so infamous, so mean, so base, that they excited the scorn and indignation which every generous mind must feel; but this has passed, and I look forward with calmness to anything which may occur, and I have that firm self-reliance which can only be derived from pure motives and upright actions. At the same time, I am not the least inclined to become a martyr, and I always mean to speak out and hit hard.[18]

So he may have claimed, but it was far from true. St John noted, 'The savage attacks to which he was subjected roused his anger, and did him permanent injury. He never was again that even-tempered gay companion of former days. He thought too much of these attacks and longed to answer every petty insult and calumnious insinuation.'[19] Sometimes there were flashes of the old self-mockery so that he could make a joke of the whole thing. 'I shall take to wearing moustaches and carry a pocket-pistol concealed in my vest, which shall peep forth whenever I meet nursery-maids, or other nervous persons, and I shall affect a lowering brow and eye unquiet – that sort of satanic Lord Byron hero sort of look, dear to youth of both sexes, and if Cobden disappears in some unaccountable manner, I shall at once gain the credit of having smothered the jewel of freedom between two blankets, and buried his remains in some unholy place.'[20] But on another occasion, when he received a particularly sharp savaging from Cobden and Hume, he cried out in agony and unconscious anticipation of Errol Flynn: 'I wish I had the two before me, sword in hand, on the sands of Santubong.'[21]

In the long, dark, tropical nights, a swelling strain of paranoia took root in his mind, and wit gave way to anger. It was not yet noticeable to any but sharp-eyed St John and it would grow only very slowly, feeding on a sense of outrage and grievous wrong – generously nourished over the years by the British government – until it poisoned James's every generous impulse with its bitterness. James Brooke had already become one of those people who write twelve sides of closely reasoned personal resentment to newspaper editors in a spidery and obsessive hand. 'I am a man of one idea – Borneo; everything else in my life is a little snuff which tickles my nostrils.' He began to feel that history itself was conspiring against him. 'I will not have a repetition of Sir Stamford Raffles' fruitless labours revived in my person.'[22]

One possible consolation was the arrival of the Rajah's heir. James was no longer a solitary ruler but the start of a dynasty, for he did not seek just to succeed but to be succeeded. Born in 1823, John Brooke Johnson, James's elder nephew, son of his sister Emma Johnson, was known as 'Brooke'. When enticed into the Sarawak service and adopted as heir, he changed his surname to Brooke too, to mark the new formal relationship that conferred continuity on the little state. He thus awkwardly became Brooke Brooke, but was sometimes also known as 'Captain Brooke' to avoid a little of the confusion this caused. (His younger brother, also to join the Sarawak administration, remained, for the time being, Charles Johnson.) In view of later disputes, it is important to note that there was no doubt in anyone's mind about this arrangement concerning his ultimate inheritance of Sarawak. Brooke Brooke soon became another favourite of Harriette, despite his shy diffidence and – it must be said – deep mediocrity.

Poor Harriette. While she was convalescing from the loss of one of her babies, her young Harry caught diphtheria in Singapore and also perished. 'The flowers all died along my way,' she sighed. But so did sturdy shrubs. Some years later, even Charley, her eldest, apparently safely tucked away in England, would find sudden death in Ipswich after being smacked on the head by a cricket ball. Some time after the death of the baby a box of presents for the infant arrived from England. She quietly unpacked it and hid it all away without mentioning it to Frank – to spare him the terrible pain she herself felt. In tribulation, her great comfort was the mountain of Matang, visible from the mission house. 'How dear a mountain becomes to you is only known to those who live in hilly countries. One gets to think of it as a friend. It seems to carry a protest against the little frets of life, and by its strength and invariableness to be a visible image of Him who is "the same yesterday, to-day and forever."'[23]

(The Malays had a different view of things. In the silhouette of the mountains they saw the profile of the Rajah, and so read into the land a sure sign of his right to rule; and as for 'invariableness', everyone knew there was a rock just down the new road they were building that was alive and grew day by day. In later times, the Malays even got up a petition to protect it.)

The new ironwood church was steadily rising a few hundred yards from the Ark. Furniture was brought from Singapore, stained glass with the new Sarawak flag. Babies were baptised in a huge pink clam shell on an ebony pillar, and this became standard practice in all the Dayak churches. The pillar was intended to simulate coral, but the skill of the carver was not equal to the task so it became simply fluted. Dayak initiands entered Christianity poetically, like Botticelli cherubs emerging from the waves.

A Chinese rebellion, over the border in Dutch territory, forced thousands of turbulent Chinese refugees into Sarawak and Kuching, where they invaded the new church, so that Frank had to drive them out like money lenders, while James, eager for their entrepreneurial skills, gave them food and tools. But there were new souls too. Ten of their children were delivered up to the McDougalls for ten years of free education, and by the end of the year the school numbered over thirty. The Borneo Church Mission objected that these were Chinese, not the Dayaks intended, but the McDougalls doted on their charges and could not bring themselves to give the children up. As long as necessary, they paid the costs out of their own pocket. Harriette sewed them neat uniforms and fed them breakfasts of rice pudding and treacle and whipped them when they were wicked. A proper Chinese teacher called Sing-Sing, who had illegally smuggled his wife out of China in a box, was engaged to teach them their letters, and Harriette trained them up as a choir that impressed visitors and remote villages alike. Meanwhile Frank, who had been in a winning Oxford crew, turned the boys into a rowing eight who enjoyed some success at the Sarawak regatta, which he had instituted to encourage the different peoples to make sport, not war.

The McDougalls were less successful with the Rajah's Dayak hostages, who fiercely resisted all attempts to lay hands on their children. James himself did his best to minimise the sufferings of children in the fighting, but many were very firm-minded. There was a little boy of eight, Ranjah, whose father and brother had been killed in the wars.

For several days he seemed very happy with the Rajah, to whom he had been brought, and then he told him confidently that he knew a place where certain valuable jars belonging to his tribe were hidden, and that if he were sent there with a party of Malays he could point out the place. The Rajah believed the child, the jars were found, and taken on board the boat; then the boy again went to the Rajah, and bursting into tears, he said, 'I have given you the riches of my tribe, and now in return, give me my liberty, set me down in a path I will show you in the jungle, give me some food, and in two days I shall reach my home and find my mother.'

The Rajah answered, 'My poor child, I would willingly do as you ask me, but I fear you will be lost in the jungle, and will die before you reach your home; for how can such a child as you know the way?' However, the boy persisted and the Rajah gave him whatever he wished for – a china cup, a glass tumbler, a gay sarong, and some food, and the little fellow set off, on the jungle path, with his bundle on his back, joyful enough; and as we afterwards heard, rejoined his mother and friends in safety.'[24]

The original plan had been to send a catechist to every one of the forts James was erecting to safeguard the rivers, but there were never enough people and the converts continued to be mostly Chinese. James was undismayed, realising, in the usual architectural metaphors, that hasty evangelisation would be 'building the super-structure on a foundation of sand'. Yet whenever Dayaks came to Kuching, the McDougalls offered them hospitality, with Harriette stoutly playing the harmonium and working the magic lantern. While they never stole, they begged her piteously for the cups and plates that were a Dayak obsession. 'You have so many more than you could possibly want.' Anyway, the mission's scriptural tableaux were perhaps no match for the Rajah's livelier pictures. In the *astana*, a favourite of the Dayaks was a magic-lantern scene of English bodysnatchers being pursued from a cemetery by skeletons who pelted them with skulls. They found it hilarious.

Frank discovered a Javanese who could cast brass and bought up a hundredweight of broken gongs to melt down into a bell. But the principal effect of its ringing was to drive the Muslims to resume the discarded habit of calling to prayer, and even to increase the number going on pilgrimages to Mecca.

Bishop Wilson of Calcutta was very different from his lissom great-nephew, William Brereton. He was seventy-two years old, huge and fat and eccentric and, by the obscure rules that govern Church geography, he was nominally in charge of the Sarawak mission. Like many deaf men he shouted and accused the rest of the world of mumbling and this excess of volume somehow strengthened his own opinions and made those of others seem pale and indeterminate and even more in need of his constant direction.

When the bishop made his first visit, Frank had struggled into unaccustomed ecclesiastical black and gone downriver to pilot in the boat. He normally did this anyway if it was anything more than a small local craft. It was one of the reasons the McDougalls always ended up housing the junior officers of visiting warships – some of them quite ungodly men – which task might more properly have fallen to the Rajah. And if it wasn't the Navy drinking up the medicinal port, it was the Dayaks gobbling the rice. Later would come wild-eyed, haggard men from the out-stations whose clothes had rotted away on their backs and who had to be wooed back to civilisation. Frank called it 'docking and tinkering' and worried that these men, so irked and chafed by unaccustomed shirts, looked more like pirates than churchmen. Money and supplies were a constant headache. And now the Bishop of Calcutta. Well, they would all have to be filled up with heavy puddings and the remains of the Christmas venison. The mission house was too far from the landing stage for Bishop Wilson to walk, so he had to be borne in triumph on an improvised palanquin by muscular Chinese coolies, trained in the transport of rice sacks and the occasional procession of joss-house figures. By the time they struggled up the curving path to the mission house, their thin blue trousers and shirts were soaked in sweat and clung to their bodies to the point of indecorous physical revelation. From the top of the hill Harriette could hear the bishop at the bottom favouring Frank with his views on the Indian castes, cattle-raising and the problems of ecclesiastical marriage, and ear-trumpeting back shouts of 'Eh? What? Who? How much?'

He had not come unattended. He had a physician, Dr Beale, and the Rev. Moule from Singapore, both good eaters. There was Archdeacon Pratt, accompanied by his tall, icy wife. The Malays stared at her in awe. White women were still a novelty in Sarawak, a new species whose general characteristics remained to be defined and generally agreed. Over the next weeks they would flock to the house, not to see the bishop, but simply to look on Mrs Pratt's white

throat, set off by jet beads and flounced bodice. There was something about that throat that strangely stirred and fascinated them.
Having silently stared their fill, they would go home nodding,
quietly satisfied. There was a pale young missionary, Mr Fox, paper-
skinned and trembly from a recent attack of fever, who would be led
into debauchery with local women by that ill-named hound St John
and later defect to a purely secular administration.

Frank proudly showed the bishop around the mission. The soil
had been too thin and sour for the projected fruit trees so there was
now only grass that fed the cattle and provided milk for the little
ones. They were tended by a Hindu syce. Harriette had never told
Frank how, one afternoon, going into the cowshed, she had come
upon Abdullah engaged in an act of blatant and absorbed adoration,
prostrate in the semi-darkness before the placidly munching and
garlanded Brahma bull, muttering prayers and whispering strange
and melodious incantations.

Bishop Wilson had come to consecrate the bright new church of
St Thomas. It was not finished, of course, but the funds were and it
would serve. Frank had found a Chinese craftsman in the bazaar
who could do gilding, and godly words gleamed out against the
darkening wood. Almost all the letters were the right way up. The
flag of Sarawak shone bright in a stained-glass window and the
building was decked, not with seasonal boughs of holly, but palm
fronds and lush banana leaves. It was trim and tight and purposeful
and its little Tyrolean tower stood firm against the wind and the
rain like one of Frank's boats. As the last nail was driven home, the
termites had arrived and swarmed over every surface in a complete
tour of inspection. Satisfied that there was nothing to eat, they
withdrew.

The bishop and his party were less fastidious than the ants. They
installed themselves in every available room of the mission house,
driving the McDougalls into a small unused corner. The Indian servants took over the verandahs and talked loudly all night while the
Malays came to see Mrs Pratt all day. Perfidious Rev. Moule crept
into the mission library and that of the Rajah and declared them to
be hotbeds of doctrinal subversion. By the time of the consecration,

Harriette and Frank were worn to a frazzle. It was as much as he could do to struggle through the service, which lasted from eleven in the morning to half-past two in the afternoon. Yet when the spirit was upon him and he was preaching, he struck the pulpit so hard with his hand that the gentle Datuk Bandar feared violence from this strange new faith and fled. That was against protocol. After all Brooke Brooke was there, representing the Rajah, and diplomatic protocol decreed that he had to leave first.

Chapter 10

The Inquiry

As part of his wider duties as British Commissioner in the east, James was requested to try to re-establish good relations with the Thais. The King had recently expelled all foreign traders in petulance at being sold a leaky cruiser. James hung around in Bangkok for week after week, behaving with considerable haughtiness and bad temper, which he justified by a claimed specialist knowledge of 'oriental ways'. The old King simply prevaricated with royal elegance and finally James admitted defeat. The mission was a total failure, without even the usual meaningless piece of paper to show for it. The voyage added, however, to Sarawak royal pomp. The Crown Prince had been met and a basis laid for future good relations. James declared him 'a highly accomplished gentleman for a semi-barbarian' and recommended the British simply put him on the throne. He would later, as King, without British interference, send to Sarawak a copy of the heavily carved and gilded Thai royal barge to be used as James's own formal vessel. One other thing came of it. The Borneo Company, founded in 1856 to develop Sarawak, became involved in Siam and the King asked them to send him an English governess, which they most famously did.

The Liberals' campaign against James Brooke – 'sometimes styled Rajah Brooke' – would rumble on like chronic indigestion for years. In March 1850 there was the battle over the payment to the Navy. The lack of British casualties was invoked as proof that this was no normal warfare but a one-sided massacre. Unfortunately, despite his own liberal and humanitarian programme, James's military conquests naturally attracted the support of just the sort of reactionary Queen-and-country Conservatives he abhorred – which, in turn, further inflamed the Liberals. The northern merchants would favour him as would the major ports as 'good for trade', so that humanitarians would also accuse him of having sordid commercial motives; he would point in vain to having invested £10,000 in Sarawak without obvious hope of return. In short, every faction in the House might find him useful for their own agenda.

In July, Hume rose again. Matters were worse than he had thought. He was now convinced, he revealed, that the alleged pirates massacred by James Brooke were actually a part of the royal navy of China. A few weeks later, when funds for Labuan came up in the House, he was on his feet again, quoting awkward extracts from James's letters, provided by Wise. Once more he was voted down and Lord Palmerston wrote to James expressing government support.

Then, out of the blue, came a letter from the American President requesting a treaty of friendship with Sarawak. It called James Brooke 'Great and Good Friend', and 'Your Highness'. James was delighted and referred it back to Palmerston, eager that he should know all about it and its unqualified acceptance of Sarawak sovereignty.

It was time to go to England in person. James was in delicate health, largely from the diseases that pullulated on Labuan, whose salubrity he had lauded. He needed to convalesce. Anyway, he always wanted to meet his enemies face to face. Passing through Singapore, he was outraged to hear that his old foe, Woods of the *Straits Times*, had been appointed Deputy Sheriff. James tried to use his influence with the Governor and get him fired, but failed. In response, Woods promptly got up a petition among the Singapore merchants demanding a sweeping inquiry into all the doings of James Brooke.

James arrived in England in May 1851, and this time he would stay nearly two years. There would be dinners in his honour and expressions of regard and support from the highest in the land, and the comfort of renewed acquaintance with friends. But his coming stirred Hume anew to heights of righteous fury. Twice in the next few months he raised James's actions in the House, first using the petition of the fifty-three Singapore merchants raised by Woods, and then other doubtful letters from traders in the east who had suffered at James's hands. Colonel Thompson scored a definite hit when he declared in the House that James Brooke might act like St George but he himself did not believe in the dragon. But Henry Drummond, MP for West Surrey, was a powerful and well-prepared defender of the Rajah. Of particular importance were the charges of a merchant of Labuan and Singapore, William Henry Miles. Drummond was crushing in his mockery. 'Mr. William Henry Miles is a gentleman who follows the occupation of a butcher, to which he unites the more honourable occupation of a boxer. It so happened that, owing to a little misfortune, he went abroad at the Queen's expense. Lord Bacon said that there were two ways of making a man wise – by books and by travel –. It has been Mr. Miles's fortune to profit by the latter.'[1] The total discrediting of the characters from whom Hume's missives derived – that they were convicted felons, bigamists, pimps, thugs, even the fact that one was most inconveniently decapitated by the pirates Hume claimed did not exist – in no way stilled his strident voice and his busy pen. 'The fact is,' wrote St John, 'that H.M.'s officers in half-civilized countries are brought in contact with wandering ruffians whose only object is to make money – honestly if they can, but at all events to make money; and where we endeavour to check their illegal acts, we are exposed to shameful abuse, which sometimes finds an echo at home.'[2]

Hume then produced another forged letter of complaint from the Sultan of Brunei. Despite the unstinted support for James Brooke from both the government and the House, Hume twice returned to his theme in March of the following year and bombarded the government with letters in a tireless moral crusade. James was philosophical: 'I have been held up as a prodigy of perfection, and I have been cast down as a monster of iniquity.' He avenged himself on Wise and the 'calumniators' by taking them to court and voiding the charter of their Eastern Archipelago Company. He toyed with the idea of a libel action, but thought better of it, and then with becoming an MP, the better to defend himself. And then in early 1853 the government fell and was replaced by a patched coalition that included the troublesome Liberals. They were no longer a mere butt of oppositional humour but crucial allies who had to be placated. Nineteenth-century British governments were notoriously more interested in power than policy. Hume would have his inquiry.

Three times the proposal for an inquiry had come up in Parliament. Three times it had been heavily defeated. James had already resigned his governorship of Labuan in the hope of an appointment to a clearer administrative position, and was packed and about to embark for Sarawak. He heard of the reversal of the government's position only days before he was due to sail. Since Lord John Russell had told the House, a mere two weeks before, that no inquiry would be instituted by him before the Rajah's return, he was now convinced that the plan had been to get him out of the country before announcing the decision, and he regarded this stealthy change as an act of fearful political treachery. Moreover, it seemed that the inquiry would be held in Singapore, not London, by the Governor-General of India, thus making it impossible to call major British figures to testify, and yet it would not bother to visit Sarawak, whose condition James saw as the real issue and his greatest justification. Once more the British government seemed to be insisting on total power over his sovereign state while accepting no responsibility whatever for its fate. He had a markedly free and frank discussion on the subject with Lord Clarendon, the new Foreign Secretary, who would not forget or forgive what was said to him or the language in which it was put.

*

James arrived back in Aden to troubling news. A letter from Brooke Brooke revealed that the recalcitrant Skrang chieftain called Rentap had attacked Brereton's fort. In the ensuing pursuit, Lee, a government officer from Lingga, had been slain and his head lopped off. The good news was that most of the Dayaks under his old enemy and new friend, Gasing, had remained loyal, attacked Rentap and forced him to retire to a hilltop fort in Sadong. It would take the rest of James's reign to winkle him out again. Charles Johnson, James's younger nephew, was sent out to replace Lee. Sarawak was becoming a family business. Charley Grant joined James in Singapore, where 'the papers teemed with letters and articles; the *Free Press* upholding him, the *Straits Times* denouncing him. His name was like a shell thrown on any dinner table, and questions in the Chamber of Commerce were decided by Brooke or anti-Brooke majorities.'[3]

Woods had published a letter from Hume revealing that he had known about the decision to hold an inquiry weeks before James had been told. Government treachery it was, then. The word was like a flare in James's mind. As soon as possible he sailed for Sarawak, straining for a sight of the honest mountains of Santubong. But as they hove into sight, with the welcoming flotilla of little boats, he was suddenly taken ill. It was smallpox.

Frank McDougall was in England and everyone else was at a loss what to do. James sent away all who had not had the disease, went to bed and sent for Sherip Moksain, a local healer, a man so modest of his own skills that he several times confidently announced James's imminent death at his hands. Meanwhile he was cared for doggedly by Inchi Subu (the public executioner), three Malays, the indefatigable Arthur Crookshank and the Rev. Horsburgh, a new and very anxious missionary. Horsburgh wrote:

> I got another note from him [Brooke Brooke], asking me to
> come over and nurse the Rajah. Sherip Moksain had said
> that he was dying, and suggested that it should be given
> out that he had gone back to Singapore, that so the change
> of Government to Captain Brooke might take place

Charles Johnson (later Brooke) in 1864: Bodleian Library

without any disturbance. This, however, I did not then know.

I had been reading in some medical publications that it was now the custom to treat fevers with wine and brandy, and I explained to Captain Brooke what I thought, and showed him the authorities on which I formed my opinion, for Mr. McDougall, who was then in England, had a medical library which we missionaries all studied. I accordingly proposed that he should have some brandy, and, Captain Brooke assenting, I mixed some with water and put in some things to make it taste like medicine, and brought it to him. He resolutely refused to take or even look at it. Captain Brooke, Mr. Crookshank, and I think, the present Rajah [James's nephew Charles], were in the room. 'For God's sake, Rajah,' said Captain Brooke, 'do take it,' and he pleaded earnestly that he should. He at last was so far moved as to ask what it was, so I told him there was quinine in it. 'Anything else?' 'Tinc. Cardammons.' 'Anything else?' I fenced with the brandy as long as possible, but before his eager and half-angry questioning I was obliged at last to confess it. This was enough, he turned his face to the ceiling, held up his hands, and exclaimed, 'Who ever heard of brandy in smallpox!' Abashed and disappointed as I was, and deeply anxious both at my own responsibility and at his evident danger, I could not help feel the thoroughly ludicrous nature of the scene, and had to turn my back to conceal a silent laugh; but I saw plainly that there was nothing more to be done, at least, at present, on this side of the question. The gentlemen then left the room and I remained alone with the servants, but as I saw he did not take kindly to me, I kept pretty much out of sight, merely coming forward and showing myself when he wanted anything. In the afternoon he seemed to be getting weaker, and I made up a stimulating prescription, which was given in one of the medical books, told Captain Brooke of it, and begged him to use his influence to get the Rajah to take it.

At Captain Brooke's entreaty, he took it, and it soothed
him and gave him a little rest. At midnight Sherip Moksain
thought him dying, and urged me to tell Captain Brooke so;
it seemed to me that he was going on well, but I went with
Sherip Moksain to the Captain's room. He told me
afterwards, that when he heard our knock he thought it was
all over. I told him that I myself thought he would live
through the night, and that there was still a hope of
recovery. This seemed to give Captain Brooke some
comfort, and my prognostication was right. I continued to
give the Rajah food and stimulants, but he did not like my
pressing the medicine on him, and from the hands of Mr.
Crookshank especially he would take what he would not
from me.[4]

Medicine in Sarawak would continue to be a rather hit-and-miss
affair for some time. Even just before the Second World War, a
District Officer in a remote station noted,

One of my daily tasks was dispensing medicine. In a case
alongside my desk were sundry bottles known as Winchesters
labelled 'Stomach Mixture,' 'Cough Mixture,' 'Liniment for
Sprains' and so on; pots of Boracic Ointment, pots of Goiter
Ointment of a beautiful pink hue, and of course quantities of
castor oil. Dayaks crowded round, plonked down two cents,
and when their ailments accorded with the labels on the
bottles it was plain sailing. If there was any difficulty in
diagnosing a case, I was instructed to prescribe castor oil; as
far as I know it generally did the trick . . . One varlet mixed
them all together. Cough Mixture was so popular that the
Medical Department limited our supplies; Dayaks used to roll
up for a morning's dose, just as we might call in at a Bar for a
morning glass of beer.[5]

Despite the medical care, James Brooke, like the Dayaks, survived. The Malays had prayed in their mosques and made

surreptitious offerings at more trusted but less official shrines; the Chinese, the Hindus, the Dayaks and the Christians had each invoked their own spiritual powers. The *astana* was heaped with jars of aromatic water to scent his bath, cool plantain leaves to soothe his bed in the sweltering heat and tempting dishes to rally his fading strength, but James slept an opium sleep. When he finally rose there had been a striking transformation. His appearance now mocked that of the Grant portrait, a sort of reversal of the picture of Dorian Gray. In his fevered state he had believed himself to be Simon de Montfort at the battle of Evesham and torn at his own cheeks in a ghostly combat for English democracy. He was scarred, pocked and lined, terribly aged and shorn of much of his hair (and what remained had turned white). James had become a shrunken old man but his blue eyes were 'as fierce as a crocodile'. (Eyes were important in Sarawak. The next rajah, Charles, lost an eye hunting and replaced it with a glass tiger's eye bought from a London taxidermist. It, too, terrified people.) With time, some of the welts healed and part of the hair grew back. James wrote cheerfully, 'I shall be a good deal disfigured; but my friends will not esteem me the less for being a little uglier late in life.'[6]

They built him a hilltop retreat near his cottage at Peninjau, 'See-afar Cottage', where he sat peacefully and stared at distant, healing nature. The fever seemed to have seared the passion out of him, so that he could now speak of the British inquiry almost with detachment. But that would not last. He went on a tour of desolate Labuan and Brunei where a new sultan, Mumein, of whom he approved, had inherited the throne. But Makota, his old enemy, had returned to prominence there.

At court, James expressed himself with great bitterness on the perfidy of the British. 'He committed . . . the natural error of confounding his feelings with the facts, and describing the conduct of the English government as more hostile than it really was. It was in vain for me to point out to the Rajah the impolicy of this,'[7] wrote St John. The Bruneians were all ears, but neither the Sultan nor Makota wanted anything to do with the inquiry. For the upcoming commission, James sought the letters his enemies had written urging

the Sultan to submit charges against him to the British Queen.
Alas, they had been lost. That was unfortunate, since money could
perhaps be found to pay for them. Miraculously, they were found by
Makota and dollars to pay for them were passed back through the
bathroom window of James's quarters under cover of darkness.

More than a year would pass before the inquiry sat, and letters criss-
crossed between Sarawak and London at a leisured pace which
denied the acrimony of their contents. The British government
was ducking and diving as James chipped away relentlessly at the
whole foundation of the commission. He questioned the instructions of the commissioners, the terms in which Sarawak was
described, the availability of previous ministers as witnesses. Like his
adversary, Hume, he had the tenacity of a terrier with a rat.

In the meantime Sarawak affairs continued to boil. A plot was
detected between the high Malay official, Datuk Patinggi Abdul
Gaffur, and Sherip Masahor, another of those troublesome descendants of the prophet who ruled over the lower Rejang River.
Invoking the same procedure he had applied against Makota and
would use again against other 'traitors', James ensnared Abdul
Gaffur and a public denunciation was bulldozed through a meeting
of the Kuching Malays, making James's personal view an expression
of popular will. Since there was no evidence of treason that could
stand up in James's own court, Abdul Gaffur was sent on a face-
saving pilgrimage to Mecca to allow matters to cool down, and
Masahor was allowed to return home to Serikei.

Abdul Gaffur had been apparently emboldened by the withdrawal of the British military presence in the wake of the outcry
raised by Hume. James saw the whole affair as an act of disloyalty
encouraged by the continuation of the policy of cowardly British
indecision that had killed Hassim and his beloved Badrudeen. He
brooded on it.

There had already been one expedition against the 'pirate'
Rentap. Now, following the latest shifting of the frontier, he was a
'rebel' as well. James and his nephews mounted another raid on
him, though its wisdom might have been questioned in the light of

the imminent inquiry. Since James was no longer up to doing any of
the charging, he stayed behind to look after the boats while the
active campaigning was left to the next generation, who made a
mess of it. But the wounded were brought to him that he might heal
them by spitting on them. Politics in Sarawak always had a spiritual
dimension. As a mighty lord, James was held to be full of *semangat*,
spiritual potency, which could cure sickness, make the crops grow
and even call the dead back to life. The Hill Dayaks were forever
bringing him seed to bless or rubbing themselves against him or
begging for small personal gifts of cloth or china that would transfer a little of it from him to them. No wonder James saw them as
touchingly 'faithful' to him.

There was a nasty, sharp little battle, nearly lost, but finally the
fortified longhouse that was Rentap's headquarters was taken and
burned – Panglima Usman quietly shinned up the wall and
unlocked the door when no one was looking. Rentap himself was
wounded and carried away to his hilltop fortress by his men. It
would take another eight years of blood, worry and expense to
finally defeat him. James's old acquaintance, the chieftain Bulan,
came and watched with interest, accompanied by a huge body of
armed warriors, clothed in blood red, who settled down to chew
betel nut and spectate peacefully while remaining strictly neutral.

An outbreak of dysentery now ravaged the Sarawak forces. Many
died in pain and squalor, young Brereton among them. He had sired
a child by a local woman but Rentap sneered at him, calling him a
man who wore women's clothes. The Dayaks were astonished but
touched that this unpaid official working for love and sheer belief in
both James and Sarawak had left his few pathetic possessions to
them. James wrote, 'He was an affectionate and particularly lovable
person, able, clever, enthusiastic, and with particular tact in han-
dling the natives. Poor dear fellow, he loved me very sincerely, and
I was attached to him from his youth upwards.'[8]

When the expedition got back to Kuching, James's presence was
required immediately in Singapore. The Commission of Inquiry was
in session. The coming of the *Lily* to fetch him must have seemed
oddly ambiguous – half obsequious flunkey, half distraining bailiff.

No other steamer had been seen in the river since 1849. A more eloquent expression of British withdrawal could not be imagined. It was
clear that James Brooke had been socially 'dropped'.

The Governor General of India really did not want to be bothered,
but according to Company rules Singapore was still part of his patch
and there was nothing to be done about it. Extremely grudgingly,
two officials were shipped over to head the commission: the
Advocate General of India, Charles Henry Prinsep, and a government agent, Humphrey Bohun Devereux. For some time they sat
about and sulked that their papers had not come and that nobody
attended the inquiry they had opened.

It rapidly became obvious that Prinsep was not quite right in
the head. James called him 'A gobbling old donkey without
judgement and without dignity.'[9] A member of the House had
remarked that it was highly unusual to combine an enquiry into
policy with an accusation of murder but this did not deter Lord
Clarendon in the instructions he had sent out. The commissioners were to decide on the compatibility of all the offices James
held – which was far from urgent since they had been resigned.
They were to determine whether or not he had deliberately
impeded British traders – the implication being that he had done
so for his own financial benefit. The allegations of genocide were
hidden under the heading of 'Whether the conduct pursued by
Sir James Brooke . . . and the relations which he holds with the
native chiefs, have been such as are becoming a servant of the
British Crown'. Anyway, in the heat and endless delay of
Singapore, the issues rapidly became as blurred as the ink of the
original records.

Charley Grant was sent in to cavil and quibble and bombard the
commissioners with letters, eliciting bland secretarial replies. In
the evenings he went round the boats in the harbour, drumming up
local sailors who would declare Dayaks to be pirates in a half-dozen
different tongues. The undertaking's total lack of structure was
resolved in a rather strange way. Since a number of Singapore merchants had signed a memorial, an open letter, written by Woods to

Hume demanding a public inquiry, Woods found himself abruptly elevated to the role of unofficial counsel for the prosecution on behalf of 'the memorialists'.

Another group of merchants had signed a contrary letter, in support of James's measures to suppress piracy, and equally suddenly found themselves counsel for the defence and collectively represented by a law agent, Aitken. The case had been turned into a football match of two teams, Woods versus Aitken, with the commissioners snugly established as referees. They could now send out some subpoenas to the signatories and settle down to watch the goal scoring.

The major question lay in the identity of pirates. Were the Dayaks pirates or not? The problem was that no one knew quite what the determining features of a pirate were. The commissioners invented their own definition but left it unarticulated, which explains the extreme oddness of the cross-examinations. They homed in on sea-going ships with sails not paddles, inveterate and general animosity rather than focused war, long-distance rather than local activity, attacks on European not native vessels, the disruption of foreign rather than regional trade, the possession of cannon not spears, and the distinction between Dayaks and Malays. In a neat pincer movement, James's side would make much of the taking of Chinese heads by Dayaks, since many Chinese turned out conveniently to be British subjects, but also invoked the Brunei treaty of 1847 which committed the Navy to suppress piracy in the dominions of the Sultan of Brunei. That this had been negotiated by James himself was neither here nor there.

It was the sort of situation, rich in pettifogging terminological dispute, that appealed to the strain of pedantry in James Brooke. He had not honed his nit-picking, legalistic skills on the bench in Kuching all those years for nothing, and he could have made a very sharp lawyer. He opened the fight with the symbolism of space and furniture, an idiom he had mastered in the east. He did not like the venue in the courthouse, since it suggested a trial. Although he cross-examined witnesses himself, he violently objected to Woods doing it. Even more, he refused to accept Woods's sitting in a space separate from the spectators with a toehold on the very platform on which the commissioners themselves sat. After arguing back and forth, in a desperate effort to placate him the venue was moved to a room without a platform. He was not placated. It was all 'bosh'. If only he had a steamer. He ordered his officials to charge the government for every farthing of postage and stationery.

Thanks to Charley Grant, the range of witnesses was large and exotic: traders of every kind, Sarawak and Dutch officials, Malay, Buginese and European sailors, British, Chinese, Jewish and Eurasian merchants. They all swore their oaths and had their say through interpreters. The documents are an extraordinary evocation of the rich ethnic and cultural mix that was British Asia in the nineteenth century, all ranged beneath the panoply of Mother India and the religion that was commerce and expressing the almost desperate belief that, underneath all this cultural variation, reason could remain inviolate.

The exiled Datuk Patinggi of Sarawak, Abdul Gaffur, was called and – unlike the Europeans – disappointed by simply telling the strict truth, quite uncoloured by his recent conflict with James. A remarkably equable man, he never felt he had done anything wrong in the first place, even though James always insisted on seeing his opponents as foolish, or self-seeking, or downright evil. But then, moral relativism and a sensitivity to an enemy's view have never built empires. First, they tried to ensnare the Datuk Patinggi with vocabulary. Were Skrang Dayaks *perompak-perompak* – pirates – or merely *musuh* – enemies? He shrugged away the difference. They were the same. Transcripts held at the Public Record Office record:

Q: When not at war with the people of Sarawak, do the Saribus and Skrang people trade with Sarawak?
A: Not before. Now they are at peace and do trade with Sarawak.
Q: When did that trade begin?
A: Six or seven years ago in Sir James Brooke's time – not in the beginning of his rule – it was after the attack of 1849.

They tried to show that the conflict with the Dayaks was balanced warfare, not predation.

> **Q:** Do the Dayaks keep and adjust a sort of account of the number of heads taken from each other and take occasion to effect a balance?
>
> **A:** I do not know that they keep such an account. The Dayaks are very bad accountants.

They tried to cast James in the role of war-criminal.

> **Q:** Have the Dayaks any means of intimating or signalizing their intentions of peace or war?
>
> **A:** When they meet an enemy, they attack him at once. They make no sign. If they did the enemy would run away.

Like many terribly serious British trials, the whole proceedings constantly threatened to turn into farce.

Napier, choleric and disaffected Lieutenant Governor of Labuan, was called and tried to mask, with a front of judicious objectivity, a determined attempt to drop James in the soup. His testimony was carefully calculated to make the commissioners infer that Dayaks might be headhunters or worse but were certainly not pirates – but even he fell prey to the absurd.

> **Q:** Has the fact of piracy in these seas been long a matter of notoriety?
>
> **A:** Yes ever since I came to this place.
> . . .
> **Q:** Is piracy a peculiarity of the Dayaks?
>
> **A:** I know that of late years piracy has been attributed to some of them and that they have been attacked as pirates. I should say the predatory Dayaks of the West Coast of Borneo are a race of man-slayers and slave-hunters and that they range the coast in the vicinity for the purpose of procuring heads and slaves.

Now, about his dismissal by James . . . The court refused to hear about it and sent him away.

The 'memorialists' on the whole were equally unimpressive. Henry Allen MD declared anxiously,

> My name was attached to an address to Mr. Hume, the Member of Parliament. It merely referred to me as one of the public of Singapore and merely with the desire for a public enquiry. I was never in Borneo and can know nothing personally of the different tribes or their customs and occupations.
>
> I never attended any meeting in connection with the getting-up of the letter. I do not know what person attested the signatures of the letter.
>
> I do not know whether the allegations contained in the letter to [*sic*] be true or not true . . .
>
> I do not know whether pirate boats are propelled with paddles or not but believe they are . . .
>
> It was not from personal motives that I signed the letter but with the public asking [*sic*] for Enquiry and not making accusations against Sir James Brooke.

Others, such as George Tod Wright, were no better.

Q: Your signature appears on the memorial sent to Mr. Hume.

A: It does.

Q: Were you aware of the contents of the memorial when you signed it?

A: No.

Various groups sought to simplify matters by producing more memorials. The philoprogenitive Chinese, for example, devised a petition showing a more earthy view of British and Sarawak policy than James might have hoped:

We the undersigned Chinese merchants and Residents of Singapore, knowing the old saying, 'A well-governed country pleases the heart of the Almighty God – his people flourish under a good and impartial Governor and all men ought to proclaim their confidence in him and rejoice with the clapping of hands.' As touching Sarawak, Labuan and Borneo, previous to their being reformed, the savage Malay Pirates gathered together both in the jungle, nested in their dens[?] and on the surface of the open Sea, with the Lanoon Pirates flying about every where like Bees. Vessels, both belonging to the country, and also other navigating traders fell a prey to them – *often* and *always* ran great danger in those seas. We Chinese trading in these places always ran great danger ourselves and with great difficulty made any profit. But fortunately thro' the gracious favour of H M the Queen of England, Sir James Brooke was sent as Her Commissioner to have control over these places, viz. Sarawak, Labuan and Borneo – to govern the said places, to open up the country and reform the barbarous Malay into a moral character . . . We the Chinese Merchants and Residents of Singapore, as mentioned before, urged by a sense of Sir James Brooke's former and deep-rooted benevolence, have hereby come forward one and all to declare the deserved praise of his skilful capacity and at the same time we pray that his son and grandson may succeed him and that successful prosperity may attend them from generation to generation without ending.

Then the European residents of Sarawak sent in another petition, expressing their unalloyed adoration of their rajah and his works, clearly got up by Charley Grant. Robert Hentig, former employee of Wise's trading company and himself a signatory, was questioned about it. It rapidly became clear that he was now a sworn enemy of James, and he joined in the attack via a schoolboy definition of pirates. He knew he was right about it: he had looked it up in Johnson's dictionary.

Q: What meaning do you attach to the word pirate yourself?

A: I have always understood that pirates were those who went out from the Mediterranean and Spanish Main in fine, fast-sailing, well-built, well-armed vessels, not in small boats that paddle along the coast . . .

Q: Do you consider these roving expeditions [of the Dayaks] legitimate excursions or what name should you apply to them?

A: I should call them war expeditions, intertribal war expeditions, principally for the purpose of obtaining heads like the North American Indians who go out in war expeditions for scalps.

More helpful to James was the dogmatically phlegmatic testimony of C. F. Boudriot, the former Dutch Resident at Pontianak. 'I am acquainted with the character of the people on the West Coast of Borneo. I know of the tribes Saribus and Skrang Dayak officially. I have always known them as pirates, killing and murdering, burning houses, all along the coast.'[10]

St John summed up the whole proceeding with customary acuity:

What shall I say of the Commission? The two gentlemen sent down to conduct it were very different. Mr Prinsep, the chief, was incapable – the mental malady to which he soon after succumbed showed itself too often and the Hon. Mr. Devereux could alone do anything [*sic*] and endeavour to control his colleague. He was an able, sarcastic man, well fitted for the work. But the results were most unsatisfactory. The Eastern Archipelago Company had nothing to say to which the Commissioners could listen; Mr. Woods, the editor of the *Straits Times*, was astonished to find himself called upon to prove the case for the enemies of the Rajah – and as the silly man knew nothing, he could only involve himself in a cloud of absurdities. The Lieutenant-Governor of Labuan tried to bring on his case but that was beyond the scope of the inquiry. The only curious incident which

occurred was the stepping forth of a Dutch civil officer,
Monsieur Boudriot, . . . who said that, being on his way
home from Java on sick leave, he had accidentally attended
the Commission, and he begged to offer himself as a witness.
This gentleman's evidence of itself would carry conviction
to impartial minds, for he had held high positions on the
coast of Borneo, and knew the Skrang and Saribus Dayaks to
be savage, inhuman wretches, and undoubted pirates.

Sir James had retired from the Commission, as Mr.
Prinsep had permitted Mr. Woods to take almost an official
position during the enquiry.

The result was what might have been expected. As no
specific accusations were brought against the Rajah, no
specific answers to them could be prepared . . . Sir James
Brooke himself did not manage his part well. He was
anxious to prove the complicity of the Eastern Archipelago
Company in all the intrigues which had brought about the
Commission, and he wearied the Commissioners with a
useless and tiresome examination of Mr. Motley, the agent of
the Eastern Archipelago Company in Labuan. Nothing
could be got out of the man, as he knew little, and had only
been playing the part of the frog in the fable. We tried
ourselves to induce the Rajah to confine himself to two
issues, which were really important: first whether the Saribus
and Skrang were really pirates; and if they were, had undue
severity been exercised in suppressing them . . .

No man perhaps felt the absurdity of the whole inquiry
more than Mr. Devereux. He vainly enquired, What are the
charges, who are the accusers? and probably had he not been
hampered with an impossible colleague, he would have
closed the Commission at once . . .

In speaking of Sir James Brooke, I wish to present him
exactly as he appeared to myself, and neither to conceal nor
palliate his errors and faults. I watched him closely during
the course of this Commission, and I thought that I detected
in him the same impatience of opposition which I have

often observed in those who have lived much alone, or in
the society of inferiors, whether of rank or intellect. Sir
James had lived much alone, or with those to whom his
word was law, so that he had had rarely the advantage of
rubbing his ideas against those of his equals, and therefore
treated as important subjects matters which, to others less
interested, were but trivial . . . Sir James Brooke did not
direct the inquiry to the real issues, therefore it failed.[11]

It failed to such a degree that the two judges were incapable of
agreeing on their report, so each sent in a separate document.
James's many different offices and allegations concerning his role in
trade, they dismissed as unworthy of investigation. Both accepted
that the Skrang and Saribus Dayaks *were* pirates – regardless of
their use of paddles, not sails – whose custom and delight was headhunting. But on the measures taken by the Navy against Skrang and
Saribus Dayaks they were at loggerheads. Devereux observed tartly,
'There does not appear any reasonable ground for sympathy with a
race of indiscriminate murderers.' Prinsep, however, was damning
about the mortality involved: 'I cannot but consider this unfortunate consequence of acting in concert with savage allies, to be a
strong ground against the investing of an individual, holding
authority under a half-savage chieftain, as hereafter mentioned,
with any such official character under the Crown of Great Britain
as that held by Sir James Brooke.' While James seemed to have
genuinely attempted to prevent 'atrocities revolting to European
feeling', he had been unequal to the task.

Both commissioners wrestled with the knotty matter of Sarawak's
sovereignty. Devereux was so perplexed by the *de factos* and *de jures*
that James had thrown at him that he was quite unable to come to
any useful conclusion and produced a long appendix to prove it.
Prinsep, however, was not a man to be fooled by mere facts and
declared James roundly to be simply a vassal of the Sultan of Brunei.
But both commissioners agreed that the Navy should no longer be
involved in the defence of Sarawak and that James should have no
role in the decision of who was a pirate to be suppressed and who

not. At the end of the inquiry, the shimmering web of ambiguities that James had so carefully spun about himself over the years was torn rudely away, leaving him naked and exposed as a mere private citizen and a foreign lackey stripped of all rights of protection. But he would not actually learn that for another year.

Chapter 11

Peace at Last

James returned to Sarawak in HMS *Rapid* just before Christmas and found it at peace. 'Now commenced a really quiet life,' notes St John. James was more ironically content. 'We are quite prosperous, and quiet, dull as ditch water.'

The commission had set him in a legalistic frame of mind.

Since the departure of the Datuk Patinggi (Gaffur), we have been very successful in establishing our inferior court, in which the Datuk Bandar presides, assisted by three or four hadjis of character. The old Temonggong is likewise a judge in Israel, and sometimes he breaks into the court, upsets the gravity of all present by laying down *his* law for a quarter of an hour – krissing and hanging, flogging and flaying all offenders, past, present, or future, and after creating a strong impression, vanishes for a month or two.[1]

There was a need for more European officers, but everything went into slow limbo while awaiting the result of the commission. Many relieved their boredom with local mistresses, 'keeps', giving themselves an appetite for the communal all-male mess dinners with a swift pre-prandial gin and autochthonic. James, of course, did not, though his successor, Rajah Charles, was partial to local ladies and embarrassingly fertile. He would publicly sing the praises of miscegenation, and scandalously urge English women to accept the embraces of virile Asian husbands. Dayaks were notoriously unflustered by such passing relationships, seeing them perhaps as an even better source of discharged *semangat* than gifts of crockery. Malays preferred more fixed arrangements, being expert at the transformation of the silken bonds of affection into the steel fetters of political alliance. Moreover, they were always keen to tie up those nasty male loose ends that might suddenly lash out at their virgin daughters or chaste wives.

James cultivated the skills of a country squire and also became a passionate chess player, delighting in thrashing younger officers at the game and working out chess problems in painstaking detail. Weekends might be spent in one of his country retreats arguing clubbily over religion, science or politics. It was a sign of how much Sarawak had changed that they were occasionally stirred to controversy by visitors. Spenser St John wrote:

> We had at this time in Sarawak the famous naturalist, traveller and philosopher, Mr. Alfred Wallace, who was then elaborating in his mind the theory which was simultaneously worked out by Darwin – the theory of the origin of species; and if he could not convince us that our ugly neighbours, the orang-utans, were our ancestors, he pleased, delighted and instructed us by his clever and inexhaustible flow of talk – really good talk. The Rajah was pleased to have so clever a man with him, as it excited his mind, and brought out his brilliant ideas. No man could judge the Rajah by seeing him in society. It was necessary to get him at his cottage at Peninjau, with his clever visitor Wallace, or with his nephew Charles . . . who was full of the crudest notions, the result of much undigested reading, but who could defend his thoughts cleverly, pleasantly and gaily . . . In the morning we would catch each other looking in the library

for our authorities, and perhaps the arguments, with which
to support another discussion in the evening.[2]

James loved the idea that it was not just 'natives' who were civilised
by contact with him, but also his young men who attended the
discussions.

Wallace departed with the opinion that James Brooke was the
finest gentleman in the east, but Frank McDougall was offended
by some of the opinions expressed at these bibulous, undergraduate sessions, so he was normally replaced by the stolidly
orthodox Mr Chambers. He and James sat in the jungle and
wrote earnest and obsessive notes to each other about such subjects as the relationship between passion and reason. James,
interestingly, argued against the need for divine revelation and
took the view that

> The passions which we share in common with animals by
> their inordinate strength disturb reason and destroy morals,
> and the struggle is common to heathens and Christians
> alike, and the victory must (independently of supernatural
> aid) depend on the proportion which reason may bear
> relative to passion. The perfection of reason must be the
> perfection of morals – the improvement of reason, the
> improvement of morals in this world; for we then know
> more distinctly the duties we have to perform, and acquire
> power to perform them as knowing that they tend to
> happiness.[3]

This is a remarkably eighteenth-century view of things, and one
wonders how far it worked to control James's own dark passions.

When the printed findings of the commission finally arrived in
Sarawak, James forgot reason and raged and roared. 'Never was there
such a farce of an enquiry. Humiliation to me, disgrace to the government, injury to the natives, ruin to our policy, from a Commission
conducted without dignity or propriety, and all about nothing!'[4]
Immediately, he got into a dispute about the competence of his

courts to judge British subjects. He was stunned that his resignation of Crown offices was simply accepted and that he was not begged to resume them. Worse, Spenser St John was appointed to be Her Majesty's new Consul-General for Borneo and found it impossible to convince James that this was intended as a friendly gesture. James huffily noted, 'He abandons a life devoted to a great cause . . . for an official mediocrity.'[5] No British consul was to be allowed in independent but unrecognised Sarawak, so St John would be obliged to move – regretfully – to Brunei, where James, according to London a private citizen and vassal, was now flatteringly called upon to settle a dynastic dispute.

At the mission, too, things were in flux. The McDougalls had just returned from leave in England, and Frank was to become Bishop of Labuan. James immediately started bickering about the need for him to become Bishop of Sarawak as well. The finer points of ecclesiastical legislation fascinated him. Harriette was more preoccupied with her new baby, with Charley Grant's young brother, Alan – entrusted to them in Sarawak for his health – and with her alcoholic Muslim *ayah*, whose charitable spirit had driven her to give Harriette's possessions away and whose greatest feat was to pass out from drink before the Bishop of Calcutta. The very day after their return, to top it all, Mr Chambers arrived from Banting with seven new Dayak converts, and then Mr Gomez turned up from Lundu with a whole clutch of new souls to pillage her stores and try her patience.

Yet occasionally the Sarawak sense of torpor would insinuate itself even into Harriette's busy helpers. One attempted suicide with slashed wrists and laudanum, apparently as much from boredom as anything. Frank was away so Harriette, of course, coped with it all.

> It is . . . a common mistake to imagine that the life of a missionary is an exciting one. On the contrary, its trial lies in its monotony. The uneventful day, mapped out into hours of teaching and study, sleep, exercise and religious duties; the constant society of natives whose minds are like those of children, and who do not sympathize with your English

ideas; the sameness of the climate, which even precludes discourse about the weather, – all this added to the distance from relatives and friends at home, combined with the enervating effects of a hot climate, causes heaviness of spirits and despondency in single men and women. Married people have not the same excuse.[6]

Until the results of the commission were announced, relations between mission and Rajah were close, even intimate. Harriette wrote:

It is an established rule now that we go to the Rajah's on Tuesday evening, and he comes to us on Thursday, and we are to dine together once a month . . . You have no idea how merry we are, but there is no resisting the fun of this patchwork society. Last Tuesday, Mr. H—, a tall and immensely stout man, would persist in dancing a *Minuet de la Cour* with a little midshipman. He mounted a Dayak cap and feathers and made us laugh till we cried . . . I danced a quadrille with the Rajah, who dances beautifully and is as merry as a child. A charade was acted, which, with the dancing, infinitely amused the natives, of whom I should think 150 were present: and the evening closed with singing 'Rix Rax', the national anthem of Sarawak, the Europeans clapping their hands and the natives yelling a war yell for the chorus.[7]

Harriette and Brooke Brooke had written 'Rix Rax', basing it on an old German nonsense 'catch', and it was the inevitable end to a festive soiree. It ran:

Rix Rax, filly bow bow bow bow, filly bow bow bow, Rix Rax
Sarawak, Sarawak, Sarawak shall win,
I see from far the Dayak fleet of war. How fast!
And meet Saribus' pirate fleet! And Sarawak and Sarawak and Sarawak shall win.

Charles Bunyon presents another account of the jolly social life
of the little settlement, which gives a hint of the relations between
rajah and bishop that were later to become so soured. The joke
centres on durian fruit. After describing tiffin and the fruits which
formed part of it, concoctions of sun-made creams and 'limonade
divine' contained in red prickly caskets lined with white satin
[durian], Bunyon adds that the announcement was made that the
first durians of the season had come in.

'Their votaries,' said the Rajah, 'are always wild on the
occasion. It is a passionate fruit and must be loved or hated.'
A mixture of ambrosia and cream, tainted with the aroma of
ancient pigsties and garlic, was beyond the capacities of the
novices; but the plates of yellow pips extracted from their
rough envelopes, pouring forth fresh perfume every time the
fork ran into them, were irresistible to the veterans. With
many jokes and much laughter the spoil was seized upon,
although the indulgence carried a retribution with it. After
this it was a relief to get out of doors into the fresh air and
upon the water . . . After a renovating bath and white jacket
toilet, the correct thing in Sarawak, unless a very wet day or
special occasion calls for European costume, the royal
household, then composed wholly of bachelors, awaited the
arrival of the Bishop's family, and with pleasure, except
where conscience had made cowards of durian eaters. On
assembling for dinner some little banter followed but, 'Never
mind,' cried the Rajah, 'I'll make them all eat durian before
we let them off this evening;' and after receiving his guests
he led the way to the dining room. When lighted up for the
evening the house looked more Oriental than in the
daylight. The windows opening into the veranda served as
the framework for several half-lengths of Dayak chiefs, who,
their approach to their sovereign being one of gradation and
delay, would stand without for hours until invited to enter.
Their fine figures, some in brilliant jackets of satin or gold
embroidery, displaying their broad sinewy chests, others

covered with an infinity of brass rings and chains, their earrings being circlets of brass frequently depending from the ear to the shoulder, made a magnificent setting to the picture; while their great black eyes, as they cast admiring looks upon their lord and his guests, or flashed telegraphic glances to each other, were more suggestive than reassuring to the stranger.

Dinner proceeded until a discussion arose, which the Rajah cut short by exclaiming, 'Do help the pudding that is waiting – that is the one which the ladies will prefer;' and, that which was before him being in a glory of flame, while the other looked deliciously cool, all took the hint. The pudding was served with a very pleasant sauce like rich apple, and was greatly admired, much to the satisfaction of the host. At dessert he announced that durians had arrived and were only awaiting the permission of the ladies to enter. Oh no, they never could or would think of allowing it. 'Vile things,' ejaculated the Bishop who, being both physician and botanist, was an accepted authority upon esculents. 'Well,' was the reply, 'I can hardly ask you to eat them twice as I know that to-day you have done so once already.' Their quick denial was met by a burst of triumph, the white teeth of the Bengalee domestics bearing conspicuous witness to the laughter of the sahibs. 'You have all done it; you have all done it,' cried the votaries of the fruit; and truly it was so. The Rajah, skilful in the diplomacy of cuisine as in the management of native potentates, had contrived a sauce which, under the belief that it was apple, had beguiled us for once into becoming durian eaters.[8]

Chapter 12

The Chinese Insurrection

Before he left for Brunei in early 1856, St John went on a tour of some of the outlying districts. Around the town of Bau, with its several goldmines, he remarked on the tremendous increase in the number of Chinese – there were now some four thousand in Sarawak – and worried that it might lead to trouble. Triad activity had been reported, and there had been resistance to some of the edicts of the Brooke government, for the Chinese were used to running their own affairs and brooked no rajah. The immediate flashpoint was opium; official imports had dropped as it was being smuggled into Sarawak on a large scale, and mainly for the Chinese. The Brooke raj never put much faith in statistics but opium, together with arms and powder, was heavily taxed and that tax was a major source of government revenue.

But the trouble over opium was merely a small ripple of the wider political currents in China and Singapore, where Chinese assertiveness was strongly on the rise. When it was fined £150 and obliged to pay tax based on the quantity of opium previously imported, the *kongsi* remembered its old grudge from James's rewriting of its charter and determined to strike.

It is hard not to believe that the loudly voiced British abrogation of all defence obligations towards Sarawak was a major element in this, since it was decided that the Rajah and his officers might safely be slain but other British residents should remain untouched for fear of naval reprisals. Brooke intelligence was good, and although the Rajah was away in Singapore, Charles Johnson was warned of the plot and hurried from Skrang to Kuching, only to find it basking in deceptive tranquillity. But the forts were manned and the garrison was set on alert, with a gunboat on the river, before he left again.

When James returned in early 1857, he irritably stood down the soldiers, against the advice of Crookshank, his senior officer, and Middleton, the chief of police. Such rumours about the Chinese were as old as time, all nonsense. Since the Singapore inquiry, more and more of the world had begun to look like nonsense to James. The forts were emptied of reinforcements, the weapons locked away. And then the six hundred armed Chinese came.

According to St John:

> Roused from his slumbers by the unusual sounds of shouts and yells just after midnight, the Rajah looked out of the Venetian windows, and immediately conjectured what had occurred. Several times he raised his revolver to fire in among them; but, convinced that alone he could not defend the house, he determined to effect his escape . . . summoning his servant he led the way down to a bath-room, which communicated with the lawn, and telling him to open the door quickly and follow close, the Rajah sprang forward with sword drawn and revolver cocked, but found the coast clear. Had there been twenty Chinese there he would have passed through them, as his quickness and practical skill in the use of weapons were unsurpassed. Reaching the banks of the stream above his house, he paused as he found it full of Chinese boats; but presently hearing his alarmed servant, who had lost him in the darkness, calling to him, he knew that the attention of the Chinese would be attracted, so diving under the bows of one of the barges he swam to the opposite shore unperceived, and, as he was then suffering from an attack of fever and ague, fell

utterly exhausted and lay for some time on the muddy bank, till, slightly recovering, he was enabled to reach the Government writer's house.[1]

It won't do, of course. St John was not actually in Sarawak, so his loyal version glosses over certain difficulties. The first victim of James's derring-do was his servant, Penty, whom he tried to throttle in the darkness. James may not have been physically himself but his behaviour throughout the insurrection falls far short of bottomless courage. His reaction is closer to simple terror. And after the terror, he is a broken man. Through the window, he and Penty silently watched Nicholetts, the eighteen-year-old cadet, cut down and beheaded by the Chinese, his head then stuck on a pole and paraded round town in triumph as the head of James Brooke. Penty was obliged to 'display very unwonted activity' to slip away into the jungle once James had made his own escape through the bathroom. 'The other attacks took place simultaneously,' continued St John.

Mr. and Mrs. Crookshank, rushing forth on hearing this midnight alarm, were cut down – the latter left for dead, the former seriously wounded. The constable's house was attacked but he and his wife escaped, while their two children and an English lodger were killed by the insurgents. Here occurred a scene which shows how barbarous were these Chinese. When the rebels burst into Mr. Middleton's house, he fled, and his wife following found herself in the bath-room, and by the shouts was soon convinced that her retreat was cut off. In the meantime the Chinese had seized her two children, and brought the eldest down into the bath-room to show the way his father had escaped. Mrs. Middleton's only refuge was in a large water-jar; there, she heard the poor little boy questioned, pleading for his life, and heard the shriek when the fatal sword was raised which severed his head from his body. The fiends kicked the head with loud laughter from one to another. They then set fire to the house, and she distinctly heard her second child

shrieking as they tossed him into the flames. Mrs. Middleton
remained in the jar till the falling embers forced her to
leave. She then got into a neighbouring pond.[2]

She sat there for some time, up to her neck in water, until rescued by
a friendly Chinese who concealed her in Chinese costume. But her
Ali Baba-like sufferings were far from over. When her deliverer led
her past the ruins of her house, the first thing she saw was four dogs
ripping her child's burned corpse apart. The story was both horrific
and embarrassingly close to pantomime. In a pre-football age, the
alleged actions of the Chinese seem oddly unconvincing and Mrs
Middleton's account bizarre. Harriette's daughter, Mab, summed it up
as 'Mama, they've killed all the chickens and the little Middletons.'[3]

The stockades were assaulted and taken after fierce resistance,
only four men being on duty in one and three in the other. In an
effort to improve the odds, two prisoners, one mad, one a debtor,
were released and armed. The madman shot himself. The debtor
decamped. He was probably a certain Dayak who had formed a
peculiar obsession with the safe of the Borneo Company and could
usually be found either attacking it or escaping from custody following a previous attempt. The Chinese now had muskets, powder
and heavy guns. They roamed the town, whooping and shooting it
up indiscriminately like cowboys.

'The confusion which reigned throughout the rest of the town
may be imagined, as, startled by the shouts and yells of the Chinese,
the inhabitants rushed to the doors and windows, and beheld night
turned into day by the bright flames which rose in three directions,
where the Rajah's, Mr. Crookshank's, and Mr. Middleton's houses
were all burning at the same time.'[4]

James fled to the Datuk Bandar's house and, finding the Malays
preoccupied with placing their wives and children in a place of
safety, fell down the river, heading for Skrang and reinforcements.
He had to borrow the very clothes he stood up in from the Malays.

Later there would be a need for a hero, but candidates were thin
on the ground at the moment. St John was often at loggerheads
with the missionaries and in later years did much to drive a wedge

between them and the Rajah so that the bishop, in St John's version, seems more like a collaborator than a resistance fighter. Harriette tells the story rather differently, and in her view it is Frank McDougall who is the bold swashbuckler of the piece. Tidman, secretary to the Borneo Company, offers yet another version, with Helms, his manager, as the man of the hour.

The remaining British sought refuge in the mission house, where Frank calmly made an inventory of their weapons. There were six guns. Realising that armed resistance was useless against such odds, he dispensed blessings and opted instead for trust in prayers. We can be sure that he was quite unsurprised next morning to have them answered and receive assurances from the *kongsi* that no harm was intended him but that he must come to the hospital to care for their wounded. Learning that Mrs Crookshank was not, as at first thought, dead but lying incapacitated by the roadside, he stoutly insisted she be cared for before he would undertake a mission of mercy to the Chinese, and she was finally brought to the house. Her thick braids had protected her head against outrage from Chinese swords but the rings had been torn from her fingers.

The Chinese were now cosily installed in the courthouse, squatting on the seats of the Rajah and the Malay lords, quietly smoking and exulting in their victory. Nicholetts' head was still on display on its pole, though it is unclear whether the leaders actually believed it to be that of James. They would, they announced, henceforth assume direction of the country themselves but the bishop, Mr Rupell the merchant, and Helms of the Borneo Company were to be put in charge of the Europeans; the Datuk Bandar was to answer for the Malays.

The bishop for once did not bite his tongue: he mentioned the certainty of the imminent arrival of Charles Johnson and thousands of loyal Dayaks, eager for revenge. The Chinese seemed not to have thought of that. In fact, it cast quite a shadow over their triumph, but they said rather optimistically that they would write to Charles offering to leave him in peace to rule his Dayaks if he did not bother them. To gain time, the Europeans and Malays all swore an oath of allegiance to the *kongsi*, recorded in a document sprinkled with the blood of freshly killed chickens. The swearers were similarly sprinkled so that when Frank returned to the mission house, with hat and smock besmirched with gore, Harriette was convinced he had been fatally injured. 'After which,' noted Tidman, 'came tea and cigars, and we had to sit another half hour drinking and smoking, and when we left, were obliged to shake hands with the brutes whom with the greatest pleasure we could have shot dead on the spot.'[5]

The Christian Chinese were also attacked by the insurgents and now fled in turn to the mission house for protection and, from there, watched the Chinese ships, laden with booty, head back to Bau, fifteen miles upriver. The rebels tried to take Helms with them as hostage but he discreetly hid himself in the jungle. 'No one in Sarawak could imagine what had become of him,'[6] Harriette notes curtly and cattily, anxious to dispose of Frank's rival.

The real, though misplaced, courage was shown not by the Europeans, but by Abang Patah, the fiery son of the Datuk Temonggong, who, with a small band of lightly armed Malay followers, ruthlessly pursued the Chinese and took one of their vessels before being driven off. European writers would later appropriate this courage as being obviously inspired by James and so conceal the Rajah's embarrassing state of total funk. Irritated by this Malay belligerence and reinforced by new arrivals, the Chinese turned back and now began the systematic destruction of the town. The Malays, under the gentle Datuk Bandar, attacked the Chinese vessels again, seizing ten, though heavily outgunned, and moored them in the middle of the river as a base from which to fire on the rebels. The Rajah sent an unhelpful note to Helms urging him to 'hold the fort'. It is unclear whether this was intended literally or metaphorically.

The bishop meanwhile, taking charge as usual, had assumed command of Rupell's schooner and sent the women and children downriver to safety in the fort at Lingga so the men would be free to fight. He had also boldly run the Sarawak flag back up the flagpole, whereas the Kuching Chinese more prudently kept both a Sarawak and a white flag in stock and displayed whichever was appropriate to the particular stage of the conflict. Helms set off in another vessel and the bishop in a third to track down the elusive Rajah. When they met, there were harsh words, but James was persuaded to return to Kuching, only to find the Malay quarter ablaze.

St John writes vaguely of a general panic that gave James no choice but to retire yet again, but it is manifest that this was not his finest hour. His days of charging were long over. He was depressed and hopeless and, determined to retreat, was heard to cry out in despair, 'Offer the country on any terms to the Dutch.' At this, Frank McDougall's anger waxed hotter still. 'If the Rajah deserts his country,' he snapped, 'I must look after my diocese.' He set off huffily gathering arms while James fled ever further downstream. Tidman notes of the bishop, 'Like us all, he was armed to the teeth, with sword, double-barrelled and revolver. He recalled the good old times, when lord-bishops could strike a blow, if need were, in a good cause.'[7]

Then fate intervened again. In the gloom and the mud and the scuttling crabs of the river-mouth, suddenly there was black smoke. It was the new, boldly armed vessel of the Borneo Company, *Sir James Brooke*. The two James Brookes took each other's stock, united and returned with all speed to Kuching. They took the first Dayak reinforcements from Skrang in tow, led by a fevered Charles Johnson. These Skrang Dayaks were the very people James was supposed to have outrageously slaughtered according to the Singapore inquiry, and much was made of their present loyalty to the government. But here it was perhaps more an example of their detestation of the Chinese and the successful use the Brookes made of the principle of divide and rule – that and the lure of human heads.

> The gloom and the depression had passed away from the Rajah now, and everyone was in tearing spirits. The moment we opened the town, we were exposed to the fort, and the guns from the old fort opened up on us with grape of original composition – balls, nails, scraps of rusty iron, came whizzing round, many of which were later picked up as souvenirs . . . The next instant our long eighteen-pounder forward spoke his mind. Firing almost simultaneously with another gun of

the same calibre the roar was a good one, and then came the sharper notes of the swivels and rifles. The shot from the gun forward, which was manned by the mate, went slap into the fort and created a scare. Out scoured the Chinese like wild hares in March, some dashing up the road . . . while many ran through the bazaar, affording practice for the riflemen on board. The new fort was quickly cleared, and two or three more rounds completed the action. We steamed slowly up the river, on the sides of which the Malay kampong was still burning, and then coming back again anchored off the bazaar. And thus the Company's steamer re-took the town of Sarawak.[8]

It was at this point that the Chinese Insurrection turned into the Chinese Massacre. Many Chinese were still busy destroying the Malay settlement on the left bank of the river, and here the Dayaks and Malays landed behind them, burned their boats and coolly slaughtered them. Those that escaped into the jungle or killed themselves in despair were ruthlessly sought out and found to have between £5 and £20 sterling and quantities of silver cutlery on their bodies. An attempted stand upriver was swept aside by the newly emboldened Datuk Bandar and a total rout of the insurgents commenced. Burdened by their women and children and their considerable loot, the Chinese now straggled in panic towards the Dutch border, bearing with them the sacred stone, the *Taipekong*, from the temple that was the very core of the *kongsi*. Harassed by the Dayaks, they bought time by dropping booty and rice. Years later, an English silver cruet would turn up in a remote longhouse as a sacred relic of the time, firmly believed to turn the fields green and drive away disease. St John has the Chinese finding a mysterious and forgotten path around the gallant and loyal Dayaks at Gumbang. Other writers have them, perhaps more plausibly, securing free passage with a hefty bribe.

Once safely across the border in Dutch territory, the Chinese began a heated internal debate concerning their recent policy, fell on each other and further slaughter ensued. In all, some 1,500

Chinese probably perished in the insurrection. The Dutch disarmed the survivors and, unexpectedly good neighbours, sent their booty back to Sarawak. Since it was hard to know what was loot and what was not, the Dutch simply sent everything. Much was stuff that had never been seen in Kuching before.

Harriette McDougall had undergone a rather different adventure, sailing downriver with the children in the hope of an escape to Singapore aboard a Chinese trading vessel. Fortunately, the bishop's boat had been kitted out with supplies for an imminent journey so they had both wine and tinned soup. At the last moment Miss Coomes, an aged spinster attached to the mission, had gone back for essential items of jungle dress and returned mysteriously with a set of stays and a black silk apron. Some of the tinned food, Harriette noted, tasted as though prepared for a voyage in the Ark, but they were more oppressed by heat and mosquitoes – and the demands of etiquette. The Malays were, as always, impeccably polite and hospitable, so Harriette was obliged to indulge in social niceties, including going to greet her old friend, the scribe Inchi Buyang, a man so vast that normal Malay houses could not accommodate his weight. He advised them strongly not to try to return to Kuching, but they did so anyway and their arrival coincided most unfortunately with the return of the Chinese. They fell downriver again to Jernang and sought, with difficulty, to persuade the Malays to take in the mission Chinese. Finally, they were joined by Frank and all determined to sail for the fort at Lingga, where both they and the mission Chinese would be safe.

The night was very dark and wet, and the deck leaked upon us, so that we and our bags and bundles were soon wet through. But we neither heeded the rain not felt the cold. We had eaten nothing since early morning, but we were not hungry; and although for several nights we could scarcely be said to have slept, we were not sleepy. A deep thankfulness took possession of my soul; all our dear ones were spared to us. My children were in my arms, my husband paced the

deck over my head. I seemed to have no cares, and to be
able to trust to God for the future, who had been so merciful
to us hitherto. I remember, too, when Mrs. Stahl opened the
provision basket, and gave us each a slice of bread and meat,
how very good it was, although we had not thought about
wanting it. We lit a little fire, and made some hot tea, but
soon had a message from the Rajah's boat to put out the fire
lest we should be seen. The only thing that troubled me was
a nasty faint smell, for which I could not account; but the
next morning we found a Chinaman's head in a basket close
by my corner, which was reason enough! We had taken a
fine young man on board to help pull the sweeps, and this
ghastly possession was his. He said he was at Kuching,
looking about for *a head*, and went into the court-house.
Hearing some one in a little side room, he peeped in, and
saw a Chinaman gazing at himself in a bit of looking-glass,
which was stuck against the wall. He drew his sword, and in
one moment, stepping close behind him, cut off his head:
and having obtained this prize, was naturally desirous of
getting away from the place; so he came off as boatman in
one of the flying boats, bringing the head in a basket, which
he stowed in the side of the boat. It entirely spoiled my
hand-bag, which lay near it; I had to throw it away, and
everything in it which could not be washed in hot water.[9]

They all ended up in Charles Johnson's house in Lingga and
then moved on to Banting to the house of Chambers, the missionary, though they were irked not to be fetched by the Rajah for
several weeks. He seemed to have forgotten them entirely.

One day we were invited to a feast in one of the long houses.
I said, ' I hope we shall see no heads,' and was told I need
not see any; so, taking Mab in my hand, I went along with
Mr. Chambers, and we climbed up into the long verandah
room where all the work of the tribe goes on. This long
house was surrounded with fruit trees and very

comfortable . . . We were seated on white mats, and welcomed by the chief people present . . . As we English folks could not eat fowls roasted in their feathers, nor cakes fried in cocoa-nut oil, they brought us fine joints of bamboo, filled with pulut rice, which turns to a jelly in cooking and is fragrant with the scent of the young cane. I was just going to eat this delicacy when my eyes fell upon three human heads standing on a large dish, freshly killed and lightly smoked, with food and sirih leaves in their mouths. Had I known them when alive I must have recognized them, for they looked quite natural. I looked with alarm at Mab, lest she should see them too; then we made our retreat as soon as possible. But I dared say nothing. These Dayaks had killed our enemies, and were only following their own customs by rejoicing over their dead victims. But the fact seemed to part them from us by centuries of feeling – our disgust, and their complacency. Some of them told us that afterwards, when they brought home some of the children belonging to the slain, and treated them very kindly, wishing to adopt them as their own, they were annoyed at the little ones standing looking up at their parents' heads hanging from the roof, and crying all day, as if it were strange they should do so! Yet the Dayaks are very fond of children, and extremely indulgent to them. Our school was recruited after the war by the children of Chinese, bought by Government from their captors. This was my first and last visit to a Dayak feast.[10]

When they finally returned, Kuching lay in ruins, the very trees scorched from the flames. The Rajah's fine residence, his papers and journals, and – worse – his great library, were all burned, as were the other European houses. In the ashes James found the scorched medal presented him by the Royal Geographical Society in the days of his popularity. He sent it home to John Templer. Another loss was the bullet that was dug from his Indian wound and served perhaps as an alibi for sustained bachelorhood in after-dinner moments of male confidence.

The Malay kampongs were devastated. The church had been stripped of furniture and the harmonium broken, the mission house dusted with gunpowder ready to be fired. The dispensary was smashed, the piano had maliciously been filled with earth and backgammon counters and the silk lining cut from Frank's cassock. The Bishop of Calcutta would send replacement ecclesiastical vestments so bizarre and grotesque they could not be worn. Many of the Kuching Chinese had fallen victim to the prejudices of both sides and now the Dayaks took great satisfaction in smoking Chinese heads in front of them. Twelve Bau Chinese were found hiding in the town, and arrested. One was tried and executed.

Miss Coomes was oddly disturbed by all the upset and her exposure to the close proximity of strapping Dayak manhood in a state of near nudity. Later she would turn up at meals in her underwear and keep pigs in her room. Frank eventually totally despaired of lady missionaries.

The Dutch sent a steamer and troops to help in any way they could. The Borneo Company sent a vessel of arms, supplies and money. The British sent HMS *Spartan* with orders to protect British citizens and interests but do nothing that might inflame the opposition at home, so they did nothing at all. The sailors, in an unofficial gesture of support, at least turned Harriette's piano upside-down to empty it of debris and so restore it to a playable condition. Henry Keppel was unable to help his friend directly but ordered out a warship to huff and puff helpfully along the coast.

After the trouble, tragedy and deprivation came in many forms. The Chinese taste for European silver cutlery had stripped the town of it so that eating now involved the inconvenience of passing a spoon and fork round the table. Harriette's aged Hindu syce triumphantly returned to her a lump of melted-down silverware the Chinese had given him as his share of the mission booty, but he grieved bitterly over the tail they had cut off his Brahma bull so that he now had to spend hours whisking the flies away himself. This lump of silver seems to have been the source of the Brooke Heirloom Cup, donated much later to Magdalen College, Oxford.

With admirable consistency, the British worked hard to see the whole event as the machinations of their sworn enemy, Makota. But they had real enemies enough. Profiting from their distraction, Rentap descended from his mountain fastness in Sadok and harried local supporters of the Sarawak government with acts that may or may not have been piratical. Charles Johnson was dispatched with a Dayak force to capture him, but nothing came of it.

'It was the madness,' wrote James Brooke, 'the stark, staring folly of the attempt which caused it to succeed. With mankind in general we may trust to their not doing anything entirely opposed to reason; but this rule does not hold good with the Chinese.'[11] No one raised their voice to say that the Chinese resentment at being by far the most highly – and arbitrarily – taxed part of the Sarawak population was only reasonable. Nobody asked – as they had about the Dayaks – whether the high mortality of the retreating Chinese was justified. The Dayaks, perhaps, were small in number and romantic so that sympathy for them was permissible. The Chinese were commercial rivals and potential enemies on a worldwide scale.

The devastation of Kuching seemed to some to have revived James. Charles Grant returned from England to see him 'talking, laughing, singing, in fact as charming as ever'. Helms noted that he quickly 'recovered tone and was able to receive the Dutch with a show of becoming confidence in his own resources'. James himself swept aside the disaster and his own behaviour with the usual soldierly jocularity and squirish assertions of high principle:

A dead Chinaman is no more to be apprehended than a dead dog, and we have taught the living miscreants such a lesson that they will not play their tricks upon us for many a long year. For the future we will take such precautions in ruling them as to deprive them of the means of doing mischief. Worldly goods, you know, I care not for. I have suffered so much before, that this misfortune appears light;

and, so that the few that I love are spared to me, I care not. Through my affections, I could be deeply wounded; but the possession of money, pictures, books, etc., is but of small account. Had I valued these things, had I desired ease, sought fame as a primary object, or lived for society, I should not have exiled myself to this country. I have a duty to perform from which I may not shrink; and I have long known, with an aching and a steadfast heart, that this duty entails trials and struggles even to the end. What, then, is the yelling of a few score of Chinese for my life? I told Penty that our death was at hand. I was wound up to the resolve that knows no shrinking, and had we been surrounded I would have given them cold steel and hot shot whilst life lasted, and so have been killed with courage tingling to my fingers' ends, and despair lending me strength; but it was not so to be, and I had quite enough of common sense and lack of heroism to make my escape when opportunity offered.[12]

In the English press, despite the huge bloodshed and the embarrassingly public revival of headhunting, James bafflingly became an icon of empire again. *The Times* was typically arch:

The conspirators did not know all. Had they had the opportunity of reading recent debates in the British Parliament, then more subtle spirits might have received further encouragement from the belief that we are not only an ultra-peaceful, but an ultra-punctilious people, and that the cutting of Rajah Brooke's throat and the burning of the town, might be considered matters beyond our cognizance until the precise colonial status of Sarawak was determined, and whether a Kunsi Chinese was under the jurisdiction of any British court.[13]

Yet there were bitter fruits of the insurrection.

That the Rajah's behaviour on this occasion seemed at variance with his previous brave and chivalrous conduct, was doubtless the case; but if we consider that he was scarcely convalescent after an exhausting illness – that by a sudden blow, he, in one night, saw the fruit of years of toil destroyed, his property given to the flames, and himself a hunted fugitive in the woods, disappointed in the support he sought amongst the natives – his failure, if such it was, to meet the occasion as it required, may well be overlooked. Still, those who were with the Rajah then and afterwards could not but think that a change had come over him, which seemed to show itself in his subsequent conduct.[14]

This was Helms's view. St John, when he came down from Brunei in July, observed James with his accustomed unclouded clarity: 'I particularly noticed one thing in the Rajah, that though when in society full of mental vigour, yet when alone he showed a loss of buoyancy, a tone of melancholy in public matters, as if all ambition was dead within him. "I weary of business," he said to me.'[15]

When James rebuilt his house, he called it The Refuge. Whereas his letters were once full of a sense that life is an accretion of rich experience, they now read as if he felt it consisted of leaving parts of himself scattered about in loss and dissolution. 'He only occasionally felt able to throw off a burden of anxiety. He writes of being "weary of the world, weary of evil, weary of weakness." A cry for rest was first wrung out of him during the Inquiry at Singapore, and after that it is never long absent from his letters.'[16]

Scarce had the smoke begun to clear than new faces appeared in Kuching. Brooke Brooke had been absent in England, looking for a suitable wife. He had found one, economically and conveniently to hand, in Charley Grant's sister, Annie. More troubling to James was his beloved Charley's marriage to Matilda Hay. Yet despite the feelings of jealousy and betrayal, James did the decent thing. He had bought new furniture for them, alas now burned, but he moved Brooke Brooke and Annie into his own rebuilt house, Charley Grant and wife into the courthouse, and decamped himself into humble quarters. 'Charley has returned to his government. I lean upon him and love him.'

In the midst of his own despair, news of the Indian Mutiny reached Sarawak and moved him deeply. Indians, it seemed, were a very different breed from Chinese, possessed of honour and affections – indeed, almost Sarawakians. 'What fine and faithful fellows they were in days gone by! And what grievous errors and offences on our part must have gradually undermined their adherence! Oh wretched, wretched system – that has converted a native soldiery into a European army; which by generalization has destroyed the interest of the officers in their men, and alienated the men between them, and predominantly brought to light that they were of different races, colours and feelings!'[17] He speaks implicitly of the contract between Sarawak and himself when he writes of local Indian troops as 'faithful, with a child-like dependence on the one side, and sympathy and the means to assist on the other'. It was a sense of mission founded on his own sense of inherent superiority, but a sense of mission none the less. Indian mutineers would be accepted for military service in Sarawak. Unlike James's young men, they were found to be excellent material.

A new domesticity was also creeping over Kuching, what crusty bachelors would denounce as the clammy, jealous hand of the *memsahib*. James took a sad pleasure in watching it from without, knowing it was not for him. 'The piano sounds, the voices mingle in some pleasant song, the violin accompaniment reaches my ear from time to time, and there is merry laughter and sweet chatter in the pauses of the music.'[18] Brooke Brooke, James's acknowledged heir, soon fathered a son, whose first act was to kick the bishop in the face, thus neatly establishing the continuity of the line and the official separation of Church and State. He was named Basil, an unlikely appellation for a rajah. The local chiefs, who had been accustomed to drop in of an evening and talk freely and companionably with the British till all hours, noticed the change towards a more private life and gradually ceased to come. The door that had stood always open to locals was now closed, just as it had been in India.

Chapter 13

Reuben George Walker

'What an important year 1858 might have been for Sarawak had the Rajah known how to secure his advance step by step! But he wanted to clear all obstacles at a bound and failed.'[1] James Brooke returned to England at the end of 1857, deliberately leaving Brooke Brooke to rule in his stead and to set his personal stamp upon the administration. He was fifty-four years old, but time had not been kind to him. He was ravaged by smallpox and constant attacks of malaria. He was disillusioned, dispirited and lonely. 'The devil has laid his claw upon my visage, and some injustice has eaten at my heart.'[2] He spoke as though he was effectively retiring from Sarawak affairs.

Yet he plucked up his courage and immediately entered another exhausting round of negotiations with the British government; it seemed that there had finally been a change of heart at the highest levels. St John had been lobbying with quiet effectiveness. Hume was dead and had taken his allegations with him. After the insurrection, public opinion was back on James's side as a gung-ho, all-British national hero. Queen Victoria received him as a sign of renewed royal favour. The government at last offered the protectorate that he had so long sought – they would even set up a naval base – but instead of gratefully accepting it James now began to haggle about the money he had invested in Sarawak – he wanted a large sum refunded. Nothing is so uncongenial to governments as to find large amounts of money unexpectedly with swiftness and resolve for the benefit of other people. To the total exasperation of his friends, James prolonged the haggling until February, when Palmerston's government fell. In the mid-nineteenth century British governments swiftly wobbled and collapsed with banana-republic unpredictability. The new prime minister, Lord Derby, had a marked dislike of foreign commitments and the Sarawak protectorate was suddenly out of the question. Public meetings, petitions and the pulling of strings all did no good. Sarawak was exactly the sort of private project, dragging government involvement after it, that he did not wish to encourage. James had simply missed the boat. He began to think about asking the government, instead, for a loan.

He was by now virtually destitute; indeed, following the Chinese insurrection, he was deeply in debt to the Borneo Company, which was itself in a parlous state. There was no line between the public exchequer of Sarawak and the private fortune of James Brooke, just as he drew no line between the whole of Sarawak and himself, so that the ruin of the one was the ruin of the other. Recent events had revived the old obsession with a steamer as the guarantee of security. 'A penny saved is a screw in the new steamer.' But he badly wanted money for something else. His big secret was about to come out. It bore the name of Reuben George Walker.

Jeanine Alexander sat across from me and sipped tea. Overhead fans whispered, less to cool us off than to say that we were in the Sarawak Club, Kuching, an institution from colonial days where Brits had always been, in some sense, suffering abroad. The national motto had been '*Dum spiro spero*', rendered jokingly by ex-pats as 'While I sweat I hope'.

'There was some writer just here,' she said, and made it a sort of accusation. 'She seemed to think James Brooke was some kind of screaming queen. I soon put her straight.' The voice was Australian and very firm.

Not wanting to be put straight, I sought refuge in a notebook. 'Well . . .' I hedged. 'Parenthood doesn't preclude homosexuality – as recent Malaysian political history shows us.'

There was a loud silence in which I seemed to hear the ticking of a clock. In a sensational recent political show-trial, Anwar Ibrahim, former Deputy Prime Minister, respectably married father of children and devout Muslim, had received a heavy jail sentence for midshipman-like activities with a chauffeur and adopted brother. His mattress had been produced as evidence in court, to great dramatic effect. It was simultaneously the most and least talked about subject in Kuching. At the Sarawak Club it was not being talked about. It was not being talked about very loudly.

'And what exactly was your own link . . . . ?' I asked.

She made a face. 'James Brooke was my great, great-great-grandfather,' I thought at once of those vague rumours that James had had a child by a Malay wife here in Kuching, 'through his son Reuben.

'I have all the documentary evidence,' she said.

I raised interrogative eyebrows.

'Birth certificates,' she signed them with a finger on the polished wood, 'tracing them back, marriage certificates. There's no doubt about it.' She reeled off a litany of names of relatives, constant rearrangements of the elements Reuben, George, James and Brooke.

I tried not to look excited and stirred tea, circling up to the big question. 'And what about the link between James and the mother?'

'No,' she said, almost with pity. 'No, you couldn't expect that. But there were the cheques.'

'The cheques?'

'Yes.' She leaned forward. 'There were cheques up to my grandfather's time. Then they stopped. No more cheques. More tea?'

Reuben George Walker seems to be first mentioned in a letter from James to Brooke Brooke in October 1855, while the latter was in England. He gave him no hint of any family relationship but asked him to look up 'a youth named Reuben Walker who was my servant when in England – the lad was wild and unsteady – misguided as lads will be and often are – he was in trouble and thinking that he

might be ruined altogether I took him. He behaved well enough
with me, barring the follies of youth, and I could find no harm in
him but thoughtlessness and wildness. I hear now from your aunt
Savage [Margaret, James's sister] that Reuben Walker is in Lord
Ward's stables getting on steadily.'[3] Lord Ward is presumably Lord
Ward of Birmingham, who was blessed with a number of residences
so that it is hard to know which location is referred to. He went on
to urge Brooke Brooke to establish 'what the young fellow is like
and whether he promises to be steady. It is a hard thing with a
young head and light heart to resist temptation – but many and
many a one with no greater crime has been driven from bad to
worse.'[4]

The claim that he was James's servant is almost certainly false
and intended to disguise from Brooke Brooke that in Reuben
George he may be meeting his own cousin. James's simultaneous
knowledge and alleged ignorance of his nature seems deliberately
misleading. Despite James's comments, it is not clear that he has
actually met Reuben at this time. He mentions him again in June
1856, complaining pettishly, 'You do not tell me about young
Reuben Walker . . . ascertain whether he bears a good character,
and if he does send him out if he likes it. He was scampish but not
really evil, and he has the making of a good man in him, with abilities above the common run. He was a favourite of mine and I can
find him useful work here . . .'[5] This does not seem to have elicited
the required response so again in August he writes, 'Why do you not
send me news of Reuben Walker . . . You will probably hear of him
at Henderson's Livery Stables – Cockspur St. or Pall Mall. I write
particularly because I do not like to be disappointed in little matters
and they lay hold on my mind . . .'[6]

Tradition has it that Reuben simply turned up, out of the blue, at
James's London hotel in 1858, but this seems most unlikely. For in
February 1857 James is writing to Brooke Brooke yet again, urging
that a huge operation be set in train.

I received your kind letter of December yesterday. The
intelligence of Reuben Walker has distressed me for I
reproach myself for losing sight of him during my own

troubles. You say you will find him if in the land of the living and (I add) ascertain his death if it has occurred. Should you have failed as yet in doing either with certainty, you must at once write to Templer and Booty to use the machinery requisite for the search – giving them every information in your power.

1st. The young grooms at Lord Ward's will know something more than the older lads, and through them you may know his haunts in London where the people may be acquainted with his history and movements.

2nd. His enlistment seems certain, his death doubtful. If he enlisted in 1855 an application to the Horse Guards would provide the information wanting, as they could give the number of his regiment and the returns would supply the date and manner of his death.

Failing at the Horse Guards, a letter addressed to the Commanding Officers of regimental depots (cavalry and infantry) would elicit the information – and Aldershot would be a good place to enquire.

3rd. At the same time an advertisement in *The Times* and *Bell's Weekly Newspaper* (?) will most likely attract his attention if living, or the attention of some of his fellow soldiers if dead. He should be described thus – Reuben George Walker – age about 21 – who lived when young at Brighton and who was lately a groom at Lord Ward's stable and before in the service of Sir J.B., supposed to have enlisted in the army in 1855, will learn something to his advantage by applying in person or by writing to Messrs. Cameron and Booty and any person giving certain information respecting him, whether living or dead, will receive £5 reward.

If he be found in the army, let him be bought out and taken good care of and provided for till I send further directions. My letter should given [*sic*] to him and be directed to write me . . .[7]

It is again interesting that he gets Reuben's age wrong if he was indeed born in 1834 as his tombstone and other records allege; and that the passage about being in the service of Sir J.B. has been added in over the line. Later, the press advertisements were looked for by James and Reuben, and could not be found. Probably Brooke Brooke, not realising the nature of this attachment, simply could not be bothered to go to so much trouble.

At the time of the Chinese insurrection James had received a false report that Reuben was dead, and it is to this that he now attributes his fever. Perhaps this is, then, the true source of James's unusual apathy and despair during these events. Then Reuben is dramatically restored to life, located alive and well in the military. Strings are pulled – by Keppel and others – to obtain his release. James finally meets Reuben, 'the dear little fellow', in Gibraltar in 1857 on the way home. It is on Christmas Day, in Reuben's erstwhile home town of Brighton, at the Savages' house, that he finally comes clean in a letter to Brooke Brooke.

> Now for Reuben. I told you he might be my son. I may
> tell you now that it is as certain as any fact can be. The
> letters I received from his mother (through another hand)
> carried conviction to my mind *at once*, because they
> mentioned names and circumstances and dates which
> could not have been known excepting by her and myself.
> The second letter when his death was reported urged me
> to seek him and to protect him if to be found – that from
> me alone he might claim help and love as he derived his
> life from me and as I was his sole natural protector in the
> eyes of God. She urged me not to seek her or to blast the
> reputation for which she sacrificed her son. There was a
> good deal more to the same effect and it carried
> conviction to my mind. I was anxious to get Reuben
> quietly – to avoid exposure and judge where I should
> place him and what he was like – but these plans were
> upset by the report of his death and afterwards by the fear
> that he would be ordered to India and probably be lost

again. I cannot tell you how much I suffered mentally and
bodily – there was the dastard fear of publicity – and
worse that his character would be bad, and his manner
and habits unfit him for a higher sphere of life. My alarm
that I should never see him, cured me of these lesser
doubts, and broke through the barriers of reserve – Keppel
came to my assistance and F. Alderson's [son of Baron
Alderson, judge in the court of Exchequer and a supporter
of James Brooke, F. Alderson was briefly employed in the
Sarawak administration] vague recollections afforded me
a plea for obtaining his discharge without introducing my
own name. This is the true reason that brought me home
and if other means had failed I should have gone to
Gibraltar and carried him away . . .[8]

Elsewhere, there are further details of this extraordinarily complex melodrama, which seems to draw on a Dickensian storyline.
No wonder Charley Grant would term it a 'romance'. Often James
Brooke's letters are hard to read, the hand wild and spidery, and
having filled the page, he writes crosswise over it – not his usual
style – as if *wanting* it to be illegible.

On arriving at home I wrote to [name illegible] Alderson
and his story is that Mrs. Walker being at the point of death
sent a woman to the Baron's house to find Reuben, who said
that Mrs. W. was in trouble of mind as she wished to tell
Reuben that 'he was not her son but the son of a
gentleman' – for this she was seeking him – Whose Alderson
does not know – but this is enough – and as to the
advertisements in *The Times* (or some other papers), he
heard of it but made no enquiry . . . Besides this, Reuben's
own recollections have thrown light on the mother. The
woman Walker when angry with him used to tell him he was
no son of hers and she would not be troubled with other
people's children – he has for years had a firm suspicion that
he was not her son. There is more that I can tell you at

leisure and a clue to the mother's present home and
position . . .[9]

So it seems that Reuben's mother may be a lady but that he was
given away to be raised by a servant, which goes some way to
explaining James's enormous guilt.

The different members of the family took the news of their new
relative in rather different ways. 'Directly your Aunt Margaret was
told the fact she said she remembered now how like he was as a boy
to the caricature of me taken when young – she was surprised it had
not struck her before.' It seems, then, that Margaret knew Reuben
as a child and that he moved within the family circle, which con-
tradicts the tale of his disappearance, for allegedly the link with
mother and child was broken when they vanished while James was
away on the *Royalist* in 1837. A strong physical resemblance
remained. He continued, '[John] Templer took up my likeness from
his table remarking on the resemblance as Reuben stood before
him – the same hair – complexion – shape of face – colour of eyes –
with the same difference of size between the right eye and the
left . . .'[10] The Johnsons, parents of Brooke Brooke, refused to
believe Reuben to be anything but an impostor, while others
thought this was all a clumsy ruse by James to conceal another of his
unfortunate attachments.

Harriette took a charitable view. 'How easily the Rajah is gulled;
I don't believe he is his son a bit,' she wrote. Frank was less tactful.
'The Rajah must be as cracked as I have long feared if he carries out
his intentions about this Reuben Walker or Brooke.' Nevertheless,
James sprang Reuben upon the missionaries in a railway station in
England in 1861. 'You should have seen Harriette's face of dismay
and disgust . . . I do not believe the fellow a bit, he is not an atom
like the Rajah, nothing but a low-born cad I am sure,'[11] wrote
Frank. And while there may have been problems with Reuben's
bold revelation to the world in Brighton, these were as nothing
compared to those unleashed in Sarawak.

Brooke Brooke waxed hysterical at the mere idea that this 'son'
was to come out east:

The young man who you have publicly proclaimed your son, given your name, and taken to your heart and who you propose to take out to Sarawak, it requires less common sense than God has granted to me, to see must dispossess me and mine of my promised inheritance . . . The two or three years that would elapse before this too certain finale would be to me, years of bitter humiliation, of heat burning and disgrace. Something of this I have experienced in days gone by, and so vividly recollect that I would far prefer seeking a livelihood elsewhere, in however humble a sphere, to such degradation . . . I can't write more. The heavy burthen that you have laid on me, has too confused my hand, to write coherently. How could you write so cruel a letter without apparent feeling that you were inflicting deadly stabs to me and my unfortunate wife at every line.[12]

For once James wrote back a letter that was gentle, infinitely loving and kind, a letter such as he would never write again in his life. 'Forgive me the pain I unintentionally inflicted, but I thought you so assured of your position, and of my trust in you, that I never dreamed of your being so greatly disturbed by the intelligence of my having a son and my intention of bringing him to Sarawak. Were I to wrong you and yours what a villain I should be!! . . . Let [Reuben] George fall into his proper place, which will not be a high one . . .'[13] This soothed Brooke Brooke, but James would rapidly prove himself to be precisely the villain that Brooke Brooke feared.

The story of Reuben George Walker has all the marks of a tale told by one who is, at times, economical with the truth and, at others, excessively prone to fanciful elaboration. But what can we really know of him? The place to start James's 'requisite machinery' is the Family Records Centre. It is where people come to excavate the private past, a discreet, modern building near Sadler's Wells. Worthy publications by staff line the lobby, betraying the flourishing individual obsessions of the academically minded. In theory, they allow anyone to track down their forebears through their prison sentences or their bankruptcies, or fix their addresses on hand-drawn maps of Elizabethan England, including gibbets. There is glamour rather than shame in such distant iniquity, since it is a claim for distinction from the common herd. Noticeboards declare the presence of a rich trainspotters' subculture, with lectures at the Genealogical Society and experts on Kentish local records about to speak at the Royal Horticultural Society Hall. Like pews in a church, the shelves and shelves of entries fan out, the whole of human life reduced to volumes of green-bound birth, black-bound death and red-bound marriage – with a special annexe for the deviant Scots. Crowds of people sweep back and forth between life and death, clutching notebooks. Going back in time, the seekers get magically older and the number of volumes for each year decreases, marking the shrinking population.

Classification of births, deaths and marriages is by year and district. Central registration of births begins in 1837, just too late for Reuben, so he falls off the page of history. We know he died in 1874 but in the wreck of the ship *The British Admiral*, in the Bass Strait off Australia. So there is no death certificate. If he did not officially get born or officially die, perhaps he got married. The name Walker is distressingly common. In the nineteenth century there are plenty of Reubens, let alone Georges, a first name he later preferred. Age at death gives you a date of birth. A boy could get married at fourteen. Most were married by twenty-five. Play the percentages, flit from entry to entry. Dice with death. Snakes and actuarial ladders. Maybe his adopted father was Reuben George Walker too, but they crop up all over the UK. Two of them get married in Eastbourne alone, in 1849 and 1851. There are too many and hence it is impossible to fix his adopted mother just down the road in Brighton.

James Brooke's will, upstairs on the first floor, left Reuben £5,000 and listed his address as Walnut Tree House, Levens, Westmorland. That gives the district of registration and cuts through all the wealth of Walkers, allowing most to be discarded. And after days of searching, he finally turns up in the marriage roster, not as Reuben Walker at all but as George Brooke, in 1862, aged twenty-eight and very old for a wedding, marrying Elizabeth Mowbray. Her father's occupation is 'Sculptor'. His father's is given as 'Knight, Rajah of Sarawak'. In 1864 they give birth to a son, Reuben George Brooke, whose father is described as having the occupation of 'Gentleman'. Reuben has finally made it from poverty to gentility.

If Reuben George was in the army, he should be somewhere in the Public Record Office at Kew. Despite the confusing electronic glamour of swipe cards, pagers, terminals and microfilms, dowdy filing cards lurk on in the dark corners like disregarded great-aunts, and that is where the real work is still done. A whole section deals with the East India Company in a manner that is brutally frank but curiously humanised. 'Lt. Arthur Jones, bachelor and bastard', 'Emma Jones, bastard, spinster, widow' – this poor woman seems to have hopped from one anomalous status to another with no intervening stage of respectable marriage. Beneath the names are little drawings. One who 'died by detonation' has *Bang!* written in a cartoon balloon. Two bebustled ladies look over their shoulders at a departing soldier: *He looks a right bachelor and bastard.* A figure in dhoti with stripes tattooed on his arm decorates the card bearing details of an NCO in the Indian Native Infantry. The girl on the desk looks round nervously and whispers, 'One of our librarians did it about twenty years ago. She got all over the place before they found out. She went a bit . . . funny . . . and left.' Her voice drops even lower. 'I think they *made* her leave.'

If Reuben George Walker, bachelor and bastard, was in the army, there should be a note of it here, though it is not clear what name he might have enlisted under. Did he already know his surname might be Brooke? James's version suggests not.

James Brooke describes him as in the 'Horse Guards', elsewhere as in the '1st Horse' and '1st Royals'. Given his background as a groom, this is what might well be expected, and James no doubt initially entertained an exaggerated idea of his abilities. The muster books of the 1st Regiment of Horse do indeed show a George Walker, height five foot six inches, from London, recruited in 1854. But he is posted as deceased in July 1855. The Crimean War ensured a brisk turnover of young recruits, so if there was a false report of Reuben's death it might well hail from here, given James's initial assumption that this was the regiment of his son. Someone simply looked up the wrong record, as is clear from the age of this George on recruitment – only eighteen. Reuben was twenty at the time.

But if this is the false Reuben George, where is the real one? There is no trace of any other Reuben/George Walker/Brooke having obtained a discharge or pension from any other regiment. James's account gives a clue by suggesting strongly that Reuben was posted to Gibraltar. Only a dozen regiments were assigned to the Rock between 1854 and 1857; not surprisingly, none of them is fashionable cavalry, and the 1st Horse is not among them. The regiments from the Scottish Highlands may be safely discarded. The 55th Foot, the Westmorland Regiment, initially looks promising, since Reuben George ended up living there, but proves to be a red herring. But the colony swarms with other army Walkers. The East Yorkshire Regiment boasts three concurrently but none is Reuben George. The 96th Foot has six, the 92nd runs to seven. Walkers were to nineteenth-century army adjutants what Patels are to tax inspectors today, and often little personal notes are appended to their names as a guide to telling them apart. Yet another George Walker turns up as a good bet in the humble 54th, the West Norfolk Regiment also known as the Flamers. Tracking him back, he is registered as enlisting in Cork on 25 September 1845, standing four feet six inches high. He is fourteen years old, too old, then, to be Reuben George.

Reuben is mysteriously undocumented in an age that had already learned to worship pieces of paper. But the fanciful tale of loss, confused identities and restoration may well all be true. After all, James himself had been erroneously declared dead in India, and the false George Walker of the Horse Guards at least exists to set the whole melodrama rolling and strengthens the story that he really was searched for there. Perhaps Reuben George was not in Gibraltar at all. Perhaps it was Malta or Menorca or some other remote outcrop of empire. And what of the paternity of James? There is no reason to dismiss it out of hand. It may have been fruit of a brief phase of heterosexuality, rapidly grown out of, or of an attempt to impose on himself the conventional sexuality demanded of him by Bath society. It certainly explains the tremendous sense of shifty guilt behind the high prose in his letters about the young man. The horror of betrayal stalks his relations with the boy, and betrayal was the sin he hated and feared most in others.

The Reuben Walker affair, moreover, does not fit the usual pattern of James's homoerotic attachments. For one thing, Reuben is far too old to be of sexual interest to James and there are no signs of the usual itchy steaminess and plummy jocosity that mark such courtships, no poems, no lingering descriptions, no discoveries of unusual talents. Above all, he does not cling, as he clung desperately to Charley Grant and Badrudeen. All in all, it seems likely he really *was* Reuben's repentant and slightly disappointed father and perhaps it was the 'lost love', the clergyman's daughter, who was the mother.

In 1857 James Brooke met a new lady-friend, Angela Burdett-Coutts, coincidentally the richest woman in England. They *may* have met much earlier in Bath and she *may* have sighed at the sight of him from afar,[14] but this tradition is to be doubted as part of that fictitious romance grafted on to their relationship by later hands in order to reduce James's life to Victorian stereotypes. Stirred by the tale of his escape from the Chinese, she invited James to dinner; the Brooke charm did the rest.

James was always carefully solicitous of Angela. His letters are full of small signs of concern, plants, little riddles, etc. ('Why is a Horse at full speed like a young Lady dancing? – You will answer because she gallops – but it is not that way . . . – Because it is Gal(h)ops.'). He gave her a Sarawak parrot, Cocky, to replace the famous one she kept in the window of her house off Piccadilly, whose principal accomplishment had been to shout out, 'What a shocking bad hat!' at passers-by. (St John would go one better and send her llamas from Peru.)

Angela had come into her money unexpectedly. Her grandfather, the eccentric Thomas Coutts, had scandalously married first his niece's servant and then, yet more scandalously, the voluptuous and well-named actress Harriet Mellons. Harriet had inherited Thomas's entire fortune, used part of it to recast herself as the Duchess of St Albans and left the remainder to Angela on her own death, quite

ANGELA BURDETT-COUTTS BY WILLIAM ROSS, 1858:
NATIONAL PORTRAIT GALLERY

ignoring the rest of her family. Angela was a startlingly plain girl, thin and spotty, but whose fortune in 1837 had been assessed at £1,800,000, including half of Coutts' Bank, so that many eligible bachelors found her irresistibly beautiful. James's main virtue in her eyes was that he was one of the few men she ever met not moved to attempt to marry her and her fortune. An ongoing obsession of the newspapers was her imminent marriage to any man she was glimpsed with, or even any celebrity who happened to be passing through town, however fleetingly. Rumours of a passionate affair, even a secret marriage, with the ancient Duke of Wellington had marked the days of Angela's prime, and there is good reason to think that *she* indeed proposed marriage to *him*.

Throughout much of her life, Angela lived with a dowdy and hypochondriac companion, Hannah Brown, who finally fulfilled her dreams by marrying a medical man and thus spares biographers the need of suspecting a lesbian relationship between the ladies. Those who despaired of finding a romance between James and Angela have even suggested that it must be Hannah who was the *real* love of his life, so, one way or another, biographers have found Angela a useful explanation of James's anomalous unmarried state. Ironically, she perhaps came closest to him in spirit in the great scandal towards the end of her life when she finally married an American protégé half her age, Ashmead Bartlett, and was obliged to renounce her fortune through an obscure clause in her grand-mother's will that excluded foreign spouses.

Apart from her extreme wealth, Angela Burdett-Coutts had the distinction of being the first known victim of a stalker, in the form of a crazed Irish lawyer named Dunn. For years he pursued and per-secuted her, dogged her steps, showered her with love letters, broke into her house. He was imprisoned, released and reimprisoned, but she was horribly conscious that he might reappear at any moment and was forced to become a nervous recluse. Finally he sued her, claiming she had written him amorous verses in prison such as:

> *When to Harrogate sweet papa beats a retreat,*
> *To take spa waters supersulphurious,*

I could hear your heart thump as we stood near the pump,
While you bolted that stuff so injurious . . .

But at last I'm relenting, my jewel, repenting
Of all that you've suffered for me;
Why, I'm even grown tender, disposed to turn lender
Of cash, your sweet person to free.

Send to Coutts's your bill – there are lots in the till –
I'll give the clerk orders to do it;
Then get your discharge, your dear body enlarge,
And in Stratton-street do let me view it . . .[15]

Angela, a very serious girl, found the public hilarity at her situation, as she was dragged through the lawcourts, harder to bear than anything else. Humour was not her strong point – all her life she had suffered jokes about her name and the East End slang for fleas, 'coutties'. James, had he dared, could have pointed out to her that it came from the Malay *kuti*. Finally, Dunn switched his affections to a member of the royal house and was promptly declared insane.

Raised in a committedly Radical household, Angela took a strong interest in politics and intellectual pursuits. Regular visits were paid by Gladstone; by Dickens and Disraeli, who would put her in their novels; and by famous preachers, actors, explorers and scientists. Her bleak intelligence was much admired. She became a member of the Royal Institution, and Michael Faraday stood on her roof watching the fireworks that marked the end of the Crimean War, shouting in exultation, 'There goes magnesium, there potassium.'

Through her philanthropic activities she earned herself the title of 'Queen of the Poor', and orphanages, churches, schools, markets, colonial bishoprics and local industries all flourished under her generous support. She set up a home for fallen women with Charles Dickens. She wrote a book on practical education for the poor, full of the virtues of economy and self-discipline, but never stinted in putting her cash where her faith was. In a single act of generosity, she offered a quarter of a million pounds to buy seed potatoes for the poor in Ireland. Above all, Angela had a strong religious faith and favoured the Evangelists. Angela Burdett-Coutts was the very embodiment of a Victorian Good Woman. Given its perilous situation at that time, it is not overstating matters to call her the saviour of Sarawak.

She had much to offer James Brooke as a friend, and they are constantly meeting and corresponding at this time. Her wealth and intelligence assured excellent connections to the rich and powerful, and she was an experienced advocate of 'petticoat politicking' so that no door in the land was closed to her and her views. Indeed, her network extended all over Europe. When James despaired of ever interesting the British government in declaring a protectorate over his little country, she contacted her friend Louis Napoleon to arrange for the French to do so. However, since she was at least as opinionated as James was, they were incapable of discussion and whenever their ideas differed fundamentally it ended in a tremendous row where one of them flew off the handle. But she took on wholesale James's sense of outrage and persecution over his treatment at the hands of the British government; and his Sarawak project could be made to fit in nicely with her own ideas of practical self-help and evangelisation. Angela saw James as something of a hero – believing through him implicitly in both St George and the dragon. Following the example of her practical philanthropy in Ireland, she would be moved to set up a model farm near Kuching to teach the Dayaks the virtues of enlightened agriculture. It was described, unkindly but accurately, as five hundred acres of very bad soil seeded with crops that the soil would not grow, with machines that would not work and ploughs that would not plough. The Dayaks anyway were miles away and had no interest in what was being done. James further ensured its failure by putting one of his hopeless young men in charge of it. More importantly for the moment, at the time when he was most beset by debt and worry, when Sarawak was being ravaged by cholera, when he was desperate to provide for Reuben George and he saw no other way out, she lent James £5,000 with no strings attached so he could pay off the Borneo Company. Better yet, she bought him the steamer of his dreams, an armed vessel that he named the *Rainbow*. It made him very happy.

Chapter 14

The Malay Plot

In October 1858, James made a short speech at the Free Trade Hall in Manchester. It was the sort of thing he had often done before, a mere preaching to the converted, and – of course – all about Sarawak. As he spoke, he felt 'a creeping movement' come over him, and walked straight to a doctor's. He had suffered a stroke, from which he would never fully recover, but was still luckier than his old enemy Makota, who at much the same moment was drowning in the Bisayun country after being attacked by the relatives of some local girls whom he had abducted by force for a night of pleasure.

James was now fifty-five. The rakish swagger had long disappeared. Photographs of him at this time show him as shrunken, gnome-like and dandified, with a permanently puzzled expression which may simply be short-sightedness. Whereas he had previously been obsessed by his steamer, he must now have, at any cost, the expat dream of a small country cottage with woodbine round the door. In 1859 he finally found one, in Burrator, Devonshire, and wrote to Angela.

My little 'Box' – that is to be – is snugly situated under
Dartmoor – a stream babbles close at hand – wood in plenty

and it boasts 72 acres of land. I might have searched for ten
years without meeting a place within my limits so retired, so
near the world and so suited in all respects to my tastes. I
have in a week's stay derived great benefit from the bracing
and elastic air and I take my daily ride and walk, to distances
I little thought ever to have accomplished again. Yesterday I
was five hours on pony-back on the Moor.[1]

Visitors were appalled by its total desolation. He could not, of
course, pay for it.

Moreover, his peace was disturbed. Brooke Brooke's wife had
died horribly in childbirth. In England there was talk of Reuben
George, and of the Rajah seeking to make Sarawak over to Great
Britain, or even to foreigners. Brooke Brooke clearly suffered some
kind of mental and emotional breakdown and fled back to England,
leaving brother Charles in charge of the country. James would
always regard that as a breach of trust and an act of desertion. Worse
still, Miss Burdett-Coutts took an instant dislike to him. When he
called on her uninvited, he was shown the door. There was talk of
a public testimonial to raise money for James, and Brooke Brooke
took it into his head that James would then finally retire and hand
over the kingdom to him. The testimonial finally fell far short of the
£20,000 hoped for, totalling only £8,800. Unsurprisingly, James
immediately ascribed its failure to a conspiracy from the Borneo
Company to keep him in dependence. Angela disapproved of the
testimonial, just as she saw no reason for the Rajah to step down,
and perhaps this explains James's constant vacillation. Brooke
Brooke was sent back to Sarawak on a tight rein and it was made
quite clear he was undergoing continuous assessment. 'You must
trust to my love and judgement, and in due time, I propose formally
to transfer the government, but not to confer upon you any power
to act independently of me.' What was he supposed to make of
that?

Things were not well in Sarawak. There had been another failed
attempt to oust Rentap from his mountain fort. Kuching was again
prey to wild rumours that swept over it in waves of terror: the

Chinese were coming; James was dead and it had been hushed up; the British were to be massacred and the Bruneians restored; the pirates were back on the coast.

Real trouble, when it came, was from much closer to home – the Kuching Malays. There had long been a feud between two of the noble houses of Mukah, just up the coast. Mukah was the home of the Melanau people, and the source of sago, the rotted pith of the sago palm, and the delicious, large, edible worms that bred in it as it lay in the water. Both were important for the nutrition of Sarawak, and the rough sago was a valuable export for the Singapore refineries. The trade was crucial to Kuching. Brooke Brooke would tolerate no disruption of commerce and had imposed fines on disturbers of the peace in Mukah – even though they were subjects of the Sultan of Brunei. Charles, in his absence, went one better and even fined the Sultan's own envoy. Unlike James, who always maintained a studied façade of politeness, neither of them bothered to hide the total contempt in which they held the Brunei aristocracy.

Meanwhile a widespread conspiracy was hatched by the pardoned Datuk Patinggi and Sherip Masahor, co-ordinating this and other Malay resentments which may or may not have involved Brunei, to drive the British from Sarawak. For once no one revealed the plot. Brooke Brooke, absent in England, prided himself on his contacts with the Malays but Charles had spent time amongst the Dayaks, wore Dayak costume and found Malays uncongenial. There had been a fatal breakdown in the Brooke intelligence machine, which many attributed to the disappearance of James's traditional open-house policy. But from the first the conspiracy went awry. A precipitate rising in Kanowit and the slaying of two Brooke administrators, Fox and Steel, revealed their hand too soon. Our information is principally derived from Charles Johnson (later Brooke), and it is striking how his melodramatic vocabulary and descriptions of politics and battle differ from those of James. 'This was the first step of a foul conspiracy, which had been hatching for some time past in the minds of a few discontented, intriguing rascals, deep and subtle as men or devils could be.'[2]

According to Charles, Kanowit was inhabited by a mix of Chinese – 'rapscallions' – Malays – 'as unprincipled a set of cutthroats as could be found anywhere' – and Dayaks – 'troublesome and dangerous'. The Malay fortmen were unreliable – 'slave-born followers'. Henry Steel had lived here in total isolation from other Europeans for some eight years. Charles Johnson brought in Charles Fox to help, the former missionary allegedly introduced to the delights of native female flesh by Spenser St John and now wedded to the more secular vocation of the administration.

The sad event happened early in the afternoon. Mr. Fox had been superintending the digging of a ditch, and Mr. Steel was lounging about in the fort, both unarmed. The latter was in conversation with Abi and Talip, whom he had known and trusted for years, but their previous characters had been extremely bad. There was in a moment a simultaneous onslaught both by Steel's companions and a party of Kanowit people; the latter rushed from a Chinaman's house and struck Mr. Fox in the back with a spear; he fell into the fort moat and was killed. Talip drew his parang and struck at Steel, but the latter, being an active man, seized the weapon, when the handle became entangled in Talip's clothing. Talip was overpowered but Abi, standing by, cut Steel over the head, killing him immediately. After this the watchman fired and killed one of the murderers; a Chinaman was also cut down; and then, instead of the fortmen guarding the premises, they gave it up into the hands of the assassins, who forthwith proceeded to rifle it of all its contents and burn it down. The guns were distributed to different parties. The heads of Messrs. Fox and Steel were taken by some of the Dayak enemies, and their bodies were left half buried in the ground.[3]

In Kuching, with a sword before him, Charles swore to avenge the deaths. The Datuk Patinggi Abdul Gaffur feigned horror and surprise, and Masahor swiftly had the 'culprits' put to death before they could talk. The fortmen were executed for leaving their post and a bloody but inconclusive battle occurred between Charles's Dayaks and the Kanowits in which their fortification was fired.

> Now came the horrors of war indeed. Some were burnt, some killed, some taken prisoner, and some few escaped. So ended that fortification. Its roof fell with a crash, leaving only its smoking embers to tell where it had stood. Our Dayaks were mad with excitement, flying about with heads; many with fearful wounds, some even mortal. One lad came rushing and yelling past the stockade, with a head in one hand, and holding one side of his own face with the other. He had it cut clean open, and laid bare to the cheek-bone, yet he was insensible to pain for the time; but before five minutes elapsed, he reeled and fell exhausted. We then doctored him the best way we could, by tying his cheek on as firmly as possible, in the hope that it would unite and heal. This it eventually did, leaving a fearful disfigurement.[4]

Later, Masahor's guilt was revealed and he fled. In his boat, honest Dayaks found a kris of gold that they brought to their rajah. James sent it to the Great Exhibition in London, where it was stolen. Then the Datuk Patinggi's involvement was made known and he was exiled – yet again. This time, the Brookes had been warned by the Malays. A much-eroded stone still stands down the hill from the old mission in Kuching, marking the death of Fox and Steel and the relentless punishment of those implicated in it. 'Justice', it reads, 'was done.'

Frank and Harriette McDougall did not like the look of things and departed on hasty home leave. It was all very well for the Brookes, Frank noted; they after all lived in well-guarded forts – which would later give James a chance to crow over Frank's lack of courage and take his revenge for Frank's witnessing his own terror during the Chinese insurrection. Harriette could scarce believe all this talk of plots. After all, the Datuk Patinggi was a dear old man who had been in the habit of dropping round to the mission so little Mab could read him fairy stories. The whole affair, involving as it did the Malays, gave the British community a considerable scare and further shook the confidence of the Brooke raj. The Governor of the Straits Settlements sent over a gunboat and a contingent of marines, but presumably they were merely to protect British interests; James, in a mixture of policy and spite, continued to negotiate with the Dutch for protection.

In 1859, circumstances in Mukah deteriorated further. The British insisted on seeing this too as part of the machinations of Masahor, though one suspects that if Makota had been still alive he, instead, would have been discovered to lie behind it. James had left a permanently paranoid stamp on Sarawak politics. Trade was disrupted, the Sarawak flag fired upon. Brooke Brooke's version of events was that he went with a small force to discuss conciliation and was attacked. In accordance with local ideas of warfare, he erected a stockade and waited for brother Charles and reinforcements. They were about to take the enemy fort when, to their astonishment, a British steamer under Governor Edwardes of Labuan, long hostile to the Brooke administration, appeared and announced that it would open fire on them unless they withdrew. Spenser St John, Edwardes's superior, was in England and therefore unable to overrule him. There was nothing to be done. Adding insult to injury, Edwardes brought back Masahor. Brooke Brooke hesitated . . . and retreated. Sarawak could not afford to go to war with Britain. The boys had not done well. No wonder James, looking back on his life, groaned, 'Not a single rising man in the service – not a man fitted to rule.'

The prestige on which the whole bluff of Brooke domination rested had been fatally impugned, but St John, in London, did his loyal best to retrieve the situation. He quickly obtained an apology from the Foreign Secretary, Lord Russell. 'Edwardes disapproved,' he telegraphed James. 'Return to Borneo November mail. Will you come?' James roused himself from convalescence and sailed with him, though he had not the fare and had to borrow it from Angela

Burdett-Coutts. Ever solicitous, she also bought him some second-hand guns, shells, rockets and powder.

James might have made a new friend in Angela, but he was losing old ones fast. Those who had been loyal to him over the years noticed a further decline in his mental state, a growing unpredictability and sensitivity to opposition. St John was defensive:

> Hasty judgement sometimes, and often hasty speech, are two faults which perhaps produced his third – that is, great impatience. In manner he is often absent and careless, which, not being understood by strangers offends them; but I will add what he is – he is a man of noble thoughts and noble actions, generous, generally most considerate; affectionate, and therefore beloved by all who are intimately acquainted with him. In conversation and argument brilliant when in happy spirits, playful when playfulness is required, earnest and sincere on all great subjects.[5]

His recent correspondence with British officials had been 'not pleasant and ended in complete estrangement. Fortunately, public officials are not over-sensitive.'

The real evidence of mental unbalance comes from James himself, in his extraordinarily vindictive reaction to comments made by John Templer and Frank McDougall about him. When their concern about his *compos mentis* came to his ears his first thought was to take legal action, and then to force the bishop to write a letter declaring that 'It is with sincere pleasure that I now find him so well in mind and body, and I am most glad to be able to correct the impression I entertained and the fears I expressed concerning his mental condition . . .' In fact, the only convincing argument against James's growing senility was the suggestion that since the Singapore inquiry he had *always* suffered a sort of emotional lability. Henceforth, the intuitive alliance between Church and State was at an end, the shared experiences and struggles that held them together set at nought, and no issue was too petty for James to take advantage of in order to afflict poor Harriette and Frank.

Templer fared even worse. James bombarded him with letters of outrage, shrugged off all attempts at reconciliation, sent affidavits from five doctors about his mental condition. Templer was unwise enough to be totally frank in explaining his view that

> the noble quality of sound judgement for which you were so remarkable had become impaired, and that I attributed it to the disease with which you had been stricken – that *it* had explained to me much that I found difficult to reconcile before with your former self, and I instanced the course you had taken with regard to [Reuben] George, by which you placed your friends and relatives in a false position. Then the Testimonial – the French question – the refusal to relinquish the Raj in Brooke's favour – and still more lately, your line with McDougall and myself in this very case, strengthened the impression . . .[6]

This was too much for James. After a little more snarling and posturing, their twenty years of loving friendship was brought to an abrupt end.

James was received in Sarawak 'as one risen from the dead'. The Sultan of Brunei, also alleged to be mad – though more widely and convincingly so than James – dropped the confrontational stance into which James's nephews had driven him and was all sweetness and smiles. St John pumped up James's flagging prestige by sailing to Mukah with him in a spanking new British corvette decked out with two hundred smart marines. Using the authority of the Sultan's letters, he imposed peace, exiled Masahor – who eloquently protested his innocence – and arranged for James to purchase rights to the whole place. St John felt sorry for Masahor, an old chess opponent. Steel, he notes, had been 'an ignorant and hard man', while Fox was 'brusque in manner' from having had too much to do with the Chinese. His tone almost suggests that even if he did not doubt the reality of the Malay conspiracy, he was unconvinced about its extent. James moved in at Mukah and reorganised everything. It was a triumph of chequebook diplomacy.

In Kuching, Brooke Brooke had remarried and was a little less hard to live with. His bride had had to travel out to him, as he dared not turn his back on Sarawak and James again. Moreover, he now asked James to install him formally as Rajah Muda, heir to the throne, since 'it will not only be a pleasing sign of your confidence in me, but will strengthen my hands in carrying on the government'. There is no doubt that he had been badly shaken by James's many conflicting signals about his intentions, and compared his own situation to a 'wretched Dwarf in the hands of some giant Fate who with one hand one day puts me on my legs, the next knocks me down again with the other'. The ceremony was carried out to everyone's satisfaction and with a sufficiency of ritual and flowery language. It was allegedly Brooke Brooke – not James – who at the last received the salute of guns accorded a rajah. Only later would arguments develop about what it had all actually meant.

James resolved to leave again for England, accompanied by St John, who had received promotion to Chargé d'Affaires in Haiti. He had, after all, rescued HM Government from a peculiarly embarrassing situation and this was his reward. James's arrival was cheered by the news that Charles Johnson had finally put paid to 'the rebel' Rentap, leaving his hilltop fort ablaze like a volcano. Angela's munitions, not needed at Mukah, had come in handy after all.

James became briefly a tourist in Paris, but soon retreated from society back to the moors. As he memorably phrased it elsewhere, 'I care nothing for penny trumpets and turtle soup.' There he threw himself into farming, raised ponies, chickens, ducks and geese and made butter, but Burrator was also a place 'where he was endeavouring to bring up two young cubs for the Sarawak service. But, as usual, these cubs remained cubs to the end, and were a source of trouble and mortification until they disappeared from the scene. Strange infatuation to believe that he could do anything with such materials when gentlemen cadets were to be had by the score.'[7]

What upset St John was not the presence of boys as such, but lower-class boys who did not know how to behave.

One of the lads was William Blackler, thirteen years old when James made his acquaintance in rather odd circumstances in Totnes.[8] James explains to Angela's companion, Hannah Brown, how

> I used to take my invalid saunter in the meadows skirting the 'Dart'. A party of boys were bathing afar off, as it appeared in forbidden water, when three fishermen in their seven-league boots, rushed upon them. They fled (very scantily clothed) excepting one, who having swum further than the others lost his clothes and was himself taken prisoner and led off to the fishing house. It was not in my nature to see this, so I went to the rescue and got the poor boy off. Thus was our acquaintance commenced. Afterwards, he was always pleased to see me and I was pleased with the attention, so we gradually became friends.[9]

Another version describes poor William as shivering in soaked nakedness with the Rajah, naturally unfazed by his total nudity, detaining him in endless comradely chit-chat.

But there is more to William.

> His father is a stone mason in the town, his grandfather, with whom he lived, and four uncles, shipwrights, well to do in the government dockyards. *He* was to be a shipwright too and spoke with pride of his lot. I saw the father who was a really respectable man of the lower order – manly, intelligent, upright, struggling cheerfully to bring up a young family. So it ended. I gave the boy *a tip* and not till the other day did I think of inquiring about my young acquaintance. He had not been on the sunny wall of fortune – children had increased and wages were low. His grandfather was out of work and so the lad had returned to his father. His uncles had families and could not get him into the dockyards as

apprentice . . . so I thought I could be in the way of helping him and have determined to send him to school for a year or two and, when he has thoroughly mastered book keeping, to send him to Sarawak as a clerk in the revenue department. I am now inquiring for a fitting school. I hope even to do something for the father who is a man one likes to meet – independent but respectful – knowing his place and acknowledging the pains and privations [?] of a life of labour without shrinking or discontent.[10]

He returns to the subject with characteristic rapidity: 'The father of the lad is a mason by trade and I should like to give him aid (not charity) to become a Master. Do you know any schools where I could put William Blackler – the son? To give him a substantial education and thorough knowledge of accounts and book keeping is my object.'[11] But he is anxious that he 'not remove him from his proper sphere, excepting in a proper degree'.

Soon, James is seeking more concrete forms of assistance from Hannah Brown: 'If you would *lend* Richard Blackler [William's father] £25 – without interest – it would be a great kindness to a good man and if the Missus [Angela Burdett-Coutts] is rich i.e. has more money than her other good works demand – she will perhaps make the sum up to £50 – a handsome capital to start with and which I think would be repaid in a few years.'[12]

How this extraordinary request went down with Angela is not recorded, but we can be sure how it was received in Sarawak. Brooke Brooke had suffered greatly from the stream of useless, wayward boys sent his way by his uncle over the years. In 1861 he wrote to him in some irritation, 'If you send out new hands let them *not* be boys but men.'[13] Nevertheless, Blackler did end up in Sarawak until dismissed from the service by Charles in 1867.

It is interesting that we are finally able to compare James's own characterisation of the Blackler family, as the deserving poor, with the assessment of his own administrative officers. For James's relationship with this boy seems to go far beyond anything consistent with previous biographers' claims that his sexual interest remained merely latent, and there is little doubt that at this period of his life he was carnally involved with the rough trade of Totnes. He not only accepted physical manhandling, he invited it. St John summed up the whole business with a sad shake of the head:

> The Rajah all his life was on the lookout for an ideal which he never found either in man or woman and his singular infatuation that virtue and honesty and simplemindedness were more the attributes of the lowborn than of others receives many singular illustrations in the relations he held with such ruffians as Prout, Blackler and May or such incapables as Penty [his steward], Read [his Singapore solicitor] etc., etc. I shall not easily forget the visit Miss Coutts and Mrs. Brown paid us at Burrator, when Blackler pushed the Rajah off the sofa on which he was reclining, in order to have the couch himself. I often expressed my surprise at his permitting such conduct towards himself but he thought it proved great independence of spirit. These were however, but spots on the sun. Still they were curious in a man of as great a refinement of mind.[14]

There were even crude blackmail attempts. Arthur Crookshank, James's deputy, was at Burrator when Blackler arrived demanding entry. When refused, he wrote 'the most impudent and threatening note to the Rajah saying he was bound to provide for him and must do so or if it came to the worst he (Blackler) had letters which were sufficient to make him do so when necessity required him to shew them. We have advised the Rajah not to take any notice of him, but if he writes again to answer him through a lawyer. He's a bad lot!!'[15]

Another lad, May, seems to have been a sailor friend. After James's death a letter was found among his papers demanding £100 'as he was on shore instead of at sea, which did not agree with his health or pocket'. May ('that wretched boy') ended up, perhaps appropriately, as an inspector of police in Sarawak.[16] In his will James left him £52 per annum, as well as to William Reed (in

Crookshank's words, 'an encumbrance which should never have existed'), who is regarded as living at Burrator.

And yet, either through sheer innocence or driven by his demons, James remained throughout his life resolutely 'on the look-out'. There was an earlier protégé, Richard Lawford, shipped out to Sarawak in 1858. He is a foundling, 'intelligent, fairly educated, a good musician', awarded two medals in the army by the age of eighteen but discharged suffering from consumption. Perhaps this was a simple humanitarian act, for James was frequently genuinely moved by the troubles of boys and young men; but it is often the case that his compassion trembled on the brink of lust, and the two might compound powerfully together into something even fiercer and more corrosive that clouded his vision and exposed him to ridicule and terrible risk.

Chapter 15

The Crusading
Bishop

Like many small places, Sarawak assumed many of the characteristics of a soap opera. The same few characters reappeared in all possible combinations of relationships, became cardboard cutouts, abruptly disappeared or returned implausibly from near death. There were petty jealousies inflamed by climate and proximity, feuds, treacheries. There was a need for black-hearted villains to account for all the misfortunes that bred with tropical exuberance. After the departure of Makota and Sherip Masahor, the Brookes had only the British government to hiss at, but bitterness had so seeped into James's heart that, over the next few years, he began to turn ever more on those about him.

At the mission, they made their own villains. It was decided that the worst was Spenser St John, with Angela Burdett-Coutts in the second row, both whispering poison in James's ear. This would be confirmed by St John's publication in 1862 of his book *Life in the Forests of the Far East*. It contained a chapter that was a concentrated vitriolic attack on the mission, its works, and the character of Bishop Frank McDougall. Financial incompetence and neglect of the outlying Dayaks in favour of the slothful ease of Chinese evangelisation in Kuching were but two of the lavishly documented charges – but it is

SPENSER ST JOHN IN RETIREMENT IN ENGLAND C.1900:
ROYAL GEOGRAPHICAL SOCIETY

much more likely that it was James who had been poisoning St John's mind than the other way around. Frank and Harriette were stunned, then outraged. A rebuttal was published by the bishop. A lively controversy developed in the British press that helped neither side. James could not resist such an opportunity to torment Frank and Harriette, and he sank to the occasion. St John followed up his book with a pamphlet, *The Bishop of Labuan, a Vindication*, but it had secretly been written by James himself, sitting stewing in peaceful bile in Burrator. It is a terrible document, the picture of a formidable but morally diseased intelligence – petty, sneering and crowing by turn, endlessly spiteful and childish, scattered with pedantic footnotes, an intensified, ingrown caricature of the James Brooke that first emerged at the Singapore inquiry. 'Upon the occasion of the late disturbances in 1859,' James wrote of the Malay conspiracy, 'the Government protected *every person* who remained at his post at Sarawak. The Bishop was not one of these! . . . The well-wishers of the Mission must have observed with sorrow, mingled with contempt, the timely precautions taken by the Bishop to escape from the sphere of his duties on the approach of danger.' He quoted in the attached footnote from Frank's report of that year and remarked, 'Timidity breathes in every line; the women showed a better and more manly example!!!'[1]

James stirred up dissident members of their mission against them, accusing them of racism in the treatment of a Singhalese pastor. His pettiness extended to arranging for blacksmiths to be installed right next to the church compound to destroy the peace of their house and foul the schoolboys' bathwater. Angela wanted to turn the knife still further by installing a rival Anglican mission on her experimental farm.

At the mission, James soon became 'that crazy old man' (Harriette) and 'that hypocritical, lying old Rajah' (Frank), but, ironically, this rift occurred at the very moment when Frank was articulating his most passionate public defence of James and everything he had done for Sarawak.

In May 1862, Brooke Brooke's second wife died – like the first in childbirth – leaving him a daughter, Agnes, whom Harriette, as always, took uncomplainingly in charge. The dwarf, Brooke Brooke, had been slapped down by the giant, fate, yet again. Brooke Brooke was persuaded to get away from the scene of his sadness by embarking on the *Rainbow* for a trip to Bintulu, accompanied by Frank and a few others, including Helms, his rival in bravery during the Chinese insurrection. The *Jolly Bachelor* followed in tow. What was supposed to be a restful voyage turned into an eventful trip. Brooke Brooke sent an account of it to James,[2] and asked Frank to work up a longer public account for *The Times*, where it was published on 27 May 1862, but both he and Brooke Brooke are more frank in their letters.

Scarcely had Helms been dropped at Mukah for a little sago business than he heard that a fleet of Illanun pirates was blockading the mouth of the river. He sent a swift boat after the *Rainbow* with the intelligence, and the little vessel bravely put out to intercept them. Brooke Brooke takes up the story:

Just at daybreak on 23rd [May 1862] to our great joy, the man at the mast reported three large boats and sampans to seaward of us. Steam was immediately got up, the *Jolly* taken in tow and off we went after them. As the light increased and the distance lessened we could distinctly see that they were crowded with men and pulling with all their might for Kadumong. The first boat, a very large and fast one, took the lead and it soon became evident that she would cross our course and get ashore before we could be up to her. This she effected and grounded just as we got abreast of her at about 250 yards distance. I stopped the steamer, and as there was not a shadow of doubt of her character, opened on her with grape and musketry which she returned feebly. We kept her under a hail of shot for about 10 minutes when the crew ran into the jungle. Leaving the *Jolly* to look after the deserted boat we pressed on, turned and went at them stern on. The Lanuns jumped overboard as we approached and swam for the shore. The captives only remained. Luckily the steamer struck the boat so that she canted alongside and we took the unfortunates aboard. Nothing could have been more touching than to see the poor emaciated wretches holding

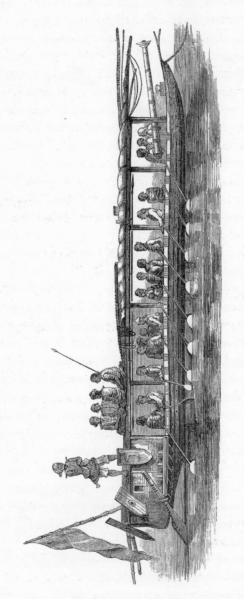

ILLANUN PIRATES: BRITISH MUSEUM

up the ropes with which they had been lashed, and entreating our compassion. In this last we found no less than five Dutch ensigns, some evidently belonging to large vessels, and one Spanish flag. Our boats were lowered and but few of the pirates escaped to the shore, but a crisp fire of grape from the *Jolly* and steamer told frightfully, and when within a few hundred yards way was got on the steamer and she went clean over her. In a moment, the steamer was surrounded by the unhappy captives floating on pillows built of planks and every thing that came to hand. Those that were Chinese holding up their tails to show their nationality, women with children clinging to them. It was not difficult to distinguish the captives for each had round his neck a rope with which they had been lashed and entreating our compassion [*sic*]. Our ladder was lowered, and beginning with the women and children all were got aboard. Our decks were now pretty well crowded, and the Bishop (who by the way had been most industrious with his new Terry rifle) took the wounded in hand – and ghastly wounds many of them were. The swimming Lanuns were intercepted by the boats and few got to shore. The Destruction of the first division of the Lanuns being as complete as possible the question was what had become of the rest. We had destroyed three, Haji Matima had reported six. The captives were consulted and reported that they had pulled straight out to sea on the previous evening as they heard of the steamer being at Bintulu . . . *Rainbow* steamed to eastward in search of the missing three. By the most wonderful luck after running 20 miles we came straight upon them – three large boats full of men, with sampans towing astern. No one had any doubt what they were. The sea was smooth, the wind had died away, and as we approached the enemy closed on each other and evidently had a conference. They formed only so that their guns might all bear, and awaited us. We knew that this betokened a determined resistance. I ordered Hewat to put the steamer abreast of them at about 200 yards distance and stop her. They opened the battle by a general discharge of *lelahs* [swivel guns] and musketry. The balls flew by us – then came our turn. The Mate commanded the forecastle gun and I turned the 12-pounder midship and I took the poop gun myself. Scarce a shot misfired. As each gun was fired you heard the grape crash into them tearing everything to pieces. Still the rascals fired away and some of us on the poop would have fared hardly, but I had luckily made a breastwork of planks and mattresses.[3]

Frank's version stressed the centrality of his own role: 'My dress attracted the particular attention of the enemy and the balls fell smartly about my station on the poop. Once I was returning to my post after helping a wounded man on the quarter-deck, and as I was near the top of the ladder, I saw a fellow in the prahu nearest to us take a deliberate aim at me with his rifle; the ball whizzed by my ear and went into poor Hassein's heart, who was standing behind and above me.'[4] Frank fought on, half medic, half warrior and – it seemed – only a little bit missionary. Brooke Brooke continues:

As the *Rainbow* got away, the rascals thinking we were going to bolt, reloaded and opened upon us again. Terrible must have been their feelings when they saw her come leisurely around, single out the first and largest boat and charged clean at her, back out of the wreck, charged the second and cut her in two, then at the third. The third boat disappeared under the steamer. Then we set to work to pick up the captives, some of them frightfully wounded. Besides the captives, we picked up about thirty Lanuns who were carefully pinioned and put down in the hold. We then went after the flying sampan and in a trice she was bottom uppermost. The Lanuns in her we left to their death, I did not dare take more on board for we had already thirty desperadoes and about 40 captives besides between 20 or 30 wounded in the *Rainbow*. Then we steamed back to Kadumong, picked up the *Jolly Bachelor* and towed her to

ILLANUN PIRATE: BRITISH MUSEUM

Bintulu. Then on to Mukah, which we reached at daylight, and landed the Mukah captives to the number of 15 out of upwards of thirty carried off a few days before. This has been the severest defeat these devils have received for many a day. According to the account of the captives each boat had from 30 to 40 Lanuns and from 60 to 70 captives on board. – in all say 200 Lanuns and 360 captives. Of this number we have thirty Lanuns in irons and probably 30 or 40 made their escape to Kadumong where the Bintulu people will hunt them up; the rest are drowned or shot.[5]

Most of the Illanuns were later executed. In his *Times* article, Frank was careful to tone down the massacre and note that the captives told terrible tales of suffering, rape and torture and that many of their injuries were from the pirates. He then commented:

Not a man flinched from his work, and, although never in action before, they showed the coolness and steadiness of veterans. We could not have had more than thirty-five rifles and muskets and smooth-bore guns between us – less, perhaps than each of the pirate boats carried; notwithstanding which, our fire was so steady and galling that we very much kept down the fire of their lelahs, and so thinned their men as to put the idea of boarding us out of their heads. In short, our weapons, though few, were good and well-served, and, in justice I must mention that my double-barrelled breech-loader, made by Terry, proved itself a most deadly weapon from its true shooting and certainty and rapidity of fire. It never missed fire once in eighty rounds, and was then so little fouled that I believe it would have fired eighty more rounds with like effect without wanting to be cleaned. When we ran down the last pirate all our ammunition for the 9-pounders was expended, and our own caps and cartridges for the small arms had nearly come to an end, so that if we had had more prahus to deal with we should have been in a sorry plight, and had to trust to our steam and hot-water hose to do the work. But the whole affair was most providentially ordered in our not meeting the six boats together, when their fire might have been too much for us; and then in their departing from their usual plan of rushing us *en masse* to board, and by their separating and giving us the opportunity of running them down one after the other. We are, indeed, all most thankful to our Heavenly Father who thus ordered things for us, and made us His instruments to punish these bloodthirsty foes of the human race.[6]

He followed it up with some standard Brooke material – about the neglect by public opinion of slavery in Asia as opposed to Africa, and the immoral and un-Christian pusillanimity of the British government in their refusal to aid the anti-piracy policy of gallant little Sarawak. Much of this had been borrowed directly from James. He even finished with a hearty endorsement of the Rajah, but was careful to leaven it with praise for Brooke Brooke.

But it seemed that Brooke Brooke had learned nothing from the storm caused by James's accounts of pirate-killing. All the passages of mitigation were ignored in the furore raised by the idea of a Christian bishop slapping his gun and praising it as the instrument of God. Frank's principal enemy in this was the Bishop of Durham, though Angela is supposed to have meddled too. Finally the Archbishop of Canterbury was forced to intervene in the debate and pronounced Frank guiltless, but 'At the same time, I regret that the Bishop should have felt himself called upon to become the historian of a conflict in which he feels grieved to have been compelled to engage, and still more that the tenor and tone of his narrative should have been such as to give just offence to Christian minds.'[7] His readiness with a rifle remained 'unepiscopal' and it was suggested that Harriette's gentler pen should write any further accounts. Spenser St John termed Frank's letter 'silly, prosey, bragging, in bad taste, exaggerated and distorted', whilst James had been toying with the idea of prosecuting the bishop for treason for alleged remarks made about the Brookes' wars encouraging Dayak headtaking.

Frank himself sighed, 'I hope that I shall never have so unpleasant a duty again, for it is a strangely distracting thing to be fighting pirates one week, and confirming and ordaining the next.' Yet it had brought the faiths closer together:

> When the affair was over and I was dressing the wounded, a Malay friend of mine, Haji Mataim, came to me and said: 'Tuan, this is terrible work for you and me, men of prayer; you are all over blood,' and so I was; the decks were slippery with it, so many bleeding men were lying about on all sides. 'You can't say your prayers, there is not a pure place in the ship where one can stand or kneel; do give me a pair of your shoes, and then I can say my prayers and thank God for this great victory.' I told him that I had none to give, mine were all bloody, but that he had better say his prayers and thank God at once, as I was doing, in spite of the blood; as God looked at our hearts and not at our feet.[8]

The McDougalls were firm allies of Brooke Brooke in his war of succession but he, fearing to further inflame James's waxing paranoia, dared be only the most lukewarm supporter of theirs. He hoped to simply keep his head down and wait for time and James's ill-health to take their course and deliver his inheritance intact. As usual it was Spenser St John who put the cat among the pigeons – though this time unwittingly.

The British government had continued to blow hot and cold on the Sarawak issue but was itself by now thoroughly confused about what it was that James actually wanted. The flirtation with foreign powers had borne no fruit. The Colonial Office remarked, 'It is just the old story. We are called upon to do an inconvenient and probably expensive thing, because if we do not, the French will.'[9] If the declaration of an official protectorate was on the back burner, this was perhaps – it was hinted – not an impediment to proclaiming some form of protection for British residents, along with recognition of the independence of the little state. Via an infinity of memos and slow submissions, the Foreign Office painfully worked its way round to suggesting the feasibility of a new commission being sent from India to enquire into the theoretical possibility of perhaps recognising Sarawak. After due process this materialised in the person of Colonel Cavenagh, Governor of the Straits Settlements.

The only initial concern for Brooke Brooke was that he might fall so hopelessly in love with Sarawak as to want it entirely for himself, but his visit, in late 1862, did not come at the best of times. The recent loss of Brooke Brooke's wife had been followed by that of his eldest son and he was in a thoroughly distraught condition. Cavenagh foolishly showed him a secret report from St John, discussing James's attempts to interest foreign countries in assuming responsibility for Sarawak. It was mentioned here that, should this happen, Brooke Brooke would need to be compensated for his loss of rights and expectations. Smelling a plot between St John, James and the British government to sell Sarawak from under him and betray the natives who had placed their trust in him, he exploded in outrage. In the white heat of indignation he wrote to James:

> When St John's secret memo was shown to me in which my rights were utterly suppressed, I hesitated not one moment but resolved to take my own course, and assert my rights and those of the people of Sarawak . . . Rajah, you must blame yourself. You have overstrained the bow of my patience, and it has broken at last; we must try our relative strength, and all I can say is, that if I prove the stronger I shall always bear in mind that you were the founder of Sarawak, that you *are* my relative, and that you *were* my Friend.[10]

He also wrote to the British government, declaring the illegality of any constitutional change. In his view James had already abdicated when he was installed as Rajah Muda.

James, too, hesitated not one moment. He was always obsessive on the matter of loyalty. Raising another loan from Angela, he stormed off to Singapore, accompanied by Charles Johnson and a mysterious Mr La Touche, an envoy of Miss Burdett-Coutts. Before he left, he briefly named Angela to inherit Sarawak in the event of his death, a move which would surely have tied up constitutional lawyers for another twenty years had it come to pass. But other writing was already on the wall. Before they sailed, Charles changed his family name from Johnson to Brooke.

James was full of self-righteous bitterness, insisting on misinter-preting Brooke Brooke's words as a direct threat against his own life. 'That you would shed your own uncle's blood, and excuse civil war upon a question of your pecuniary rights, is so horrible that I dismiss it at once from my mind . . .'[11]

In February 1863 Brooke Brooke crossed to Singapore in the *Rainbow*, to avoid a confrontation with James in Kuching. James transferred all the cash in the bank to his own account and took the precaution of boarding the vessel in Brooke Brooke's absence and making the crew swear loyalty to him alone. Mr La Touche was probably there to arrange the seizure of the vessel on behalf of Angela, the legal owner, should this fail. James then issued an ulti-matum. If Brooke Brooke would submit to him, they would meet at twelve o'clock. If not, they would never speak again on earth. A melodramatic sealed letter was prepared in advance, announcing his banishment. They met in what seems to have been a stormy encounter in the presence of Mr La Touche. It ended in Brooke Brooke's total defeat. He was relieved of all authority and ordered to return to England immediately. He would receive £500 a year on condition of good behaviour. James, triumphant, returned to Kuching with seven British vessels, allegedly there to chase pirates. But again, to knowing Sarawak citizens, they must have carried a very different message, one of British support.

Brooke Brooke showed signs of fighting on from England, even threatening legal action. James pointed out logically and coldly that he could bring no action in Sarawak because, as a traitor, he was denied access to the court. Men were set to watch for him. Should he return, he was to be cut down. All his property was confiscated, his pension was stopped and James refused to take any responsibility for his surviving child, so that the overstretched McDougalls had to pay her passage home. (James spitefully insisted she must travel first-class.) Charles Brooke meanwhile 'stepped into his shoes, the measure of which he had long before taken', according to Charley Grant.

The moves were pushed through the Native Council by James, who boasted of the personal loyalty of all to himself. The locals seem not to have been greatly disturbed either way. After all, mad rajahs, children disinherited, banished and declared traitors – all this was the familiar stuff of a transfer of power and simple proof that the Brookes had turned into a normal Malay royal house. All that was needed was some strategic krissing to complete the scene. Only a couple of Sarawak administrators resigned out of loyalty to Brooke Brooke. Frank and Harriette McDougall found themselves in a very difficult position, having committed their support to him but having to accept the *fait accompli* in the interests of the infant Church. They were astonished at the intensity of James's hatred for his opponents. Harriette wrote in awe to his former heir, 'He speaks calmly of your death.'[12]

James left Sarawak for the last time in September 1863, but he had already made so many final appearances that no one could be sure he would not return yet again. Frank's ingenuity was severely strained when he had to make a farewell speech of gratitude and congratulation to his rajah on behalf of the British residents. James, for his part, seems to have intercepted the bishop's letters and wrote his own, heavy with menace, speaking of 'mischief' and 'accusations'[13] that might arise from unguarded communications.

The disinheritance of Brooke Brooke struck particularly at the friendship of James and Charley Grant, since Brooke Brooke had married his sister. Charley finally broke off his relations with the Brooke raj, but there remained a residue of sad, chastened affection between the two men. In 1863, having composed a stern and formal rejection of James's treatment of his erstwhile heir, Charley wrote across it, in an outburst of feeling, 'Oh, Rajah, I wish you would make a real effort to restore things as they were in the days when we all loved each other and have some of the confidence in your fellow men that you had then . . .'[14] But it was not to be. James Brooke no longer had much faith in anything. He was eloquent that it was all

Brooke Brooke's fault: 'He has rubbed off the bloom from the tender
flower of Trust.' It was betrayal again.

On his way home to England in September 1863, James crossed the
news that Lord Russell proposed formal recognition of Sarawak as
an independent state. It was little enough to show for a quarter of a
century of campaigning, but it was something. Perhaps John Grant,
Charley's father, wrote truer than he knew when he described this
obsession with the recognition of Sarawak as 'having this child
acknowledged'.[15] The leitmotif of orphans, foundlings and abandoned boys continues to run through James's life, and parallels
between his blinkered fixity of purpose in the Reuben George
Walker affair and his dogged determination in the matter of diplomatic recognition are clear. Actual British protection would not
finally come until 1888 – and be shown to be totally worthless in
the Japanese invasion of 1941. A British consul was appointed to
Kuching but could not find enough work even for a diplomat. Still,
at his first report, James commented, 'I am purring with content-
ment,' thinking perhaps of his favourite cat, reared from a kitten,
who survived the Chinese insurrection and was now installed at
Skrang, where it 'enjoys a sleek and quiet old age'. As usual James
was not sleek and quiet but worrying about the need for a new
steam gunboat.

The newly minted Charles Brooke was anxious to make his mark.
There had long been trouble with the Kayan people of the head-
waters of the Rejang River. Protected by a series of rapids which
were held to make their country impregnable, they had staged a
series of raids on Sarawak Dayaks and – worse – harboured the
killers of Fox and Steel, slain in Kanowit. A war spear was sent
around the Skrang longhouses. The Rajah was calling out his forces.
  Some three hundred boats and twelve thousand men set off over
the boiling Pelagus rapids with European guns and support. Even
today, after the expenditure of much British dynamite, it is still a
formidable barrier. Charles is described as seated on a rock during
the boat-hauling, rattling off a rendition of *Il Trovatore* from the

manuscript. He had a passion for opera equalled only by that of the Dayaks for revenge, and they had much to avenge since the Kayan had a taste for taking captives and having them elaborately and slowly tortured by their women before they were mutilated and finally decapitated. In the ensuing warfare with Charles, the Kayan were defeated and fled rather than fight to the end; their long-houses were set ablaze. No longhouse could long withstand a siege once the enemy was close enough. If the fire did not consume it, the attackers scattered large quantities of chilli on the flames and pro-duced a smoke like tear gas. A Kayan captive was given a Sarawak flag and a 12-pounder shot to take to her chief, meaning 'Is it peace or is it war? Choose.' The forces returned to Kanowit.

After a month, the news was brought that a deputation was coming down the river. No one quite knew when it would arrive, since Dayaks told time by the moon and the stars or how long it took to cook rice or for their hair to dry. In the fort, they strained to see the boat as it swept round the distant curve of the coffee-coloured torrent. It was carrying the Sarawak flag. It was peace.

In two months' time they again held the great ceremony of 'drying the eyes and wiping the face', where a line was drawn under old enmities and ancient feuds were buried in the squealing death of a pig. It was attended by the great Kayan leader Akam Nipa. The main gift brought from the other side of the rapids was the heads of two of the slayers of Fox and Steel. Akam Nipa wore the Sarawak flag over his shoulders like a shawl. Underneath he was decked out in the tattered splendour of James's old uniform of the Governor of Labuan, cast aside in rage when he saw himself betrayed by the Singapore Commission of Inquiry.

Charles Brooke nestled in snugly as heir in Kuching, and repelled all attempts to incite him to guilt or loyalty or family feeling con-cerning his elder brother. He replied to such missives with bland and owlish non-comprehension. Brooke Brooke fell into a slow decline, while Angela's relations with James were poisoned by signs that he might ultimately agree to a reconciliation with his erst-while heir. She declared slanderously that Brooke Brooke was a drunk – not falling-about drunk but, she announced authoritatively, it didn't take much to confuse a weak head such as his. When James suffered another stroke in 1866, Brooke Brooke rushed – sober – to the scene but was denied access through her good offices. He died in 1868, but the claims of his son Hope were felt to be sufficiently strong for them to be bought off with a tax-free pension of £1,000 per annum, charged to the Sarawak exchequer.

James spent his time visiting friends and engaging in country pursuits, and maintained a stream of letters to Sarawak, favouring Charles with his views on just about everything. Between bouts at Angela's houses in London and Torquay, he retired largely to his cottage in Burrator, where he retained his interests in animal husbandry and home improvements. He participated in local affairs, was made a churchwarden and, assuming himself as omniscient here as in Kuching, caused the local church to be stripped of its ancient rood screen and clumsily rebodged by a local builder in cheap materials. He got the money from Angela. Locals behaved obligingly, much as the Dayaks had, with suitable awe and reverential hand-touching, and James was universally benign as in Sarawak. Sarawak had always been run like a gentleman's country estate, and now his estate was run much like Sarawak. He was known for his charity and approachability. James was also busy designing postage stamps and currency, bearing his own head, for the newly independent state of Sarawak. They would be used only after his death but would be avidly collected by generations of schoolboys.

And James was still acutely interested in boys. In 1866 he read in the newspaper of a thirteen-year-old youth, Samuel Bray, who had saved a friend from drowning in Devonport, and he became unhealthily excited. He traced the lad, sent him a half sovereign and tried to open a correspondence with him.

In 1866 Charles Brooke published his *Ten Years in Sarawak* and James was asked to write a preface. It is both his testimonial and his own obituary.

I once had a day-dream of advancing the Malayan race by enforcing order and establishing self-government among

ANGELA BURDETT-COUTTS WITH MRS BROWN, 1864:
MANSELL COLLECTION

them; and I dreamed, too, that my native country would derive benefit of position, influence, and commerce without the responsibilities from which she shrinks. But the dream ended with the first waking reality, and I found how true it is that nations are like men; that the young hope more than they fear, and that the old fear more than they hope – that England had ceased to be enterprising, and could not look forward to obtaining great ends by small means, perseveringly applied, and that the dependencies are not now regarded as a field of outlay, to yield abundant national returns, but as a source of wasteful expenditure, to be wholly cut off. The cost ultimately 'may verify the adage, and some day England may wake from her dream of disastrous economy,' as I have wakened from my dream of extended usefulness. I trust the consequences may not be more hurtful to her than they have been to me.

Since this I have found happiness in advancing the happiness of my people, who, whatever may be their faults, have been true to me and mine through good report and evil report, through prosperity and through misfortune.[16]

At the end of 1867 came a great, but inevitable, falling-out with Angela. Although staying at her house in Torquay, James stormed off and moved into a hotel. Angela was perplexed but unforgiving. 'Nothing could have exceeded the hardness and cruelty of their conduct to him during the last six months of his life.'[17] The trigger seems to have lain in Mrs Brown's jealousy of his influence with Angela, but two such egos could never easily rub shoulders together.

On Christmas Eve of that year, James suffered another stroke, and in June 1868 a final one, dying on 11 June. It was described much as it would have been in Kuching: 'When a little while later, the poor people stole in sorrowfully and reverently to take their last look, they found that the weary anxious expression which had touched their hearts the more because of the smile ever ready to light up the face, had entirely passed away, and the Rajah lay in death as Sarawak had known him in the full vigour of his manhood.'[18]

The obituaries came thick and fast. Readers of *The Times* were treated to an extraordinary mishmash of muddled ideas. The writer was unsure whether James had been born in India or Bath, but confirmed him to be 'from a good old Somersetshire family and the son of a plain retired official'. He came to power in Sarawak when 'Muda' was appointed Prime Minister and recommended James as his successor, at which point 'the honour and dignity of Rajah was laid at the feet of the Englishman'. There had been calamities, notably when 'his books and private papers had been destroyed in an insurrection in Borneo, which he was not on the spot to quell'. At least, the writer soothed his readers, British rule had now been assured.

Perhaps the most discerning was that in the *Monthly Packet*. Significantly, it was by Tidman, who had worked for the Borneo Company and seen James at his lowest ebb during the Chinese insurrection.

The Rajah Sir James Brooke was no demigod, triumphing unaided and alone over the so-called injustice of his country. He was one of the really great men of his time. – with high noble aims – courageous, ambitious, and at times unscrupulous. Capable of the greatest things, he could yet under the influence of prejudice and an over-weening trust in himself, commit gross injustice and become the sport of contemptible imposture. But his work that will live when his faults are forgotten, is perhaps without a rival. He came to a disorganised crowd of savages, and left them a compact nation. He gave peace in their borders and taught them for the first time the meaning of Justice, Mercy and Truth. When his Biography comes to be written, there must be in it, dark chapters as well as bright ones, but while those who loved him the best, could fondly and sadly wish it had been otherwise, they will ever be able to think of their leader, as the Father and Founder of a nation and as one of England's greatest sons.[19]

James Brooke was laid to rest in Sheepstor Church, near his beloved cottage, in a spot he delighted to point out to visitors as his future tomb. The gravestone read:

SACRED TO THE MEMORY OF
SIR JAMES BROOKE KCB, DCL
RAJAH AND FOUNDER OF
THE SETTLEMENT OF SARAWAK
WHO DEPARTED HIS LIFE AT HIS RESIDENCE
BURRATOR IN THIS PARISH THE 11TH DAY OF JUNE 1868
AGED 65 YEARS

Angela, litigious to the end, disliked the word 'settlement' and vainly tried to have it rechiselled to read 'state', which she found more to her taste. Frank and Harriette McDougall, though in England, were not invited to the funeral. Charley Grant came, though: for him, as for James, loyalty was all. In Sarawak, Charles Brooke was declared Rajah and the waiting guns finally fired off the royal salute. Having eventually attained royal dignity, Charles would remain Rajah for another fifty years.

James Brooke led an extraordinary life but in the past he has been so enwrapped by the unavoidable myths of empire, positive and negative, that the man himself has been hard to see. For as our views of the imperial programme have changed, so necessarily have our ideas of its great icons, and it is only with the final banishing of that romantic vision and its aftermath that he can emerge again as an individual. James Brooke dedicated himself to a cause that he genuinely believed to be greater and more important than his own life or happiness, and it is not surprising therefore that it brought him both his greatest satisfactions and that caustic bitterness and sense of failure that poisoned his later life. His critics have debated whether he was benevolent or arrogant. He was both. He was a giver and a taker. For him, Sarawak and himself were each absorbed in the other. Without Sarawak, he would have had nothing to live for and, without him, Sarawak would either have become a neglected Dutch possession or remained a despised backwater of Brunei. He offered it identity, self-respect and a firm independence. So he kept his sacred promise, made many years before, to Sarawak as incarnated in the orphan Situ. Perhaps it does not matter, then, that the noble urge to nurture, protect and cherish that he frankly expressed seems now unbearably patronising, that it drew its strength from vanity and hypocrisy and was ultimately rooted in expiation and displacement of a desire that is – if anything – even less acceptable now than it was then.

To say such things is not to belittle his achievements and reduce them to a mere mask of magnanimity. James Brooke is a prime example of the ways in which darker instincts may be employed to drive high motives, converting the compassionate lust of his private life into the 'tender philanthropy' of his *Athenaeum* address and the therapeutic usefulness of imperialism to the rulers, if not the ruled. In its wake followed a sense of paranoia, betrayal and obsession that left its mark on those who believed in him but also a genuine sense of selflessness that he inspired in others, both European and local. To call him a racist is irrelevant – he lived in a racist age. More importantly, he knew himself to be a member of the ruling class and it is not clear that he treated his Devonshire neighbours and tenants as well as he did his beloved Dayaks, or held himself to be closer to them. The blood he spilled was spilled in the name of peace, while his compulsive imposition of his own views went hand in hand with a manifest and modest respect for local ways of life. Such contradictions confound the simplicities of good and bad, for they are the contradictions of love in its many forms. For he did love Sarawak and its inhabitants, just as he loved Charley Grant and Badrudeen, and each form of love informed and justified the others. His model of Sarawak was one blatantly transplanted from the English shires – small is good, the valorisation of face-to-face relationships, the local over the metropolitan, tradition and emotion over rationality – but perhaps these are the values of all small communities everywhere, which is why Sarawak never became entirely absurd and evoked a sort of piquant antiquarian nostalgia from the very start. And the first and last of virtues was that of loyalty.

JAMES BROOKE TOWARDS THE END OF HIS LIFE: BRITISH LIBRARY

Yet behind the agreeable Toytown façade there always lurked the harsh economic and military reality of the wider British Empire on which he covertly relied at the same time as he publicly rejected it. It seems ironic and inevitable that after all the tumult and the fury of the Second World War, the empire finally took over the Brooke dynasty as the acceptable and caring face of itself, and exiled the last of his royal line.

The stabbing in 1949 of Duncan Stewart, the despised British Governor, was perhaps the final desperate attempt to prevent that act of mythic appropriation. As the conspirators spent their final days in the condemned cell, listening to the workmen hammering together the expensive new scaffold on which they would hang, rumours swept again through the little town of Kuching. It was confidently expected, even by some of the prisoners themselves – patriotic fighters for their independence – that they would never pay the price for their crime. Surely the Rajah, or the Tuan Muda – anyway *one* of the Brookes – would miraculously intervene and save them, just as they always had? But the Brookes had gone.

Epilogue

There was a serial killer loose in Kuching. The third headless body had just been found under the suspension bridge. The police deduced from the absence of a smallpox inoculation scar that the victim was an Indonesian illegal immigrant. I found that interesting.

'Your lot must have done it.' I pointed out the article to Tong. He was a Bidayuh, what James Brooke would have called a Hill or Land Dayak. Tong had received a Christian education but gone back to the old ways.

His morning risings were now quite complicated and required the participation of his wife and the sun and the sacrifice of several eggs. Tendrils of beautiful, swirling blue tattoos peeked out at wrist and neck from under his modish designer wear.

He studied the newspaper and pouted. 'No. This is Chinese stuff, mafia, you know. Just business, not like in the old days.'

'What,' I asked tentatively, 'do people think of the old days, when the Brookes were in charge of Sarawak?'

He smiled. 'You'd have to ask my grandad, but I think he'd say that the Chinese liked them as good for business. The Malays disliked them at first then supported them because they kept them in power. We Bidayuh liked them because they protected us from the Iban. The Iban couldn't agree and fought amongst themselves.'

'And what about when Sarawak became part of Malaysia?'

He smiled again and poured beer. 'The Chinese liked that as good for business. The Malays were against it but then changed their minds because it kept them in power. We Bidayuh liked it because Malaysia protected us from the Iban. The Iban couldn't agree and fought amongst themselves.'

That seemed pretty conclusive.

'Anyway. The best argument for Sarawak is to visit Brunei. If it hadn't been for the Brookes we would be part of Brunei. Have you been?' He sipped, shuddered at the coldness or perhaps the mere thought of Brunei, reached out and poured more.

'Yes,' I said. 'I went one weekend from Miri. It was hard because no one ever wants to go *to* Brunei on Friday night, just get away from it. When I arrived, every flat surface was covered by migrant workers, Pakistanis, Indonesians, Filipinos, sleeping, bored out of their minds. When they got up, they staggered around yawning, staring with blank empty eyes, just wanting beer and sex and Brunei had made both illegal. Instead, they had a free funfair.'

He nodded. 'So . . . you see. Brunei is hostile to *life*. People don't cross the border to Sarawak to have wild orgies and mad drugs. They just want to have a beer and walk along the beach holding a girl's hand. What can be wrong with that? And things are so laid-back here compared to the rest of Malaysia. The Brookes gave us that.'

'What about James Brooke?' I asked. 'He was . . . That is he didn't . . . Look . . . He was . . .' I couldn't remember a polite term. In my very Indonesianised Malay I would have to call him an *orang sakit*, 'a sick person'. I wasn't going to do that. Then I recalled the punchline of a joke. '*Pondan*,' I said. 'He was a *pondan*.' Then, in English, 'It's obvious he was gay.'

Tong raised his eyebrows. 'Really? They never told us that in the history books. Are you sure?'

'Well,' I hummed and ha'ed, not wanting to go into the whole thing. 'He was strongly drawn to young boys and had no interest in women. Work it out for yourself.'

There was something tickling at the back of my head. 'Hang on,' I said. 'Let me read something to you.' I had brought along one of my favourite books of all time, *Nine Dayak Nights* by W. R. Geddes, a delightful, gently affectionate study of Tong's people by a man who had obviously known them and lived with them and fallen totally in love with them. I dug in the index and found the passage I was looking for. 'Here you are, Tong. Listen to this. Is it true? "The Land Dayaks are highly homosocial but they are rarely, if ever, homosexual, and I believe that in the first fact may lie at least part of the reason for the second. From the beginning of their lives to the end they can indulge freely their affectionate feelings, especially the protective parental affection the older persons have for the younger, and these feelings therefore never reach the intensity which inspires sexual desire."'

I felt a moment's doubt. Perhaps, after all, this had been what James Brooke had been all about. The Land Dayaks had always been his favourite people. Perhaps their charm had lain in uniquely permitting this form of love, which lay at the core of his being, but was of a simple chastity unimaginable to dirty-minded Europeans such as myself. Perhaps . . .

'Total crap,' laughed Tong. 'All the unmarried men have to sleep together in a Bidayuh house. What do you think they do at night when there are no girls around?'

'But it says here . . .'

'You'd better come with me,' he sighed. 'I have something to show you.'

We rattled off on Tong's motorbike through the middle of the Kuching night. Rain gleamed wet on the streets and fog ghosted across the river by the old Brooke fort – now a disco – and the Chinese temple. Across the river gleamed the white-painted Brooke palace, the *astana*, with its crenellations and towers and leaded windows, but what looked ridiculous was not this blatant English anomaly so much as the hi-tech concrete mosque added on the back by the new tenant, the Chief Minister. There were statues of cats everywhere on the roundabouts, simpering and cutesy or noble and independent. The whole city was in love with its name, Kuching – 'cat'. 'Have you been to the Museum of Pussy?' Tong shouted over his shoulder. 'In the Town Hall. You would like. It is very horrible.' On our left, we flashed past the Chinese bazaar, then Rajah Charles's mossy courthouse, like a prop from *Gone with the Wind*, then Rajah Vyner's grandiloquent Post Office. On the hill was the National Museum, designed to look like a Normandy farmhouse by Rajah Charles's French valet. Tong pulled up in a roar and a swirl of dust. It had not been raining here and the sudden still air was like a warm flannel over the face. He dumped his clattering helmet and led me up a Busby Berkeley staircase with gushing fountains and glowing, benodorous flowerbeds, towards a pillar lit in shades of deep red and green. It was the heroes' monument.

In the museum, further up the hill, were the received ortho-doxies of Brooke rule as I had read them at school, but here was the revised, post-colonial version, with new heroes and the Brookes as inevitable villains. 'When we joined Malaysia,' nodded Tong, 'they just couldn't leave it alone. They wanted us all to feel resentful about the past, but that's stupid. That's just the way it was then. Maybe they thought that if we hated the Brookes we would have less time to be resentful about what they are doing to us now. So they took all the people who fought against Rajah James and Rajah Charles and called them national heroes and put them up there.'

And there they all were, memorable from the pages of the white rajahs, with passport-type pictures cast in bronze. There was stub-born Rentap; Sawing, the killer of Fox and Steel; Liu Shanba, who led the Chinese insurrection which burned down the town; inter-fering Sherip Masahor; and for good measure a few contemporary political hacks had been tacked on to soak up some of the glory. At least they had put in James's friend, the Datuk Patinggi Ali, but they weren't at all happy about him. There were snotty remarks in Malay about 'the Brooke regime'. And there, snuggled in amongst them, was Rosly bin Dhobie, assassin of Governor Duncan Stewart.

Tong frowned. 'Who is he? There is some theatrical troupe named after him that does stuff on Independence Day.

'Come on. There is more. The children from Bishop McDougall's school come here during the day to eat their noodles – I was a pupil – but at night it is different.'

He took my hand and led me back down the steps and abruptly off to one side. At first I thought the sounds were mice and other creeping things. But the dark was busy with furtive doings, quite simply the place where love of the state gave way to the state of forbidden love. Young couples arrived every few minutes, mostly by motorbike, the girl on the back holding on tight. Some sat on the benches, clutching hands stickily, and gazed at the pale moonlight reflected in each other's soft, brown eyes, but from the giggles and rhythmic thrashing of the shrubs it was clear that others indulged less lunar and more earthy passions.

'There is more. This is a happening place.'

'A happening place?'

'Yes, very happening. Careful now.'

We stumbled further, over knee-jarring rough grass and past a row of ancient Chinese tombs, and toed our way down some steps in the darkness under the rustling trees. A line of young men were sitting, smoking demurely, on a low wall as at a tea dance. Tong peered along the row and gave a grunt of recognition, picked one up by the shoulders and hugged him.

'My little brother, James,' he said and introduced us. We shook hands and touched them to our hearts in greeting. 'My brother,' he explained, 'is one of those gay Bidayuhs you anthropologists say don't exist.' He hugged him again. 'Everybody knows, nobody minds. There is only one sadness, that he cannot know the joy of babies, but that is all right. James and his friend have adopted two of mine.'

'James?' I asked. 'Was he named after . . . ?'

Tong laughed. 'No – after my uncle.'

'Welcome to Sarawak Cultural Centre,' said James with a huge grin. He was small, dark, very handsome. 'The whole of Sarawak is here.'

He walked down the row, marking each off by a pat on the shoulder. 'Iban, Bidayuh, Melanau, Malay, Chinese, Kayan – I'm sorry, I don't know you . . .'

'Filipino,' laughed a stocky little man. 'I came across from Sabah.'

'. . . Filipino . . . and this one . . .'

The man at the end sat with the darkened visor of his crash helmet pulled down. 'I'm not taking it off,' he said with grim stubbornness, as though James had asked him to. 'I'm well known in Kuching and I'm a married man.'

James did a what-to-do? gesture with both arms. We sat. We smoked. I asked whether they knew about the private life of James Brooke. They didn't – except one.

'I heard something at university in Australia,' he said airily. 'Have you seen his portrait? Handsooome-lah.'

I told them.

'So our rajah loved us,' said a quiet scholastic Malay, after a bit. 'That makes me feel good.'

'At least he wasn't Australian,' said James irrelevantly. 'I was just telling about my trip to Bali. You know the Hulu Bar and that old Australian who does the act as a very ugly lady?' He leaped lightly up onto the wall and strutted in fake arrogance amongst the gleaming eyes and teeth. 'He did this biiiig number . . .' his hips began to swivel and the wiry shoulders to rotate, 'with a snake . . .' he plucked an invisible serpent from the air – perhaps the ghost of one Frank McDougall had killed just yards from this spot – drew it up between his legs and caressed it with practised eroticism. 'Ooh, he did the most disgusting things with that snake . . .' He began to belt out the chorus of 'I Will Survive' in a light disco voice as the snake explored his gyrating body and wiggled from one hand across his chest and out over the other. Some of the girls appeared quizzically out of the darkness, smoothed their hair and began clapping and swaying. Their boyfriends followed, struggling into tight jeans and looking annoyed and frustrated. James writhed and grasped the back of his head in ecstasy, twined the snake around his neck and worked through a couple of hand-clapping verses – strutting and spasming towards the big diva finale. 'I will survive. I will survive.

Hey HEY—' He stopped dead, grasped the snake with both hands, inserted the head in his mouth and made gagging, choking noises. The audience froze. He held up his hand and took the head out again.

'The problem was, his act was so good, he did *three* encores. The poor snake couldn't take it any more. It died. Maybe it died of shame.' James's assistant went suddenly limp in his hand and he flung it whirling into the bushes. The crowd erupted in cheers and screams of delight. Tong glowed with pride as his little brother danced sure-footedly along the wall, bowed and blew superstar kisses at his adoring public.

'You shouldn't laugh at animals like that,' said the Iban, annoyed. 'There will be a terrible reckoning for laughing at animals. You should never laugh at animals.'

'That's all right,' smiled Tong, applauding hard and nodding up at the museum. 'Relax. There is no harm in it. Look, he's just following his rajah.'

Chronology

Notes

Chapter One
1 British Library, Add. 45906.
2 G. Jacob, *The Raja of Sarawak*, Vol. I, p.2.
3 S. St John, *The Life of Sir James Brooke, Rajah of Sarawak*, p.2.
4 Jacob, op. cit., p.10.
5 St John, op. cit., p.5.
6 Jacob, op. cit., p.47.
7 S. Brooke, *Queen of the Headhunters*, p.133.
8 A. Ward, *Rajah's Servant*, p.196.
9 E. Hahn, *James Brooke of Sarawak*, p.20.
10 Ibid.
11 F. Marryat, *Borneo and the Indian Archipelago*, p.4.

Chapter Two
1 G. Jacob, *The Raja of Sarawak*, Vol. I, p.21.
2 Ibid., p.14.
3 Ibid., p.21.
4 Ibid., p.23.
5 Ibid., p.26.
6 Ibid., p.27.
7 S. St John, *The Life of Sir James Brooke, Rajah of Sarawak*, p.182.

8   C. Brooke, *Ten Years in Sarawak*, p.xiii.
9   R. Norton, *Mother Clap's Molly House*, p.132.
10 Jacob, op. cit., p.33.
11 St John, op. cit., p.376.
12 Ibid., p.92.
13 Jacob, op. cit., p.45.

Chapter Three

1   N. Tarling, *The Burthen, the Risk and the Glory*, p.13.
2   G. Jacob, *The Raja of Sarawak*, Vol. I, p.33.
3   Ibid., p.37.
4   Ibid., p.39.
5   Ibid., p.49.
6   S. St John, *The Life of Sir James Brooke, Rajah of Sarawak*, p.9.
7   Jacob, op. cit., p.47.
8   Ibid., p.69.
9   G. Jacob, *The Raja of Sarawak*, Vol. II, p.277.
10 G. Jacob, *The Raja of Sarawak*, Vol. I, p.91.
11 Ibid., p.54.

Chapter Four

1   H. Keppel, *The Expedition to Borneo of HMS Dido for the Suppression of Piracy*, Vol. I, p.165.
2   S. St John, *The Life of Sir James Brooke, Rajah of Sarawak*, p.20.
3   J. Templer, *The Private Letters of Sir James Brooke, K.C.B., Rajah of Sarawak*, Vol. I, p.85.

Chapter Five

1   H. Keppel, *The Expedition to Borneo of HMS Dido for the Suppression of Piracy*, Vol. I, p.157.
2   Ibid., p.154.
3   Ibid., p.163.
4   Ibid., p.165.
5   Ibid., p.145.
6   J. Walker, 'This Peculiar Acuteness of Feeling', *Borneo Research Bulletin*, 1998, p.164.

7 J. Templer, *The Private Letters of Sir James Brooke, K.C.B., Rajah of Sarawak*, Vol. I, p.269.
8 Keppel, op. cit., p.208.
9 Ibid., p.171.
10 Ibid., p.77.
11 Ibid., p.195.
12 Templer, op. cit., p.137.
13 Keppel, op. cit., p.227.
14 Ibid., p.50.

Chapter Six

1 J. Templer, *The Private Letters of Sir James Brooke, K.C.B., Rajah of Sarawak*, Vol. I, p.116.
2 Ibid., p.131.
3 G. Jacob, *The Raja of Sarawak*, Vol. I, p.179.
4 S. St John, *The Life of Sir James Brooke, Rajah of Sarawak*, p.65.
5 Templer, op. cit., p.123.
6 H. Keppel, *The Expedition to Borneo of HMS Dido for the Suppression of Piracy*, Vol. I, p.139.
7 J. Templer, *The Private Letters of Sir James Brooke, K.C.B., Rajah of Sarawak*, Vol. II, p.17.
8 Keppel, op. cit., p.321.
9 St John, op. cit., p.69.
10 Jacob, op. cit., p.70.

Chapter Seven

1 G. Jacob, *The Raja of Sarawak*, Vol. I, p.189.
2 H. Keppel, *The Expedition to Borneo of HMS Dido for the Suppression of Piracy*, Vol. II, p.13.
3 Ibid., p.18.
4 Ibid., p.43.
5 Ibid., p.55.
6 Ibid., p.63.
7 Ibid., p.65.

8   Ibid., p.68.

9   Ibid., p.70.

10 F. Marryat, *Borneo and the Indian Archipelago*, p.15.

11 J. Templer, *The Private Letters of Sir James Brooke, K.C.B., Rajah of Sarawak*, Vol. I, p.283.

12 Marryat, op. cit., p.90.

13 E. Hahn, *James Brooke of Sarawak*, p.101.

14 J. Templer, *The Private Letters of Sir James Brooke, K.C.B., Rajah of Sarawak*, Vol. II, p.2.

15 Keppel, op. cit., p.79.

16 Ibid., p.92.

17 Ibid., p.95.

18 Ibid., p.110.

19 Ibid., p.120.

Chapter Eight

1   H. Keppel, *The Expedition to Borneo of HMS Dido for the Suppression of Piracy*, Vol. II, p.158.

2   G. Jacob, *The Raja of Sarawak*, Vol. I, p.307.

3   S. St John, *The Life of Sir James Brooke, Rajah of Sarawak*, p.110.

4   Ibid., p.111.

5   Jacob, op. cit., p.321.

6   R. Mundy, *Narrative of Events in Borneo and Celebes, Down to the Occupation of Labuan: From the Journals of James Brooke, Esq., Rajah of Sarawak, and Governor of Labuan*, Vol. II, p.93.

Chapter Nine

1   J. Templer, *The Private Letters of Sir James Brooke, K.C.B., Rajah of Sarawak*, Vol. II, p.167.

2   R. Reece, *The Name of Brooke*, p.63.

3   S. St John, *The Life of Sir James Brooke, Rajah of Sarawak*, p.127.

4   Ibid., p.124.

5   J. Templer, *The Private Letters of Sir James Brooke, K.C.B., Rajah of Sarawak*, Vol. I, p.244.

6   Ibid., p.255.
7   St John, op. cit., p.133.
8   Basil Brooke Papers, Rhodes House, Oxford, MSS Pac.s.90, Box 1, File 1.
9   Ibid., Box 5 item 6.
10 Ibid., Vol. IV, f.57.
11 Ibid., Vol. IV, f.56.
12 E. Hahn, *James Brooke of Sarawak*, p.127.
13 H. McDougall, *Sketches of Our Life at Sarawak*, p.113.
14 G. Jacob, *The Raja of Sarawak*, Vol. I, p.224.
15 Jacob, *The Raja of Sarawak*, Vol. II, p.24.
16 Ibid., p.25.
17 Templer, *The Private Letters of Sir James Brooke, K.C.B., Rajah of Sarawak*, Vol. III, p.60.
18 Jacob, op. cit., p.2.
19 St John, op. cit., p.212.
20 Templer, *The Private Letters of Sir James Brooke, K.C.B., Rajah of Sarawak*, Vol. II, p.292.
21 St John, op. cit., p.213.
22 Jacob, *The Raja of Sarawak*, Vol. II, p.2.
23 McDougall, op. cit., p.23.
24 G. Jacob, *The Raja of Sarawak*, Vol. I, p.376.

Chapter Ten

1   G. Jacob, *The Raja of Sarawak*, Vol. II, p.46.
2   S. St John, *The Life of Sir James Brooke, Rajah of Sarawak*, p.239.
3   Jacob, op. cit., p.77.
4   Ibid., p.79.
5   A. Ward, *Rajah's Servant*, p.51.
6   Jacob, op. cit., p.83.
7   St John, op. cit., p.250.
8   Jacob, op. cit., p.161.
9   N. Tarling, *The Burthen, the Risk and the Glory*, p.186.
10 Public Record Office, FO12/19–20.
11 St John, op. cit., p.270.

Chapter Eleven

1 G. Jacob, *The Raja of Sarawak*, Vol. II, p.187.
2 S. St John, *The Life of Sir James Brooke, Rajah of Sarawak*, p.274.
3 Jacob, op. cit., p.225.
4 N. Tarling, *The Burthen, the Risk and the Glory*, p.183.
5 Ibid., p.194.
6 H. McDougall, *Sketches of Our Life at Sarawak*, p.118.
7 C. Bunyon, *Memoirs of Francis Thomas McDougall and Harriette his Wife*, p.128.
8 Ibid., p.130.

Chapter Twelve

1 S. St John, *The Life of Sir James Brooke, Rajah of Sarawak*, p.296.
2 Ibid., p.298.
3 M. Saint, *A Flourish for the Bishop and Brooke's Friend Grant*, p.71.
4 St John, op. cit., p.300.
5 Saint, op. cit., p.64.
6 H. McDougall, *Sketches of Our Life at Sarawak*, p.133.
7 E. Hahn, *James Brooke of Sarawak*, p.217.
8 L. Helms, *Pioneering in the Far East*, p.183.
9 McDougall, op. cit., p.143.
10 Ibid., p.151.
11 G. Jacob, *The Raja of Sarawak*, Vol. II, p.235.
12 Ibid., p.241.
13 Hahn, op. cit., p.219.
14 Helms, op. cit., p.213.
15 St John, op. cit., p.319.
16 Jacob, op. cit., p.245.
17 Ibid., p.249.
18 Hahn, op. cit., p.221

Chapter Thirteen

1 S. St John, *The Life of Sir James Brooke, Rajah of Sarawak*, p.320.

2 G. Jacob, *The Raja of Sarawak*, Vol. II, p.263.
3 Basil Brooke Papers, Rhodes House, Oxford, MSS Pac.s.90, Vol. 2A.
4 Ibid.
5 Ibid.
6 Ibid.
7 Ibid., Vol. 2A, f.120.
8 Basil Brooke Papers, Vol. 2A.
9 Ibid., Box I/I, File I, f.146.
10 Ibid., Box I/I, File I, f.147.
11 M. Saint, *A Flourish for the Bishop and Brooke's Friend Grant*, p.100.
12 E. Hahn, *James Brooke of Sarawak*, p.226.
13 Ibid., p.227.
14 Ibid., p.25.
15 E. Healey, *Lady Unknown*, p.126.

Chapter Fourteen

1 O. Rutter, *Rajah Brooke and Baroness Burdett-Coutts*, p.64.
2 C. Brooke, *Ten Years in Sarawak*, Vol. I., p.336.
3 Ibid., p.338.
4 Ibid., p.353.
5 S. St John, *The Life of Sir James Brooke, Rajah of Sarawak*, p.320.
6 E. Hahn, *James Brooke of Sarawak*, p.245.
7 St John, op. cit., p.350.
8 J. Walker, 'This Peculiar Acuteness of Feeling', *Borneo Research Bulletin*, 1998.
9 James Brooke to Hannah Brown, British Library, BL, Add. 45275.
10 Ibid., f.143.
11 Ibid., f.148.
12 Ibid., f.150.
13 Basil Brooke Papers, Vol. V, f.396.
14 Ibid., Vol. XV, f.64.
15 Ibid.

16   Walker, op. cit.

Chapter Fifteen

1   J. Brooke, *The Bishop of Labuan, a Vindication*, p.10.
2   Basil Brooke Papers, Vol. III, f.318.
3   M. Saint, *A Flourish for the Bishop and Brooke's Friend Grant*, p.223.
4   C. Bunyon, *Memoirs of Francis Thomas McDougall and Harriette his Wife*, p.245.
5   Saint, op. cit., p.225.
6   Ibid., p.114.
7   Bunyon, op. cit., p.234.
8   Ibid., p.245.
9   N. Tarling, *The Burthen, the Risk and the Glory*, p.427.
10   Basil Brooke Papers, Vol. V, f.488.
11   Ibid., Vol. III.
12   Saint, op. cit., p.233.
13   Ibid., p.142.
14   Basil Brooke Papers., Vol. II, f.155.
15   Tarling, op. cit., p.388.
16   C. Brooke, *Ten Years in Sarawak*, Vol. I, p.xii.
17   Tarling, op. cit., p.429.
18   G. Jacob, *The Raja of Sarawak*, Vol. II, p.367.
19   P.F. Tidman, *Monthly Packet*, 14 September 1874.

Bibliography

Baring-Gould, S. and B., *A History of Sarawak Under its Two White Rajahs 1839–1908*, London, 1909

Brooke, C., *Ten Years in Sarawak*, 2 vols, London, 1866

Brooke, J., *The Bishop of Labuan, a Vindication*, London, n.d. Published under the name of Spenser St John

Brooke, S., *Queen of the Headhunters*, Singapore, 1970

Bunyon, C., *Memoirs of Francis Thomas McDougall and Harriette His Wife*, London, 1889

Geddes, W., *Nine Dayak Nights*, London, 1957

Hahn, E., *James Brooke of Sarawak*, London, 1953

Healey, E., *Lady Unknown: The Life of Angela Burdett-Coutts*, London, 1978

Helms, L. *Pioneering in the Far East*, London, 1882

Jacob, G., *The Raja of Sarawak*, 2 vols, London, 1876

Keppel, H., *The Expedition to Borneo of HMS Dido for the Suppression of Piracy: With Extracts from the Journal of James Brooke, Esq.*, 2 vols, London, 1846

   A Visit to the Indian Archipelago in HMS Maeander, 2 vols, London, 1853

McDougall, H., *Letters from Sarawak, Addressed to a Child*, London, 1854

    Sketches of Our Life at Sarawak, London, n.d.

Marryat, F., *Borneo and the Indian Archipelago*, London, 1848

Mundy, R., *Narrative of Events in Borneo and Celebes, Down to the Occupation of Labuan: From the Journals of James Brooke, Esq., Rajah of Sarawak, and Governor of Labuan*, 2 vols, London, 1848

Norton, R., *Mother Clap's Molly House: The Gay Subculture in England 1700-1830*, London, 1992

Payne, R., *The White Rajahs of Sarawak*, London, 1960

Pringle, R., *Rajahs and Rebels: The Ibans of Sarawak Under Brooke Rule 1841–1941*, London, 1970

Reece, R., *The Name of Brooke*, Oxford, 1993

Runciman, S., *The White Rajahs*, Cambridge, 1960

Rutter, O., *Rajah Brooke and Baroness Burdett-Coutts*, London, 1935

Saint, M., *A Flourish for the Bishop and Brooke's Friend Grant*, 1985

St John, S., *Life in the Forests of the Far East*, 2 vols, London, 1862

    The Life of Sir James Brooke, Rajah of Sarawak, Edinburgh, 1879

Tarling, N., *The Burthen, the Risk, and the Glory: A Biography of Sir James Brooke*, Kuala Lumpur, 1982

Templer, J., *The Private Letters of Sir James Brooke, K.C.B., Rajah of Sarawak*, 3 vols, London, 1853

Walker, J., '"This Peculiar Acuteness of Feeling": James Brooke and the Enactment of Desire', *Borneo Research Bulletin*, Vol. 29, 1998, pp.148–89

Ward, A., *Rajah's Servant*, Cornell, 1966

Unpublished Sources

Army Records, Public Record Office, Kew, WO 12, WO 14, WO 97

Correspondence between James Brooke and Angela Burdett-Coutts and Hannah Brown: British Library, BL Add. 45275

Correspondence of Charles William Brooke, British Library, BL Add. MS 45906

Correspondence of James Brooke: Basil Brooke Papers, Rhodes House, Oxford, MSS Pac. s. 90

Papers relating to Singapore inquiry, Public Record Office, Kew, FO 12/19–20

Index

Note: Page references in *italics* indicate illustrations. JB = James Brooke.